CONTEMPORARY LANGUAGE STUDIES

GENERAL EDITOR: Professor F. M. Willis, University of Bradford

Based on an original plan, this series is a new venture, in publishing for modern language students, and aims to promote the interdisciplinary study of language and of the sociocultural context in which language is used and evolves.

Its predominant concern at present is with French studies, and this governs the selection of themes. At the outset, however, the programme provides for a general text on linguistics designed for students not only of French but of other European languages also.

The books are of an introductory nature and devised, with appropriate adjustments in each case, on the following general plan:

- a section, in English, with chapters of description and analysis
- illustrative texts, in French, at the end of each chapter, and bearing directly on it
- a section, in French and English, of linguistic exercises followed by bibliographical guidance

The series is addressed to all who are concerned with the study of France and its language, and is of special value to two broad categories:

1. Modern language students who are engaged in a new discipline (e.g. economics, politics, business studies) involving new concepts and requiring them to acquire a new technical lexis and a new style of writing or speech.
2. Students of social sciences and business studies taking a modern language course requiring application of the principles or theory already acquired in their primary discipline.

PUBLISHED

Linguistics for Language Learners by Anthony F. Hartley
Contemporary French Society by Linda Hantrais

IN PREPARATION

The Contemporary French Economy by Graeme M. Holmes and Peter D. Fawcett
Contemporary French Politics by

[illegible]

[illegible]

[illegible]

PUBLISHED

[illegible]

IN PREPARATION

[illegible]

[illegible] Malcolm Slater

Linguistics for Language Learners

Anthony F. Hartley

M

First published 1982 by
THE MACMILLAN PRESS LTD
London and Basingstoke
Companies and representatives throughout the world

ISBN 0 333 26683 8 (hard cover)
ISBN 0 333 26684 6 (paper cover)

Typeset in Great Britain by
Multiplex techniques ltd, Orpington, Kent

Printed in Hong Kong

For Elizabeth, Eileen and Frank

Contents

List of Figures

Acknowledgements

I would like to express my thanks to all those friends, students and colleagues who helped and encouraged me in the writing of this book. I am most grateful to Jenny Finder, John Horton and the staff of the Social Sciences Library, and to Helga Wagner, Winfried Haag, Richard Pollock and Rafael Sala for the wealth of information they gave me on German, Russian and Spanish. Any misapplications of it are my doing along. Jeanette Pugh, Professor Frank Knowles and Professor J. C. Sager commented on early drafts of some of the chapters and gave generous advice on shortcomings of content and of style. My thanks go also to Professor Frank Willis for his support and general editorial guidance. The warts that remain are, of course, all mine. My greatest debt is to Elizabeth Murtha, for her encouragement.

University of Bradford ANTHONY F. HARTLEY

General Editor's Foreword

The present volume is one of a series based on the fact that language as a means of communication is bound up inextricably with the society that uses it. While the others concentrate on particular facets of the sociocultural context in which the foreign language is used and developed, this book focuses on communicative competence in it. Starting from sociolinguistic discussion and problems of language acquisition, the author then moves on to formal linguistic description.

It is this particular treatment, with its constant emphasis on language in its social setting, that marks off this work from so many on the same topic that examine linguistic theory in detail and treat sociolinguistic discussion and the problems of acquiring a second language as matters of only peripheral interest.

The presentation follows the general pattern of the series in that the author's description and analysis are followed by suggestions for practical exercises and annotated bibliographies which, it is hoped, will provide the stimulus and guidance for readers to undertake further independent study.

Although designed primarily to meet the needs of those intending to specialise in modern languages, communication studies and linguistics, this introductory book offers a useful initiation to students of sociology, psychology and literature who recognise the relevance of linguistics to their own particular fields.

FRANK M. WILLIS

Introduction

The central themes of this book are not so much 'linguistics' as 'language' and 'learners'. It is designed for a particular audience – learners of modern European languages who are not content with merely 'getting by' but wish to use those languages with a high degree of proficiency, and who are interested in the users of languages and their social setting.

It is written in the belief that informed learners can direct their efforts more effectively towards their particular goals. Learning a language is not easy, especially for someone who is for most of the time outside the foreign community where that language is spoken. This book is intended as a starting-point for an exploration of the reasons for this difficulty. It contains chapters on aspects of the learning task and on the different facets of language itself. The choice of subject-matter is necessarily wide, and the discussion can do no more than skim the surface of the several branches of linguistics which are represented in these pages. The problems faced by advanced linguistic research and the conflicts of opinion surrounding many issues receive little attention. The emphasis is, instead, on establishing a number of fairly clear landmarks which will guide learners in their task and stimulate further their curiosity about language.

Chapter 1 is intended to provoke thought about some of the questions which are taken up later in the book and to outline briefly the main fields of linguistic investigation. It should be read first. Thereafter, the book divides into two main sections. In the first (Chapters 2–6) the emphasis is on the social setting of language; in the second (Chapters 7–10) the emphasis is on linguistic structure and approaches to its systematic study. Chapter 2 illustrates something of the historical and social background to the present situation of the languages of Europe. In Chapter 3 the processes of learning a first and a second language are compared. Chapters 4, 5 and 6 deal with the uses of language, its users, their social organisation and the contacts between them. Chapters 4 and 5 should be read before Chapter 7, which bridges the two sections. Chapters 8, 9 and 10, which discuss phonetic, lexical and textual structures, can then be read in any order. The final chapter attempts to draw together these several threads in a discussion of two practical skills of language manipulation - translating and interpreting.

Each chapter closes with recommendations for further reading. Many of the books listed are themselves introductory, assuming little prior knowledge of the subject but going to greater depths than is possible here. There are also open-ended suggestions for inquiry which generally relate aspects of each chapter to language-learning activities. They are intended as a starting-point for project work and discussion. Titles and publication details of the works of the authors cited in each Further Reading section will be found in the Bibliography (pages 198 - 202).

The special, **bold**, type used in the index enables the reader to locate quickly the page on which a given term is defined or explained.

The phonetic symbols used throughout the book are not explained in detail until Chapter 8. The reader who wishes to refer quickly to their values will find at the end of section 8.2 an illustration of the consonantal symbols and in sections 8.3.1 and 8.3.2 illustration of the vowel symbols.

The symbol * preceding some examples in the text indicates that the word or sentence is in some way anomalous.

The main language of exemplification is English. Where appropriate, examples are also given in other languages, especially French, Spanish, German and Russian. This choice is not meant to imply that the notions presented in the book are applicable only to these five languages; it is simply a reflection of the fact that they are among the languages most widely studied by English-speaking learners.

Finally, the use throughout the book of the personal pronoun *he* does not imply that the world of the language learner is male-dominated; it should be read as an abbreviation of *she/he*.

1

Linguistic Inquiry

> A conversation is one of the commonest phenomena we encounter, yet it is one which raises very great scientific problems, many still unsolved. It is so often our commonest experiences, which we take for granted, that are most elusive of explanation and description.
>
> C. Cherry (1978) *On Human Communication*, p.10

Linguistics has something to do with languages. That much, at least, is implied in the title of this book. It also implies that linguistics is *relevant* to the learning of languages – unless, that is, it were in the vein of *Quantum Physics for Pigeon Breeders*, which is not the intention. It is common to begin a book on a scientific topic – linguistics claims to be a science – with a definition. We will start instead with a question which will give some idea of what inquiry into a language can involve. In subsequent parts of the book we will look at some possible answers to the problems raised by this initial question and try to assess their relevance or otherwise to language learning.

1.1 Can we construct a machine that talks?

Talking machines already exist, of course. There are synthesisers which replicate more or less the sounds of the human voice and which produce whole, recognisable utterances. There is a computer programmed with the symptoms of a host of medical complaints and which answers the questions of young doctors being trained to diagnose correctly different illnesses without putting an agonised patient at risk. Many such systems are already in operation. So the prospects look promising, and the tentative answer is 'yes'. . . But – and this is the first of many questions as we embark on the project – how big is our research budget? And what are the requirements of potential customers? A machine which is to answer time-table inquiries over the telephone will require sound-receiving and producing units unnecessary in a machine which reads invoices and prints the information in tabulated form. Let us look, then, at the kinds of features which would have to be incorporated in the ultimate model, one which would be capable of conversing with human beings and match their ability to produce and understand speech. Let us imagine, too, that the machine is to be English-speaking.

The basic arrangement might well resemble that of a computer, with input and output devices, a memory and a central processor. Just what hardware, in terms of pieces of equipment, do we need and what operations must the software - the programs - be able to carry out?

First of all, do we include an on-off switch? Is the machine to speak only when spoken to, or is it to be allowed to initiate conversations? In the first case we could envisage a voice-activated on-switch, in the second it would require a sensor to detect the presence of a possible (but willing?) conversation partner within hearing and speaking distance. Let us set aside the sensor for a moment to consider further the voice receiver. Humans make all sorts of noises in addition to speech with their vocal tract - they yawn, sneeze, cough, etc. Is the machine to register these and store the information that its interlocutor is tired (or bored?), has a sore throat (or wishes to interrupt?) or has a cold? Is it to respond with *Bless you*, or to seek clarification of the speaker's real physical and emotional state? The cost is already mounting. Let us filter out all these noises. That should not be too problematic in that they sound distinct from speech itself. The filter might also serve to tell the machine the sex of the speaker, as female voices tend to be higher pitched than male voices. That would avoid the unfortunate mistake of saying *Sir* when *Madam* is required. Or is it *Miss*? Somehow the machine has to acquire information on the sex, age and marital status of the addressee. Well, the sensor might supply these details if it can be made to see, which would have the added advantage of recording the gestures that speakers often rely on to illustrate what they are saying. Alternatively, all messages sent to the machine will have to be entirely verbal and entirely explicit.

We have decided that the machine must filter out non-speech sounds when 'listening' by checking all sounds against a description of possible speech sounds of English which is stored in its memory and which presumably serves as the basis for its own ability to utter whole words. The more storage space is used, the more expensive the system becomes in terms of both hardware and running costs, since it is likely to take longer to search for, locate and communicate the required information. Some thought must therefore be given to an economical and efficient organisation of the 'sound bank'. Let us look at the solution of the printer to the similar problem he faces. Stocking all the words of the English language would be a costly business, especially when we consider that even a modest dictionary contains something in the order of 50,000 entries, and an admission that this represents only a selection. Of these words, some, like *a*, *the*, *is* and *of* are used many times in a single page, while others, like *recondite*, may not be encountered in a year of reading. All these thousands of written words can be reduced to different combinations of a mere twenty-six letters, which is a vast saving of storage space. Admittedly, the printer will need a bigger stock of the letters *e*, *u* and *s* than of *q* and *x*, but these are minor details. As with letters, so with sounds. It would be equally economical to establish a 'sound alphabet' for composing spoken words. For English, at least, it is not possible simply to use the written alphabet since there is not always a one-to-one correspondence between a letter or group of letters and its pronunciation. The sequence *-ough* in *cough*, *through*, *bough* and *tough* is illustration enough. The 'sound alphabet' could be streamlined by omitting from it all indication of sounds which do not serve to distinguish one word from another. The *p* in *pun* is aspirated quite strongly [p^h], yet since no two English words are differentiated by the presence or absence of aspiration after *p*, we could choose to disregard this feature.

We seem to be aiming at the description of the largest possible number of units – in this instance, words – in terms of the smallest possible number of components – letters or sounds. Yet the other side of the coin to the economies of storage space is an increase in time due to a need to 'compose' the words. Furthermore, we will have to take up some of the machine's memory with instructions on just how to combine the members of the phonetic alphabets. For example, it needs to know that the initial sound [ʃ] in *sugar* cannot be combined, in English, with the initial sound [t] in *tap*. That is, * [ʃtep] – **shtep* – is an inadmissible sequence. Clearly an optimum balance has to be found between the space devoted to holding basic information, the space for holding instructions and the time allowable for processing.

Designing a machine to produce English speech sounds in acceptable combinations does not appear to pose any insuperable problems. The interpretation of speech sounds by the machine is more problematic. How, for example, is it to distinguish between (1) and (2)?

(1) Beautiful ice-cream!
(2) 'Beautiful!' I scream

Obviously it will need to be able to draw on sources of information other than sound.

Further, how is it to cope with hearing a variety of accents? If it is to understand Scots, Irish, Australian and American accents, then we will have to invent a system which 'translates' from one accent into another. We might also ask whether the machine will sell better if it has an Oxford or a Washington accent. It would seem sensible to construct the 'voice box' so that it is flexible enough to produce the sounds not only of different English accents but also of languages other than English. This would immediately open new markets, but since the sounds of one language are rarely identical to those of another we are again faced with the choice of having a separate entry in the memory for each, or, on the other hand, finding a single set of sound components from which all the actually occurring speech sounds of the world's languages can be 'built'.

Pronouncing words entails more than simply stringing sounds together in an appropriate order. Once they exceed one syllable in length they show a *stress* pattern. For example, it is the second syllable which is stressed in *repeát*, the first in *úndertaker*, though the third syllable is usually more prominent than the second and fourth. We cannot neglect this fact and opt for a (boring?) monotone delivery, because stress is the basis for some important distinctions in meaning, as between *gréen hóuse* and *gréenhouse* or *Frénch místress* and *Frénch mistress*. In addition to word rhythms there are sentence rhythms, or *intonation* patterns which can convey information. *You'll do it* with the stress on *you* and a falling intonation indicates that the speaker has confidence in the other person; placing the stress on *do* with a sharp rise in pitch indicates his incredulity. Do we try to cope with this source of difficulty, or do we inform the machine's interlocutors that it only understands as questions those utterances where there is an inversion of subject and verb auxiliary?

This discussion leads us now to envisage another part of the machine, to be responsible for joining words together to form complete utterances. While we recognise (3) as a jumbled-up English proverb and (4) as being a scrambled version of (5) rather than of (6), we remain at a loss to sort out (7) –

(3) Broth too the spoil cooks many
(4) The the ate hamburger man
(5) The man ate the hamburger
(6) The hamburger ate the man
(7) The the saw man dog

– and we must ensure that the machine does not set any such puzzles for its listeners. We therefore, have to supply a set of rules which it can follow.

A reasonable effort-saving step might be to feed into the machine the grammar rules laid down in an already published textbook of English. This might tell us that, given two sentences like (8) and (9) and provided it is the same man who is being referred to in each, they can be combined to form the single sentence (10):

(8) The vicar blamed the man
(9) The man went mad
(10) The man the vicar blamed went mad

We can easily instruct the machine to perform this operation. But if it is further given the information in (11) and (12) -

(11) The reporter interviewed the vicar
(12) The policeman warned the reporter

- what is to prevent it from reapplying the same rule in logical fashion to come out with (13)?

(13) The man the vicar the reporter the policeman warned interviewed blamed went mad

The machine's human partner is capable of fathoming out the structure of this utterance, probably after requesting at least one repetition, but it is stretching his attention to sentence structure and his short-term memory beyond the limits normally tolerated in conversation. What is feasible for a machine may be unacceptable to a human. Can we devise some safeguard to ensure that the machine does not place too great a burden of comprehension on its interlocutors?

Let us turn now to the machine's own processing of word order in speech addressed to it. What is it to make of an utterance like *Er, would you, mind, well, let me put it like this, er, give me, that is, lend me five pounds*? It would seem an impossible brief to construct a machine to filter out these false starts in a similar fashion to the coughs and other noises, yet human speakers do so constantly.

How is it to interpret an utterance like (14)?

(14) Fighting heavyweights can hurt

It may not be able to decide, any more than could a person, whether (15) or (16) is intended -

(15) Fighting heavyweights do sometimes hurt
(16) Fighting heavyweights does sometimes hurt

- but it must be able to spot the ambiguity and search elsewhere in the conversation for information which can solve the problems. Failing that, it could be programmed to ask *Do you mean 'fighting heavyweights do hurt, or does hurt'?*

Conscious that there is a premium on memory space, we must again explore possible economies. A moment's thought will tell us that there can be no question of storing ready-made sentences, even if this appears an attractive way around having to take time combining sounds to form words and words to form sentences. First of all, the number of possible sentences of English is in practical terms unlimited. Let us consider sentences (17)–(19):

(17) The dog sees the rabbit
(18) The dog will see the rabbit
(19) The rabbit saw the dog

Already, if both *dog* and *rabbit* can function as subject or object and we wish to allow for any of the fourteen tenses of English, we are committed to feeding in twenty-eight sentences. And that is with only one article, one verb and two nouns. A modest dictionary contains 50,000 words, remember. But a saving suggests itself – why not specify a basic sentence pattern into which words of an appropriate part of speech and and appropriate meaning can be slotted? This appears to be a reasonable approach, especially in view of a second fact that even if the machine contained a million sentences it would doubtlessly very soon encounter a situation where not one of them corresponded to the message it wished to convey. Human speakers are constantly uttering new sentences they have never uttered before and interpreting utterances they have never heard before. Our machine must contain at least the rudiments of a similarly *creative* system. By providing it with a further three sets of instructions which would operate on the basic affirmative pattern of (17)–(19), it could be made to transform the order of the words in order to produce interrogative, negative and passive sentences, as in (20–(22):

(20) Will the dog see the rabbit?
(21) The dog won't see the rabbit
(22) The rabbit will be seen by the dog

The three rules can be applied cumulatively to give (23):

(23) Won't the rabbit be seen by the dog?

Performing the same operations on (24) gives (25) –

(24) The boy will kick the ball hard
(25) Won't the ball be kicked hard by the boy?

– which is perfectly comprehensible, of course, but which is somewhat unnatural. It is hard to imagine a person actually saying just that. So are we to tolerate this as machine 'jargon', or can we afford the extra cost of insisting that its output be closer to authentic human speech?

So far we have begged the question of meaning, though it is the basic issue: we speak in order to be meaningful. It is the intention to convey to an interlocutor a request for information, for example, which may favour the use of an interrogative rather than an affirmative sentence pattern. It is the intention to deny some state or event that determines the use of the negation rule, as in (21). But meaning is not confined to word order, it is a characteristic of words themselves. We have looked briefly at the physical properties of words, their expression in letters or sounds. It is now time to consider how words and their intangible meanings can be stored.

Shall we simply give priority to their physical shape? A machine which is to compose poems must be able to locate words according to their ending and number of syllables. Yet these are marginal applications. A conventional solution would be to list them in alphabetical order, using either the conventional or the phonetic alphabet. But given the way computers work, tracing the word *warm* which has been used by its interlocutor, may entail scanning a large number of entries between A and W.

Arranging words by frequency may save time. But apart from the 'function' words mentioned earlier, like *on*, *in*, *and*, *is* and a few 'full' words like *go*, *take*, *make* which are used anywhere and everywhere, how are we to determine a word's frequency? *Scalpel* is frequent in the operating theatre and *tee* on the golf course. The reverse is probably not true. We could adopt, then, an initial grouping by sphere of activity, which amounts essentially to relating words by reference to some common aspect of their meaning. Each group will the be internally ordered according to some principle of shape, frequency or meaning. We might in this way be able to relate *short* to *tall*, *kangaroo* to *marsupial* and *censor* to *film*, while keeping *shatter* and *trilby* apart so that the machine is not tempted to say *His trilby shattered*. We can perhaps economise even more by exploiting the fact that the suffix *-ion*, for example, can be added to many verbs to create an equivalent noun. We need store only a noun-ending rule and the verb forms, with an indication that this particular rule can be applied to these particular verb forms. Similarly, *-ness* can be added to many adjectives to create nouns indicating human qualities: *open-ness*, *kind-ness*, *selfless-ness*, *good-ness*. But what of *warm-ness*? The rule in this case is to add *-th*, it seems. And *charitable-ness*? Can we accept it, or is *charity* the proper form? This question is similar to the issue in (13); sometimes we cannot be sure in our own minds if a rule should be made to apply or not.

Providing the machine with a vocabulary interrelated on several levels is not enough. It can only hold a conversation and answer questions on topics where it possesses a relevant stock of knowledge. Setting up an information file consisting of, say, the *Encyclopaedia Britannica* is not specifically a language problem, yet it is not unrelated to our ponderings here. Is the machine to remember only what is explicitly taught, or will it be able to add to its knowledge of its language and of the world by asking for explanations or even guessing the meaning of a new word from its context? For example, if it heard (26) and did not know what *kumquat* was, then it could be made to respond as in (27) –

(26) I ate a kumquat yesterday
(27) What sort of food is a kumquat?

– rather than asking the very general question *What is a kumquat*? This facility for guessing from the context would be extremely useful in enabling the machine to discover whether the speaker had in mind *flower* or *flour*, *tale* or *tail*, and perhaps allow it to choose between (1) and (2). It would be judicious to instruct the machine to ask not only for the meaning of a word but also for an indication of its acceptability in different situations. *Knackered* may refer to the same state as *exhausted* but they can hardly be used interchangeably in polite company.

We must now consider the machine's ability to take turns in a conversation, which has been taken for granted. First of all, it will need to recognise what *we, it, he, this,* etc., refer to and to use them correctly. To repeat the noun on every occasion the same idea or object is evoked would be another instance of inauthenticity. Then we must guard against *non sequiturs* of the kind *Do you know her*?, *Yes I will* or, even worse, *Yes, I was*. Next it will, ideally, respond to an utterance like *Can you spell 'brain'*? with not only the answer *Yes* but also the information indirectly requested. If it were to reply to questions of the form *Will you tell me* . . . ? by *No*, its chances of selling at all would be extremely slim.

The complexity of the task is daunting. It was remarked upon in the seventeenth century *Discourse on Method* (1637) by Descartes who foresaw even then the thorny problem of ensuring appropriate responses:

> [It is easy] to understand a machine's being constituted so that it can utter words, and even emit some responses to action on it of a corporeal kind, which brings about a change in its organs; for instance if it is touched in a particular part it may exclaim that it is being hurt, and so on. But it never happens that it arranges its speech in various ways, in order to reply appropriately to everything that may be said in its presence, as even the lowest type of men can do.

We may not have progressed very far in the construction of the machine, but we have glimpsed something of the complexity of 'holding a conversation'. This common experience, at least, should no longer be taken for granted. It would seem wise to leave the drawing-board for the time being in order to see how contemporary researchers have approached the study of this possibility for self-expression enjoyed by 'even the lowest type of men' and which we call *language*.

1.2 Language and languages

Language, to give the barest of definitions, is a means of verbal communication. To communicate by speaking is not a gratuitous act; it is purposeful, and thus language has an instrumental aspect. Communication can only take place successfully if the means of communication is agreed upon by its users, and thus language has a social, conventional aspect. Society as we know it could not exist without language, and indeed, for some, it is a defining characteristic of the human race itself, far exceeding in sophistication any animal communication system (see 2.4).

To *language* viewed in abstract terms we can oppose the many thousands of *languages* – Hopi, Quechua, Basque, English, etc. – spoken in different parts of the world in specific communities (see 2.1). Linguistics concerns itself with both language and languages; its central task is to describe the characteristics of language, which unavoidably entails reference to a given language, if not several. Sometimes a distinction is drawn between *linguistician*, a practitioner of linguistics, and *linguist*, a person who studies languages in order to gain a practical command of them. But in this book we shall avoid using the longer term and mean by 'linguist' someone interested in understanding the particular features of a particular language and the general principles of language. Where the emphasis is on the ability to speak or write a second langauge, we talk of a *language learner*.

1.3 Linguistics – general

Human beings, not only scientists, have a natural inclination to differentiate and categorise persons, things and events in the world around them. For instance, we class people by income, by shape, by personality, describing them as rich, poor, fat, thin, outgoing, introvert, and so on. For the layman the dividing-lines between categories and within categories are fuzzy. The economist, the doctor and the psychologist, on the other hand, strive for a better understanding of 'richness', 'fatness' and 'extroversion' and thereby for a precise and professionally agreed definition. At the same time, the medical doctor and the psychologist try to establish the limits of their respective science. This is not to say that their concerns should remain entirely separate and without overlap, though it is not uncommon to hear specialists in one field accusing colleagues in a neighbouring discipline of encroaching unlawfully on 'their territory'. Such a parochial attitude is less productive than a readiness to learn from other disciplines and co-operate across established boundaries, so helping gradually to redefine them and to extend human knowledge. But it does illustrate that the need to explore a particular problem is sometimes in conflict with an overrigid frame of reference.

Linguistics, too, attempts to determine which phenomena lie within its province and which fall beyond its scope. By our initial definition, the province of linguistics is language. To describe language linguists develop models and assign labels to the components of these models, just as a cartographer models an area of the Earth's surface by drawing a map and providing a key for its interpretation. Labelling is a use of language to describe language, in other words a *meta-language*. There are many schools of thought as to what language is, each having therefore its own model and its own meta-language. It would be neither appropriate nor possible to enter here into the many debates that are taking place. We will confine ourselves to examining in outline the components of a broadly accepted model of language and looking briefly at some of the differing but complementary approaches to the complex behaviour we attempted to simulate on our machine.

1.3.1 A descriptive framework

The machine project caused us to consider three different types of relationship, all of which are recognised fields of linguistic inquiry. First, there is the relationship between words – the meaningful units of language – and the outside world. Its study goes under the heading of *semantics*. Semantics is also concerned with describing how all the words of a language relate to one another, that is, with describing the lexical system of that language (9.4.1). Second, there is the relationship between words themselves in so far as they can be combined into sentences of the type, say, subject + verb + object: *Boris buys butter.* Its study is known as *syntax*. Third, we have the relationship between language and the situation in which it is used. We call this area of study *pragmatics*. If we take, for example, sentence (25) above, a semantic analysis will attempt to establish the meaning carried by each of the words. A possible question for investigation might be to ascertain why nobody understands *ball* to mean 'dance'. A syntactic analysis describes a construction in terms of auxiliary, article, noun, verb, adverb, etc., and shows how word order contributes to meaning. It may also relate (25) to (24). A pragmatic analysis may question what effect the speaker was trying to achieve by uttering this string of words and why he was or was not successful in achieving that effect.

If we now return briefly to our hypothetical machine, we can pick out from our reflections in 1.1 four aspects of its specification:

(a) A *system* of rules which governs the combination of sounds and words and which relates these to meanings. To describe such a system of interrelated rules for a given language is to write a *grammar* of that language. Using the terms introduced so far, we can say that grammars show how speakers use syntactic structures to achieve semantic and pragmatic goals.

(b) A system of rules which governs the *appropriateness* of the use of the grammar rules. These are, then, pragmatic rules and would operate for example, to select the use of short, simple constructions, familiar words and a gentle voice when talking to children.

(c) The *producing* of the output. Establishing rules (a) and (b) is one thing; making them function as intended is another. A gap in our technological expertise may mean that the execution of certain operations is just not *feasible*. Machines are liable to crossed wires, short circuits and breakdowns, the result being that the rules are imperfectly obeyed. Humans likewise suffer from interference – lapses of memory, tiredness, stress, lack of breath – with similar results. They 'um' and 'ah', stutter, forget to end what they are saying, mispronounce words.

(d) The *actual* output. It is the only physical manifestation of the rules and their execution. The output may contain errors, as in (3) and (4), which lead us to conclude that either the execution has gone haywire or that the grammar rules need revising as they cannot be considered an adequate description of English. Humans often correct themselves both in writing and in speech: *I weren't, sorry, wasn't ready*. If they do not, we can ask a speaker who says (6) if that is what he really meant to say, since to us it seems anomalous. We can thus decide whether our judgements of what is 'correct English' and what is not are in agreement. Judgements by different speakers do not always coincide, as in the case of *charitableness* earlier or of *The government have resigned*. Is it *have* or *has*? Differing answers will result in differing grammars.

Let us now see to what extent these four constructs have been considered worthy of attention by linguists.

1.3.2 'Langue' and 'parole'

The fundamental distinction between the system and its physical manifestation characterises much of linguistics today. This insight is credited to the Swiss linguist Ferdinand de Saussure, who is generally held to be the 'father of modern linguistics'. The modern era dates from the posthumous publication of his lecture notes by two of his former pupils, in 1916. He termed the physical manifestation of the system *parole*. This covers both (c) and (d) above – 'speaking' and 'speech'. He makes no mention of aspect (b) – rules for use – but we can assume that it too would be relegated to *parole*, which de Saussure sees as individual, heterogeneous and accidental. De Saussure rejects all this potential subject-matter as too disparate for profitable study. For him the object of linguistics is the description of *langue*, which is 'a self-contained whole' (1974, p. 9). His treatment of *langue* concentrates on semantics and phonology to the exclusion of syntax (which for him may conceivably be part of *parole*); so *langue* is not quite identical to our system (a).

It is worth devoting some time to the notion of 'self-contained whole', which is related to that of *system*. Now a commonplace, it was at the time revolutionary. If we take de Saussure's own analogy of a chess game in progress, each piece has a theoretical potential to move – the rook along the diagonals, etc – but its actual freedom to move, its real value, is determined by the position of all the other pieces on the board which block its path or threaten vacant positions. As one piece moves or is removed, so the value of all the other pieces changes. The semantic, phonological and syntactic dimensions of a grammar can also be viewed as systems in which the elements are mutually defining. Moreover, the medium in which the elements are expressed – their substance – is irrelevant to the system. That the pieces are of wood or of ivory does not alter their values. The important property of speech sounds is not their physical substance but the fact that they are consistently *different* from each other. Relations – form – are all-important. Language is form, not substance.

1.3.3 Competence and performance

Noam Chomsky has been arguably the most influential figure in linguistics since de Saussure. His views on language and his particular conception of grammars are widely publicised by both his supporters and his detractors, but again these wider issues lie beyond the scope of this book. We can equate *performance* with *parole* and with our constructs (b) – (d). Chomsky, like de Saussure, effectively disregards performance in order to study the *underlying* system which makes performance possible, and which he terms *competence*. However, he sees competence as dynamic, in contrast to de Saussure's static view of *langue* as an 'inventory', and accords prime importance to syntax. More important is his statement that competence is 'the speaker-hearer's knowledge of his language' (1965, p.4). For Chomsky a grammar is not just an abstract, relational system in the sense of *langue*; it is an account of competence, therefore of linguistic *knowledge*. But as such it is wanting in two respects. First, a speaker's judgement of what is or is not 'English' is often indecisive and ill-defined, whereas competence is said to be well-defined. Second, a speaker's knowledge of his language obviously includes a knowledge of (c) above, that is, when to use it and when to remain silent; but this is ignored by Chomsky as 'mere' performance. Chomsky's grammar holds great interest as a partial description of a particular language but is inadequate as a model of the place of language in the mind.

1.3.4 Communicative competence

It would be wrong to imagine that all linguists agree with Chomsky in thinking that 'linguistic theory is concerned primarily with an ideal speaker-listener, in a completely homogeneous speech-community, who knows its language perfectly' (1965, p. 3). Dell Hymes approaches language from a socio-cultural viewpoint with the aim of embracing the tremendous variety of ways of speaking which are found within the individual and within the community. Speakers vary their performance not at random but in a regular way. Thus there is no reason why the notion of competence, restricted by Chomsky to a *knowledge of grammar*, cannot be extended to incorporate the pragmatic ability for its use. We refer to this extended idea of competence as *communicative competence*. The goal of a theory of communicative competence is 'to show the ways in which the systemically possible, the feasible, and the appropriate are linked to produce and interpret actually occurring [speech] ' (in Pride and Holmes, 1972, p. 286). The four aspects of communicative competence specified here by Hymes match our features (a) – (d) outlined earlier. They are all relevant to the language learner.

The language learner is not content to *know* the grammar of a language, as the linguist may be. Yet he cannot communicate without this systematic formal knowledge of the relation between sound and meaning. His goal is to develop a functional ability to *use* language as an effective instrument in a given situation, that is, to use language appropriately. Impinging on the feasibility of achieving proficiency in a second language there are many factors connected with memory, personality, age, motivation, teaching and contact with the other community.

What data does the learner need in order to acquire communicative competence? The rules of a grammar produce *sentences*, free from slips of the tongue and sudden changes of construction or topic They are not related to any particular speaker or situation, nor even to any particular function. Real speakers produce *utterances*, containing many or few 'blemishes', in real situations and for a purpose. The language learner is faced with the problem of filtering out – on the basis of non-native intuitions – what is pertinent and what is not in order to extend his knowledge of the systems which underlie performance. This means being attentive not only to what is said and what is not said, but also to the actions and intentions of the persons involved and the situation in which communication takes place.

Linguists are only just beginning to investigate the 'rules for use'. Even if these were better understood, it is difficult to see how they could be taught in a classroom. They can be investigated adequately only in the community where they apply, and they can be learnt adequately only in that same setting. The fact that we are unable to give an explicit account of these pragmatic rules does not mean that it is impossible to learn them. We speak our native language without knowing how we form the sounds or what meaning is, and it is no less possible to acquire a 'feel' for a second language without knowing how this comes about.

1.4 Linguistics - plural

There is not one linguistics, there are several. We should consider it a plural rather than a singular noun. From their differing viewpoints they create different pictures of language, just as an infra-red photograph of a tree, distinguishing dead from living cells, is different from a colour photograph of the same tree which highlights the shades of colour in the leaves. The two views are equally real. Their interest depends on the photographer's goal.

De Saussure's goal was to establish the autonomy of linguistics, giving it a well-defined object and freeing it from reliance on other disciplines. With its coming of age linguistics is developing integrative links with other sciences. The central goal of describing the underlying system remains; this is the province of general, descriptive linguistics. But since language has both individual and social aspects, it is naturally of interest to psychologists and sociologists among others.

Psycholinguistics investigates the interrelation of language and mind, in processing and producing utterances and in language acquisition, for example. Chomsky goes so far as to define linguistics as a branch of psychology, thus denying it any autonomous status.

Sociolinguistics is an umbrella term which covers a variety of different interests in language and society, including the social functions of language and the social characteristics of its users. Here again there are overlaps with objectives which are seen by some as more particularly anthropological, ethnographic or social-psychological. One focus of this last hybrid is on attitudes to languages and their users. The boundaries are fuzzy, but that need matter little to the language learner, who wishes simply to gather eclectically any information which has a bearing on his goal of communicative competence.

The findings of linguistics, mathematics and artificial intelligence contribute to the construction of machines which are responsible for the storage and retrieval of information and its processing in various ways, which include automated abstracting and translation.

There are many applications of the results of psycholinguistic, sociolinguistic and grammatical studies. The elaboration of remedial exercises for people with speech handicaps and of educational programmes for multilingual communities are but two examples. Generally, however, the term *applied linguistics* is reserved for applications in the teaching field - not only foreign-language teaching, but also first language courses in schools and adult-literacy programmes. In this domain the emphasis is on *prescribing* the learner's performance rather than describing usage.

Linguists often find themselves working, therefore, in close co-operation with researchers in other fields. In common they have an interest in language and the same scientific approach. Whether it is the speech habits of an individual or the languages of Europe that are under investigation, the approach must be systematic, using a clearly defined descriptive system which will not exclude any of the data and which is free of internal contradictions. The model constructed should not only account for the data from which it is derived; it should have predictive power. In other words, if we claim to have described how an individual talks to colleagues at work on the basis of a recorded sample of utterances, we should expect that any utterance produced at a later date should also be adequately described within the terms of our model. The more precise the prediction, the better. A prediction that the individual will speak after lifting the telephone receiver is of virtually no value. But to predict that he will address male colleagues, female colleagues and superiors in differing, specified styles is of more interest. A failed prediction necessitates the revision of the model, so that when he addresses a superior in the same style as a male colleague, we must introduce a new hypothesis - that membership of the same club or age group overrides status, say - and test that. In this way individual idiosyncrasies can be distinguished from behaviour patterns which are widespread throughout a community. Such an approach is known as the *hypothetico-deductive* method and it is characteristic of many sciences. It is important to remember that the model and the phenomenon it purports to describe are not one and the same. Models are partial, in both senses of the word, and their characteristic precision which distinguishes 'possible' from 'impossible' without an intermediate 'perhaps' finds no total counterpart in language use itself.

Linguistics has served as a model for many other spheres of inquiry seemingly as far apart as art and genetics. Crick, one of the 'breakers of the DNA code', and François Jacob talk of the 'four-letter language' of nucleic acid molecules, of 'message', 'information', 'alphabet', 'ideogram', 'sentence', 'writing'. At a more abstract level linguistics and genetics *are* linked, by a common interest in communication.

In outlining a 'total science of communication' to interpret society as a whole, Jakobson proposes three provinces of inquiry of increasing generality (1973, p. 36). The most specific is *linguistics* – the study of communication by the exchange of verbal messages – and it is the model for the other two. Second, there is *semiotics* – the study of communication by the exchange of any messages, whether pictorial, choreographic, theatrical, vestimentary or verbal. Finally, there are *social anthropology* and *economics* – the study of communication by the exchange of mates, money, goods and services, often involving verbal messages, such as cheques, marriage licences and contracts.

Such wide horizons can only be glimpsed here. We look more closely in Chapter 2 at languages and language before pursuing in the following chapters our concern with the various facets of communicative competence.

Further reading

Note: Here and in the Further Reading section of each of the following chapters, the title and publication details of the works by the authors cited are given in the Bibliography at the end of the book.

Hartmann and Stork (1972) provide succinct explanation of unfamiliar terms. Crystal (1974) gives a concise and lucid account of what linguistics is and is not, and presents in another study (1971) a fuller account of its development and major themes. Aitchison (1978) is a general introduction for beginners. Other accessible discussions are to be found in Stork and Widdowson (1974), Fowler (1974), Pilch (1976), Cherry (1978), and Fromkin and Rodman (1978). Lyons (1968) and Robins (1971) are classic and comprehensive treatments of general descriptive linguistics. Expositions of the work of de Saussure and Chomsky are given in Culler (1976) and Lyons (1977) respectively. Smith and Wilson (1979) offer a well-illustrated account of post-Chomskyan developments. For readers with some knowledge of linguistics Robins (1979) traces the history of the subject from Greece to the twentieth century. Finally, Magee (1975) is an introduction to contemporary scientific method.

Suggestions for inquiry

1 Order the following words according to their relative frequency in English: *computer*, *tea*, *class*, *chip*, *allay*.
2 List ten ways of getting someone to finish what they are drinking.
3 Are they all appropriate in the same situation?
4 Each member of a group writes at the left-hand end of a strip of paper a word which can figure at the beginning of an English sentence, and passes the paper to a neighbour. Each person adds a second word which is syntactically and semantically compatible with the first. The process is repeated; each time a strip of paper is passed on, it is folded so that only the last word is visible. The aim is to produce English sentences.
   (a) How do the participants know when to stop?
   (b) Are the sentences grammatical?
   (c) Do constraints on word choice operate only between adjacent words?
   (d) What would be a better way to plan and produce sentences?
5 Is it possible to refer the design of the individual components of the talking machine discussed in 1.1 to either grammatical or sociolinguistic or psycholinguistic studies alone?

2

Shared Heritage

> Except as an abstraction from reality, language does not exist in a vacuum; it is a human activity performed in time and space and in almost constant interaction of one human being with one or more others.
>
> W. Winter (1973) 'Areal Linguistics: Some General Considerations', in Th. A. Sebeok (ed.), *Current Trends in Linguistics*, vol. II (Mouton: The Hague) p. 147

In the previous chapter we made a distinction between languages and language (1.2). Here we propose to consider at some length contacts between the languages of Western and Eastern Europe and their degree of relatedness to each other. Then we will look briefly at some deeper similarities between languages, features which can be thought to underly language in general and distinguish man, as the possessor of this particular capacity for self-expression, from beast.

2.1 Back to Babel

The number of languages spoken in the world today runs into thousands, possibly as many as ten thousand, certainly more than five. They are no more equally distributed than is wealth, and this link between the vitality of a language and the power of its speakers is by no means accidental. According to Katzner, fewer than 100 languages are spoken by over 95 per cent of the earth's population (1977, p. viii). The language with the greatest number of native speakers is Chinese, with an estimated 800 million speakers, some 20 per cent of the world's population. In second place is English, with in excess of 300 million native speakers, but as the world's most widely spoken second language it is also its leading means of communication, numerically speaking. Third is Spanish, which is the native tongue of over 225 million people in Europe and South America. This number is increasing rapidly. Within the Soviet Union there were in 1970 some 184 million speakers of Russian, making it one of the world's major languages. Arabic is the mother tongue of approximately 120 million people and, as the language of the *Koran*, it reaches an audience of many more millions. The 100 million speakers of German are concentrated mostly in Europe, while some 75 million native speakers of French are to be found in Europe, Africa, South-east Asia and North America.

We know that in the recent past many other languages have become extinct because those who spoke them have died or been assimilated into a social group possessing a different tongue. This is especially true of the Indian languages of North, Central and South America. But the process can also be witnessed in Europe among the dwindling community of North Friesian speakers living in Schleswig, along Denmark's southern border. Welsh is not dead, but its survival hangs by the tenuous thread of a further revival of Welsh nationalism in the face of English economic and political dominance. It is impossible to predict the destiny of the world's surviving languages. We can simply point, on the basis of our knowledge of the past, to the manifold social forces which together determine the fate of groups of speakers united by a common language (see 4.5 and 5.3).

This decline, fast or slow, in the number of human languages does not remove the need to explain how such a bewildering diversity of tongues came to be. Even ignoring the thousand American Indian languages, the hundreds of Malayo-Polynesian languages and the forty Caucasian languages, how can we account for the 'crazy quilt of languages' which covers the comparatively small area of Western and Eastern Europe shown in Figure 2.1? Why does the number of human languages exceed the number of human races by a thousandfold? Some have put forward a theory of 'the survival of the fittest' which would seek to explain the diversification of languages as an adaptation to differing ecological factors and their subsequent reduction in number as a consequence of selective survival. But, as we shall see in 6.1, no language is dependent on its milieu in the same way as a plant which has evolved over the millennia in adaptation to a certain environment and which will wither if re-rooted in a hostile climate: 'With the simple addition of neologisms and borrowed words, any language can be used fairly efficiently anywhere; Eskimo syntax is appropriate to the Sahara' (Steiner, 1975, p. 55). The presumption of the *inherent* suitability of a given language for its particular setting is an invalid foundation for any account of this great diversity. What could be the evolutionary justification for placing in the way of communication between men a barrier which can be surmounted only by translation, with the inefficiencies and inadequacies which this entails?

Figure 2.1
The European languages quilt

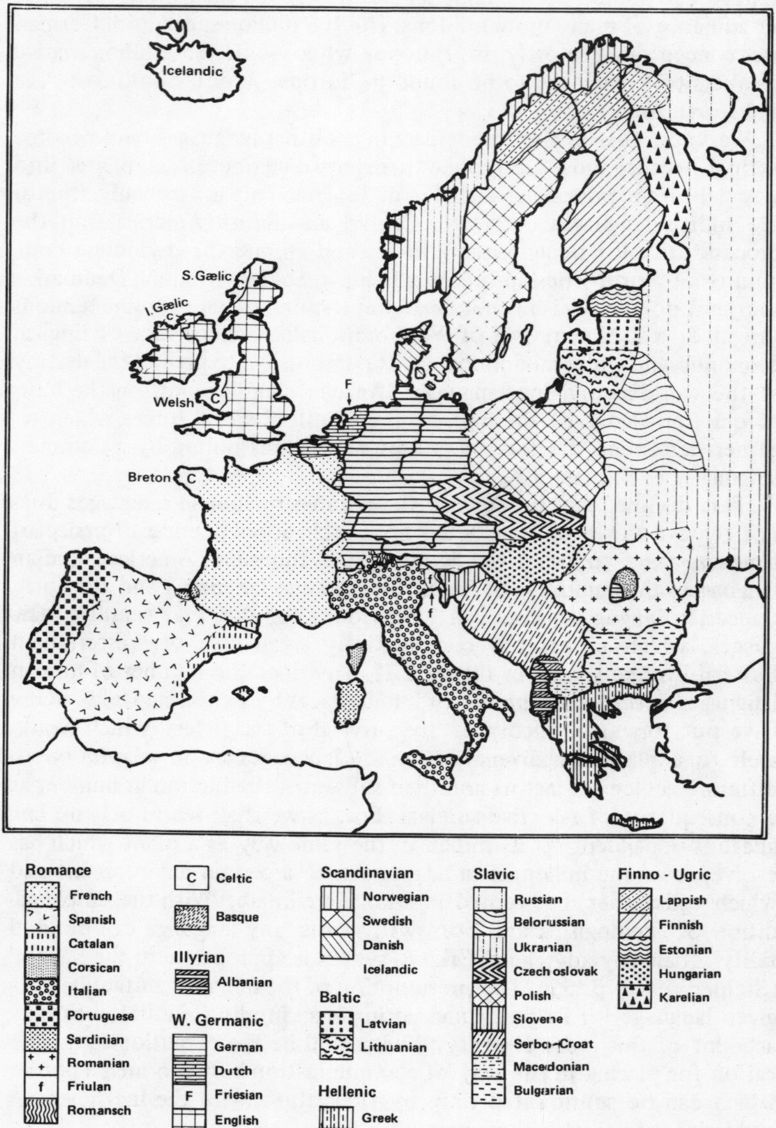

Since, therefore, the evolutionary model suggested for plant and animal life does not apply to languages, let us turn to mythology for an answer. *Genesis* (11:1-9) describes the attempts of man, at a time when 'the whole earth was of one language and of one speech', to build a city and a tower which came to be known as Babel 'because the Lord did there confound the language of all the earth, and from thence did the Lord scatter them abroad upon the face of all the earth'. Thus diversification is seen as a divine act of punishment, and man's quest is to rediscover this unitary language of Eden, a pure and direct mode of communication with God.

Over the centuries many thinkers have maintained that the tongue spoken prior to Babel must represent a primal *Ursprache* from which have sprung the languages of the world. There was much speculation about the nature of this mystic tongue of God, some people claiming that it must have been Hebrew or one of its ancestors.

2.1.1 Language families

Whether they have shared these particular beliefs and motivations or not, there has been great interest among linguists, especially in the late eighteenth and nineteenth centuries, in demonstrating historical connections between languages. The branch of linguistics concerned with tracing the changes in languages over time is known as *comparative philology*, and at that period it was the main preoccupation of linguistic inquiry in general.

It is easy to see from Figure 2.2 that there are greater than random similarities between vocabulary items in the five languages. Column 1 shows a threefold division: the similarity is very high between English and German, and considerable between French and Spanish, while Russian is isolated. Column 2 no longer shows Russian to be so dissimilar, and although the other groupings remain, the gap between them has narrowed. Columns 3 and 4 show distinct similarities between all five

Figure 2.2
Word similarities in some European languages

	1	2	3	4
English	*hand*	*give*	*mother*	*month*
German	*Hand*	*geben*	*Mutter*	*Monat*
French	*main*	*donner*	*mère*	*mois*
Spanish	*mano*	*donar*	*madre*	*mes*
Russian	*рука* (ruka)	*давать* (davat')	*мать* (mat')	*месять* (mjesjat')

languages. On the basis of extensive language data linguists have concluded that where such similarities between pairs or groups of languages are regular and systematic, these languages can be said to be related. The isolated fact that the word for 'black' in Hausa, an African language, is pronounced [bakl] is no basis for assuming a genetic link with English. The degrees of relationship vary according to the number of features taken into account, as we have just seen. The languages spoken today in Europe are traditionally classified into eight groups: (1) Germanic; (2) Romance; (3) Celtic; (4) Hellenic (Greek); (5) Illyrian (Albanian); (6) Slavic; (7) Baltic; (8) Finno-Ugric. It is accepted that the Finno-Ugric languages are distinct from the language groups (1)–(7), which, moreover, show a high degree of interrelatedness. They constitute the *Indo-European* language family, and, as the family name indicates, they are related to the languages of India, like Hindi, Urdu and Gujarati, and also to Persian and Kurdish. Many such family groupings have been established, though several languages, among them Basque, Japanese and Vietnamese, have not been conclusively related to any other language.

2.1.2 Linguistic reconstruction

In classifying the languages of Europe into the above groupings 'here and now' we have adopted a *synchronic* perspective, that is, we have looked at a *system* of relations (see 1.3.2) at a given point in time. Naturally, it is impossible to carry out any analysis of a language at literally 'one point in time' after the fashion of an instantaneous snapshot; no study can claim to be any more than relatively synchronic. However, the evidence on which the classification rests is gleaned from investigations of the development of these languages over much longer periods of time, in most cases over centuries, in some cases over millenia. To look at language change over time, whether the span is of 20 or 2,000 years, is to adopt a *diachronic* perspective. A diachronic comparison of, say, the English language of Chaucer in 1400 and the English language today presupposes the establishment of synchronic analyses of the language at those two times. Let us give some attention to the data and the methods used in these tasks.

The oldest records of an Indo-European language are Anatolian Hittite texts from Syria dating back to the seventeenth century BC. The sacred Indo-Aryan scriptures of the Vedic Sanskrit of the *Rgveda* are appropriately 3,000 years old. There are some Greek tablets which may date from 1400 BC, but the oldest lengthy Greek texts are the Homeric epics of the eight century BC. The earliest Latin inscriptions are about 2,500 years old, and the age of the first literary texts is some 300 years less. Informative records of Germanic are young by comparison, dating back only to the fourth century AD. No records of Celtic survive from before 700 AD, and the earliest Slavic texts in Old Church Slavonic date from 800 AD onwards. The oldest substantial material in Baltic comes from the late fourteenth century.

It is evident that these data are only fragmentary. However, considered together with archaeological findings, they can be used to help piece together the history of peoples and civilisations. In addition, techniques have been developed in order to supply the missing pieces in this linguistic jigsaw-puzzle. *Internal reconstruction* works on the assumption that language change is gradual, that it affects not just isolated elements but the whole of the system, and that changes leave remnants in the form of irregularities which can be traced back to earlier regularities. On this basis linguists attempt to establish for a given language a chronological sequence of changes which resulted in its earliest documented linguistic state and thereby reconstruct a prior stage in its development. For example, many English words ending in the unvoiced sound [f] simply add [s] in the plural, thus *reef*: [rif, rifs]. Others, like *leaf*, add [z] and also give the preceding consonant the value of voiced [v], hence [livz]. We can postulate that at an earlier time even *leaf* had a plural pronounced [lifs], which simplified and regularised the pattern. We can further surmise that it was the same alternation of unvoiced and voiced final consonants in singular and plural forms of nouns that affected words like *sheath* and that its plural form was once pronounced [ʃiθs] and not [ʃiðz].

The logical extension of such reconstructions and of the existence of regular correspondences between related languages is to attempt to trace the members of a language family back to a 'parent' language. The model adopted is that of the family tree showing a chain of downward transmission of inherited features from one stage to the next, and in which the closeness or remoteness of the branches is a reflection of the relatedness of the languages. This *comparative method* aims to reconstruct *proto-languages*, which are unattested by actual texts (reconstructed forms are marked *). Thus, on the evidence of Old English *cyning* ('king') and Old Saxon and Old High German *kuning* linguists assumed a Proto-Germanic form * *kuningaz*. The validity of this informed guess appears to be borne out by the Finnish *kuningas* ('king'), which must have been borrowed from Germanic at a time which predates our records of the language.

This last example illustrates that a genetic model of vertical transmission cannot account for all the facts of relationships between languages. Features are also transferred horizontally from one group of speakers to another with whom they are in communication. The 'borrowing' of 'foreign' elements occurs in response to a need which may be material – the establishing of trade links, for example – or because the linguistic behaviour of the other group is seen as prestigious or fashionable (see 5.3 and 6.2). This *wave model* of linguistic change emanating from a prestigious centre is interesting in that the nature and direction of the transfers can shed light on the relationship between the communities. However, the notion of geographically related languages suffices only to explain changes in the permeable area of vocabulary (see 6.2.3). It is no more than a complement to the notion of genetic relations which account for the transmission of syntactic features.

Attempts are also made to determine the relative chronology of the branchings of the family tree and to date their emergence. Of course, languages do not suddenly 'split'; the drift apart is a gradual process. Moreover, the method used, which assumes a regular 'turnover' of the basic vocabulary of each language, may not be wholly reliable For these two reasons any date must be taken as an approximation, unless corroborated by archaeological or palaeontological evidence. It is thought that the Anatolian, Indo-Aryan and Greek families of Indo-European branched off between 3000 and 2000 BC. These are descendants of a proto-Indo-European tongue spoken by a population traced back as far as the fifth millennium BC and which inhabited a region east of the Dnieper, north of the Caucasus and west of the Urals. This culture spread westwards to span, by 3000 BC, an area from eastern central Europe to northern Iran. As the culture broke up, so the speech diverged more and more until distinct languages emerged.

It is probable that the Indo-European languages are related to the Uralic family, of which Finnish and Hungarian are members. But the existing evidence is insufficient to allow the reconstruction of 'Indo-Uralic'. Thus to go back even further in time is out of the question, and the rediscovery of the lost *Ursprache* (if indeed it ever existed) must be forever beyond our reach.

2.2 Linguistic diversity in Europe

To follow the migrations from the Russian steppes and the splitting of the many groups over a period of 5,000 years would require more space than is available here. So we will now focus on some of the vicissitudes, in terms of prestige and official status, of the languages and major dialects spoken in Europe today. We shall see that the threatened survival of certain of these languages is due not to any inherent inadequacies but to a lack of autonomous political and economic power on the part of their speakers.

2.2.1 The Romance languages

French is a modern development of the Latin introduced to Gaul after Caesar's conquest of the area in 58–51 BC. Standard French is based on the Francien dialect of the Île de France which achieved pre-eminence after Paris became the capital in the twelfth century. Francien gradually displaced the Norman and Picard dialects and in 1539 was declared the sole official language. Many dialects survive today, the most prominent being the *Occitan* group situated in the sourthern half of the country. Occitan took its name from *la langue d'oc* in contrast to *la langue d'oil* spoken in the northern half of the country (*oc* and *oil* are the equivalents of *oui*). Although some ten million people know some Occitan, only an estimated two million use it with any regularity, and this in rural settings among older speakers. All can use French if required. The idea of an independent Occitanie is still dear to the heart of many *Méridionaux* but the process of decline shows no real sign of being arrested. Since the *Loi Deixonne* of 1951 Occitan has been taught in some schools but its prestige remains low compared with that of the politically powerful Parisian speech, despite attempts by regionalists to boost it. Its hope lies in the devolution of powers to the regions. One Occitan dialect, *Provençal*, has a small number of speakers in an area which extends across the Alps into Piedmont in north-eastern Italy. In the opposite corner of Occitanie *Gascon* is somewhat isolated from the other dialects in the group. It is less close to them than is Catalan, probably because the inhabitants of Béarn used their own standardised official language until after 1620 when the region was incorporated into France. They are also thought to have had close ties with the Basques. French is spoken by the Walloons of Belgium, where it is an official language, a status it enjoys in Luxemburg and Switzerland also. Its use is widespread in the Aosta Valley in Italy, just to the north-east of Piedmont.

Italian has a large number of dialects ranging from Piedmontese, in which some claim to see a Celtic influence, to Sicilian, which may bear traces of the Greek once spoken there. These two extremes are not necessarily mutually intelligible. The standard language is based on the Tuscan dialect, especially Florentine. Italian is spoken in the Tessin canton of Switzerland and is an official language there. A majority of the population of the northern half of Corsica speaks *Corsican*, a language related to Tuscan Italian. The idiom of the sourthern part of the island is closer to *Sardinian*, which is considered to be the Romance language closest to Latin. There is no one standard form; older members of the population speak one of three dialects, which are offering no resistance to the spread of Italian, the island's other official language.

Catalan is spoken by about 12,000 inhabitants of Alghero in Sardinia, which has maintained links with Spain since 1327, when the house of Aragon established an administration lasting until the beginning of the eighteenth century. Catalan's homeland extends along Spain's north-western coast into the Roussillon area of France. To this side of the political border Catalan retains its vitality among the workers in the predominantly agricultural economy, despite the absence of any official status for it. Its survival is without any doubt due to the resurgence of Catalan nationalist feeling south of the border and the recent granting of some measure of administrative freedom to the Spanish province. Catalan had been stripped of its official status in 1938, but it is now, once again, the vehicle for a flourishing press and literature. Whether Catalan is more closely related to Spanish or Occitan is a matter of some dispute, but it is the latter affinity which is stressed by those who wish to assert Catalan independence. The language is also spoken in Andorra and the Balearic Islands.

The standard dialect of *Spanish* is Castilian. The Castilians played a major role in the reconquest of Spain, completed in the fifteenth century. Their prestige dialect was widely adopted, then developed in Toledo in the sixteenth and seventeenth centuries. It has been modified more recently by the influence of Madrid.

Portuguese and Spanish could be considered dialects of the same language since they are to a great degree mutually comprehensible. In the north-west corner of Spain *Galician*, or Gallego-Portuguese, is spoken; it is considered by the people of Portugal to be an archaic form of their own language. In fact it is from this area, originally populated in the second century BC by small communities of Celtic stock, that the language spread southwards. But as Portugal prospered and Galicia came increasingly into the shadow of Castilian, the speech of the two communities diverged, though even today Galician and Portuguese are virtually indistinguishable in print. Deprived of official status and of prestige, despite a fairly rich literature, the language remains vulnerable to Castilian interference.

Standard *Romanian* is based on a variety of Daco-Romanian centred on Bucharest. Dacia was the name of the Roman province created by Trajan in 107 AD and evacuated by Aurelian in 275AD, and whose frontiers correspond to those of today's Romania. There is some argument over the continuity of a Romance linguistic tradition in the area, but this thesis is hotly upheld by the Romanians themselves in defence of their present borders and their independent political stance within a Slav-dominated Warsaw Pact. Romanian is also spoken in small pockets of Bulgaria, Yugoslavia and Hungary, and by many inhabitants of the Moldavian SSR, an area reclaimed after the war by the Soviet Union, where it is officially known as Moldavian.

Romansch, spoken by only 1 per cent of Switzerland's population in the Grisons canton, yet one of the country's four official languages, is a dialect of the Rhaeto-Romance family, as is the *Friulan* dialect of the Italian province of Udine. The Rhaetian language was widely spoken through Switzerland and southern Austria and parts of Bavaria until the ninth century when it was overwhelmed by the advance of German and Italian dialects. The surviving Rhaetian dialects lack any standardisation and are not mutually intelligible.

2.2.2 The Germanic languages

The Goths were firmly located in southern Scandinavia and along the Baltic and North Sea coasts at around 750 BC. Over the next 1,000 years they spread throughout an area ranging from Scandinavia and Jutland south to the Danube and east through Dacia to the Black Sea. Up to 400-odd Germanic groups crossed to England and conquered much of the country, while the Elbe group spread into parts of Switzerland, Austria and northern Italy.

The Celtic tongues spoken in Britain were largely displaced by the settlement in the fifth and sixth centuries of Jutes, Saxons and Angles. *Old English* dates from this period. The Jutes settled in Kent and southern Hampshire, the Saxons occupied the rest of England south of the Thames, and the Angles took over the remaining areas of England and the Scottish lowlands. Their distinctive dialects were retained, and in the Anglian region Northumbrian and Mercian speech groups developed north and south of the Humber. The Danish and then Norwegian invasions of the eighth and ninth centuries robbed Northumbria of its cultural pre-eminence, and the West Saxon dialect of Winchester became the standard. This supremacy was, in its turn, lost after the Norman Conquest. As London became the seat of culture, the Kentish dialect spread considerably, confining West Saxon to the south-west. Northumbrian split into Northern and Scottish; and Mercian became divided into West and East Midland, the latter being recognised as a standard form of Middle English. It was the dialect of Chaucer, though Latin and French remained in wide use until 1400. Indeed, scholars continued to publish in Latin up to the seventeenth century. During the Renaissance it was the source of many borrowings, which entered either directly or via French. Modern English dates from 1500, shortly after Caxton's press began operating in London. The prestigious dialect of the Court of St James was further disseminated by the publication of the Bible in 1611, and Johnson's *Dictionary* of 1755 did much to enshrine the standard language which was already being 'exported' to South Africa, India, Australia and New Zealand. Marked dialectal differences, vestiges of the movements of people and cultures just described, characterise even today the many regions of the British Isles. (Figure 2.3, below, shows some contemporary examples of variations in vocabulary and pronunciation).

The ease with which Latin words permeated all of the early Germanic dialects indicates that they were not markedly differentiated at that time. The emergence of *High German* dates from the sixth century, when striking changes in the pronunciation of consonants occurred in the southern dialects, some of which were gradually adopted by the dialects of the north. This shift is the basis for the distinction between Low and High German still made today (see 2.3). With the transition from Old to Middle High German in the mid-eleventh century, final *b*, *d* and *g* became devoiced and the spelling changed from *tag* to *tac*, *grab* to *grap*, and so on. Modern German has reverted to the old spelling but retains the modified pronunciation (see 7.5.2). The Franks had taken over Burgundy and spread into northern France, giving Gaul its new name, but their territory had been romanised and by 1200 the linguistic frontier became stabilised at more or less its present location. To the east German was spreading into Slavic areas, and it continued to be spoken in Northern Poland, Czechoslovakia and the Volga until after the Second World War. There is still a thriving German-speaking enclave in Romanian Transylvania today. From 1350 onwards the language's development is characterised by an increasing standardisation of High German which owes much to the influence of Luther and the publication of his High German Bible in 1621. Nevertheless, spoken German is even today marked by great variations from region to region, the colloquial *Umgangssprache* of the cities being closer to the standard than is the speech of rural areas. The uniform written form of standard German has been adopted in Austria, much of Switzerland, and in Luxemburg. In all three countries it is an official language, but the strong regional dialects of *Schwyzertütsch* and *Letzeburgesch* are heard in everyday speech.

Alsace has had a chequered history which has seen it suffer or enjoy alternating periods of French and German rule. From 1871 to 1918 and from 1940 to 1945 German was the official language. Although a knowledge of the Germanic *Alsatian* dialect is still quite widespread, especially among older members of the population, many more speakers are conversant with the official language, French, than with Standard German.

The Flemings of Belgium and the Dutch of Holland have the same standard language, *General Cultured Netherlandic*. In the sixteenth century the speech of Brussels was something of a standard throughout the Netherlandic-speaking area. However, with the split between the United Provinces of the north and the Spanish Netherlands, French gained ascendency among the ruling circles of the south and the status of Flemish declined to that of an unofficial and unstandardised dialect. Nowadays Netherlandic is, with French, a joint official language of Belgium. There is a fast dwindling group of Flemish speakers on the French side of the border.

Frisian is the Germanic language most closely related to English and was once spoken from the Scheldt to the Weser. The northern dialect spoken by a tiny number of people in Schleswig has no standard form or official status to protect it from the advance of German. The West Frisian of Holland, on the other hand, is taught in schools and used to a limited extent in courts of law. Moreover, there is a Frisian Academy which has standardised the language, and literature in Frisian is flourishing. The two dialects are not mutually intelligible without effort.

The North Germanic dialect of the Scandinavian countries was fairly uniform until the Viking expansion from 750 AD onwards. *Danish* has evolved furthest from this common norm. Written *Norwegian* was, until the nineteenth century, only a variety of Danish. At that time Aasen constructed a norm, *Nynorsk*, from the Norwegian dialects. Although taught in all schools, it is not widely spoken and the predominant language is *Bokmål*, devised by Knudsen and much closer to the Danish-influenced written norm. There are many dialects in Scandinavia but the standard forms of Danish, Norwegian and *Swedish* are mutually comprehensible. Swedish is spoken by about 6 per cent of the population of Finland, where it is a joint official language.

2.2.3 The Slavic languages

The first Slav expansions from the area between the Dnieper and the Vistula took place in the fifth century as the Germanic tribes withdrew westwards. In 100 years they had progressed through the Balkans and into central Europe, slavicising territory formerly Germanic. At the end of the ninth century the Magyars seized Hungary and when the re-germanicisation of Bavaria and Austria was complete in 1200, the South Slavic group was effectively cut off. At the same time a southwards expansion of Romanian divided this group into two. *Bulgarian* and *Macedonian* were influenced much more by Byzantium and the east, while *Serbo-Croat* and *Slovene* turned to the west. The last three languages are all officially recognised in present-day Yugoslavia. The cyrillic alphabet devised in the ninth century was adopted by the followers of the Orthodox Church, while Roman script was adopted by those Slavic populations which espoused Catholicism. The only significant difference between Serbian and Croatian is a graphic one.

To the north and the east, early Slavic expansion met few real obstacles, except for the Turkic nomads of the south-eastern steppes. Local variants of the Old Church Slavonic standard developed from 1000 AD, but after the eleventh century these fell into disuse in the areas where the West Slavic dialects of *Polish*, *Czech* and *Slovak* were spoken. This led to the gradual establishment of separate literary languages. In contrast, *Russian Church Slavonic* remained in use until the middle of the seventeenth century, when it was replaced as the official language of the Russian Orthodox Church by a new variety based on the *Belorussian* and *Ukrainian*, dialects of East Slavic. The intention was to create a literary language having closer connections with everyday speech. Ukrainian itself incorporated many West Slavic elements, and this facilitated the westernisation of the Russian language so vigorously undertaken by Peter the Great. Belorussian and Ukrainian remain official languages of the republics of the same name, and have seven and thirty-five million speakers respectively. *Russian* is to an increasing extent the first language of a national population which embraces speakers of Eskimo, Altaic, Semitic, Caucasian, Finno-Ugric and Baltic languages.

2.2.4 The Baltic languages

The Baltic and Slavic proto-languages are thought to have split at around 2000 BC. The area inhabited by Baltic tribes shrank as the Slavs moved north, and in the seventh century *Latvian* and *Lithuanian* began to develop as independent languages. Both are divided into several dialects, but have a standard which is recognised as an official language, together with Russian.

2.2.5 The Finno-Ugric languages

This group is believed to have dispersed from the Volga–Ural region during the third millennium BC. The Ugrians (meaning 'Siberians') moved south, and in the ninth century conquered the area that is now Hungary. There are some twelve million speakers of *Hungarian* today in the country itself and in adjoining areas of Czechoslovakia and Romania. A sizeable Hungarian community is settled in the central Carpathians also. The Finns arrived in the Baltic no later than 500 BC, and several languages developed. *Lappish* is spoken by a population of some 35,000, still migrant to a large extent, scattered over northern Scandinavia, Finland and the Soviet Union. They are of distinct racial stock and are assumed to have once had their own, non-Finno-Ugric tongue. Like *Karelian* it is losing ground quite rapidly. *Finnish* is spoken by about five million people in Finland and over the Swedish frontier, but the extinction of this second language group seems imminent. *Estonian* has approximately one million speakers, the northern dialect being intelligible to the southern Finns.

2.2.6 Celtic and Basque

The languages discussed under this heading have in common the force with which they have made felt their protests against repression. The Celts were strongly implanted in southern Germany and the Alps in the fifth century BC and spread north and west to occupy much of Gaul. However, romanisation proved an irresistible force and the language was completely wiped out in that country by 400 AD. The Celts who had reached Britain were pushed to the west by the invading Anglo-Saxons. Celtic is thought to have reached Ireland through immigration from Scotland. These two varieties of *Gaelic* constitute the Goidelic branch of Celtic. In the sixth century Celtic returned to France following an exodus of Brittonic speakers to Brittany. *Cornish*, extinct since the eighteenth century, is thought to have been mutually intelligible with *Breton*, but the gap between Breton and *Welsh* is too wide for comprehension to be possible. Although only 3 per cent of Eire's population speak Gaelic, the language is protected by official status. In contrast, about 20 per cent of the population of Wales can speak Welsh, but the official recognition of bilingualism is a grudging one. The defence of Breton has been more militant, but for all that its days as a living language seem numbered.

The presence of *Basque* in an area which straddles the western Pyrenees and the Franco-Spanish border is something of a mystery. It is presumed to be part of a group of languages which predated the arrival of Indo-European. The French side has by far the smaller population and it is wide open to the influence of French. The Spanish Basques, on the other hand, are achieving some measure of political independence. This is not in itself sufficient to guarantee the language's survival, the autonomists' struggle for linguistic unificiation being comlicated by the existence of seven widely divergent dialects and the absence of a recognised standard.

2.3 Dialect, language, nation, speech-community

We frequently read sentences which refer to 'language *X* and the dialects which constitute it'. This implies a hierarchical relationship between language and dialect, the latter being considered *structurally similar* and *functionally inferior*. But the distinction is also made on *political* grounds. The five major 'dialects' of Chinese are less mutually intelligible than are the Norwegian and Swedish 'languages'. And we have already noted the examples of Catalan and 'Moldavian' (2.2.1). These three vantage-points may therefore offer differing, even conflicting pictures.

A *structural* viewpoint emphasises genetic relationships, but it is often very difficult to draw a hard and fast line between ways of speaking on structural grounds. Which features are we to take into account? Are Romansch and Friulan to be grouped together on genetic grounds even though the former is now closer to French and the latter to Italian? In Italy and in Germany we are faced with a *continuum* of dialects in which adjacent communities understand each other's speech, but the extremes are mutually unintelligible. Thus, as far as speech is concerned, we have an uninterrupted spectrum of dialects stretching from Holland through Germany into Switzerland and Austria. In order to mark off this spectrum into sections, linguists try to establish, thanks to field surveys, maps bearing 'linguistic contours' known as *isoglosses*. Each isogloss marks a change in use with respect to a given feature, be it phonetic, lexical or syntactic. Thus, Figure 2.3 shows two isoglosses. To the north of the dotted line speakers say *muck* and to the south *dung*. In most of the Midlands and England north of the broken line speakers pronounce *suck* [sʊk], while to the south it is generally pronounced [sʌk]. The two isoglosses do not coincide, but they follow a similar line. Where a number of isoglosses form a *bundle* in this way, we can feel justified in talking of a dialect boundary. There are many isoglosses which run from the Severn to the Wash in England, a line which coincides approximately for part of its length to the division between the Middle English dialects of South Western and West Midland (2.2.2). The slight offsetting of the isoglosses explains the feeling that dialects 'shade into' each other. A similar bundle of isoglosses can be discerned following the Garonne from Bordeaux to Toulouse and south to Andorra. They show the linguistic particularity of Gascony. A bundle of six major isoglosses running southwest–northeast across central Germany marks the transition from *Plattdeutsch* in the north to *Hochdeutsch*.

Functionally speaking, a dialect is usually restricted as regards the spheres of social activity in which it is employed (see 4.5), whereas the standard is used by the media and those who run the country, and is furthermore a sign of authority and prestige. Thus 'the French language', 'the German language' and virtually all other languages are far from uniform and homogeneous in their actual use because of their many regional and functional variations. Furthermore, there is no one-to-one correspondence between often fuzzy linguistic frontiers and political frontiers, as Figure 2.1 makes abundantly clear. 'Language' and 'nation' do not match as neatly as many *political* rulers would wish, though there have been and still are many attempts in different countries to achieve such a correspondence in order to govern more effectively and weld a feeling of national solidarity.

Figure 2.3

Examples of dialect boundaries in England

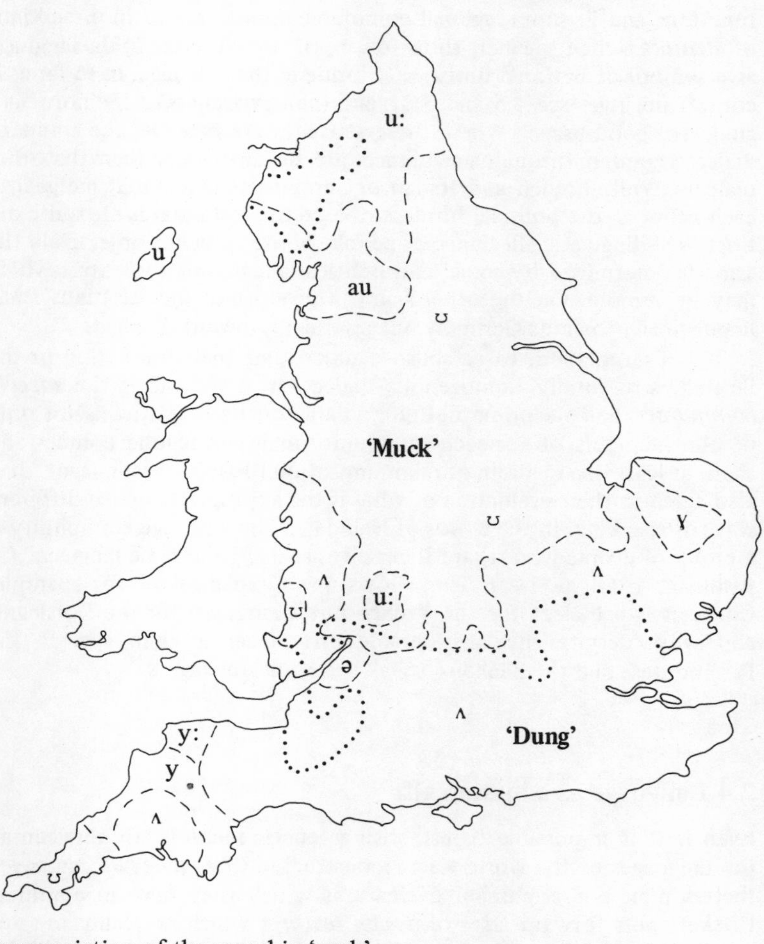

Pronunciation of the vowel in 'suck' _ _ _ _ _ _ _ _ _ _ _ _ _

'Muck' *vs* 'dung' . . . .

SOURCE: H. Orton, S. Sanderson and J. Widdowson (eds), *The Linguistic Atlas of England* (London: Croom Helm, 1978), © University of Leeds 1978. Reproduced by permission of Croom Helm Ltd.

An essential step towards this goal is the selection and codification in grammars and dictionaries of a standard form of speech and writing, or *norm*. The extent to which this norm is actually used in all social functions and in supra-regional communication is related in three kinds of *attitude* which speakers show towards it: their loyalty to the language as a symbol of national unity; their pride in the language, in so far as it confers prestige (see 4.5 and 5.3); and their awareness of the norm as a guide to 'good usage'. Where these attitudes are positive, the standard dialect acquires, through acceptance, greater autonomy than the other dialects. While French and Italian or German and Dutch may merge into each other at the political borders, the codified standards are quite distinct. The linguistic allegiance of people whose speech is objectively the same is determined by social and political allegiances to centres which may be remote. On the other hand, a group like the Alsatians leans linguistically towards Germany but politically towards France.

It is useful, then, to establish a unit other than the nation or the limited, structurally homogenous dialect area. We call it the *speech-community* and its prime defining characteristic is attitude. Not only do the members of a speech-community maintain regular contact and share at least one medium of communication (dialect or language), they also agree in their evaluation of what is the appropriate use of different ways of speaking. In the words of Halliday, 'The language community is a group of people who regard themselves as using the same language' (in Fishman, 1968, p. 140). This allows us to explain why, for example, Corsican is a dialect for the French but a language for the Corsicans, and why, despite the considerable differences in their speech, the Piedmontese and the Sicilians 'speak the same language'.

2.4 Language as a human gift

Even if it is impossible to establish a genetic relationship between all the languages of the world via a reconstructed *Ursprache*, we can nevertheless pick out a number of features which they have in common. Hockett puts forward a set of *design features* which he claims are universal characteristics of language (in Sebeok, 1968). His intention is also to demonstrate that the systems of communication used by animals are qualitatively different from linguistic communication by men, that is to say, the design features are not only species-universal but also species-specific. If this is so, then it is possible that man has an innate predisposition for language and impossible that language evolved as no more than an elaboration of the calls used by primates. We shall see that while many of these features are properties of animal communication systems, no one animal other than man possesses them all.

First, blackbirds isolated on hatching sing normally on maturity; this aspect of their behaviour is genetically determined rather than learnt. Human beings, however, will not talk unless exposed to language, and they have to *learn* the norms for its appropriate use. This is also true of the white-crowned sparrow, which will not sing if isolated from other members of the species. Other birds, such as chaffinches, produce a basic song even if isolated, but do not develop sophisticated patterns without contact with other chaffinches. Thus, in the bird species the balance between pre-planned and learnt behaviour varies.

Second, human communication takes place primarily via the vocal–auditory channel. Some animals do not use this channel for transmitting their messages. The 'honey dance' performed by bees to indicate the location of pollen prevents them from doing anything else at the same time. It also precludes 'whispering' or directing messages to selected receivers, as humans can. Humans are further able to distinguish one voice from a group of voices and to 'tune in' selectively.

Third, in a human message the individual sounds acquire meaning only by virtue of being *combined in certain patterns*; meaningless in themselves, the sounds [a], [p] and [t] can be combined variously to construct the different, meaningful words *apt*, *pat* and *tap*. This is true of the notes of bird songs, though the number of permitted combinations is very restricted, but not of animal cries. Moreover, humans recognise that *it*, *the red car* and *the car that turned the corner* occupy structurally equivalent positions in a pattern and can all occur before *crashed*, for example. No animal communication would appear to have such complex, structured units.

Fourth, the link between speech and the object or event to which it refers is a matter of *arbitrary* convention (see 8.2); the raising of a claw by a crab to signal aggression is not. As a consequence of this arbitrariness, words can be made by agreement to relate to any specific aspect of things, actions or ideas in the outside world, while it is probable that an animal's danger call signals simply 'danger' without specifying whether its source is a lion or a rhino. The number of different messages a human can transmit is therefore infinite, yet it seems that even bees and dolphins, the virtuosos of the insect and animal worlds, can send no more than a limited range of messages. Bees can give information relating only to the direction and horizontal distance of the pollen source from the hive. They cannot indicate that the source is perched at the top of a pole, as one experiment revealed, nor do they appear to communicate about weather conditions, for example.

Bees at least possess an ability to refer to something that is remote from their immediate situation, whereas most animal messages are transmitted in response to a stimulus in their direct environment. Yet although the animal's communication system is part of its immediate situation, no animal is able to use it to refer to that same system in the way that we use language to talk about language.

Because their signals are not arbitrary and are generally made as a response to a concrete situation, animals lack the human ability to create through language imaginary worlds or even theories, since theories are speculations about 'what might be' rather than statements of 'what is'. It means, too, that animals cannot tell lies. For Steiner, 'The potentials of fiction, of counterfactuality, of undecidable futurity profoundly characterize both the origins and nature of speech. They differentiate it ontologically from the many signal systems available to the animal world' (1975, p. 473). In talking of 'origins' we return to the question posed at the beginning of the chapter. Steiner maintains that the profusion of mutually unintelligible languages stems from a fundamental human need to exploit this 'fictional' capability of language in order to 'reject the empirical inevitability of the world' and create a private territory. An individual language is vital to the identity of the individual. A distinct language is vital to the identity of the group, as we shall see in Chapter 5.

Further reading

The topic of historical linguistics is perhaps best approached through Lyons (1968), Robins (1971) or Anderson (1973). The sources for much of the information on language families contained in this chapter are Lockwood (1972), which contains historical and structural data, Katzner (1977), which gives brief profiles of countries and languages together with sample texts, and Stephens (1976), which gives extensive coverage to the political situation of linguistic minorities. Haugen discusses dialect, language and nation in Pride and Holmes (1972). The notion of speech community is presented by Gumperz in Giglioli (1972). Other accessible discussions are to be found in Bell (1976), Trudgill (1974) and Fishman (1970). More detailed articles figure in Fishman (1968) and Gumperz and Hymes (1972). Dittmar (1976) offers a concise summary. Aitchison (1976) has a lively discussion of animal communication, while Sebeok (1968) presents Hockett's design features and a mass of research data.

Suggestions for inquiry

1 Make a list of twenty English dialect words.
2 What do you think are the chances of Welsh becoming an official language in Britain?
3 Why is West Frisian relatively healthy and North Frisian on its death-bed?
4 Try to account for the relative stability of the linguistic position in Switzerland as compared with Belgium.
5 Outline the territorial limits of the different language families on Figure 2.1. Note any irregularities in their distribution.
6 How many political frontiers in Europe coincide with sharp linguistic frontiers? In how many countries is only a single language spoken?
7 What would be the repercussions of requiring Estonian, Latvian and Lithuanian to be written in cyrillic rather than roman script?

3

Acquisition and Learning

> Originality of mind does not make a good linguist. In fact, a talent for languages does not imply any higher intellectual development of any kind.
>
> H. Sweet (1899) *The Practical Study of Languages*

We are all born linguists. This statement seems intuitively valid for all normal human beings, who in the space of a few childhood years and with no apparent effort become accomplished speakers of a first language. Many add a second language or even more at various ages and in various settings, from a bilingual home to a course in reading for scientists. The effortlessness of this process is not always so apparent, nor is attainment so uniformly high. This chapter asks to what extent the processes of first- and second-language acquisition are similar or dissimilar. What makes people become bilingual and what makes them proficient bilinguals? What obstacles stand in their way and what are the particular pains and pleasures of individual bilingualism?

3.1 The stages of first-language acquisition

In our discussion we will assume that the family and community environment are monolingual, though not, of course, homogeneous. In many cases one or both backgrounds may be bi- or multi-lingual (see 2.3, 4.5 and 5.3), but for the time being we exclude this complicating factor.

The use of the word 'stages' does not imply that the language-acquisition process is anything but continuous. The stages are characterised by developments which linguists have picked out as being significant milestones. It is important to note that at every stage the child's comprehension of speech exceeds its productive abilities. The ages given in Figure 3.1 and in the text below are only approximations, and individual children vary greatly in the onset and duration of the different stages.

What is constant, however, is the *sequence* of development, not only for children who grow up speaking English, but also for those born into French, German, Russian, Japanese and, presumably, any other communities. The assumption has not been falsified by studies of thirty different languages belonging to ten different language families. The striking fact is that the major steps towards proficient verbal communication take place very rapidly over the brief span of some thirty months between 1½ and 4 years of age. By this time children are indisputably members of a given community by virtue of speaking its language, even if it is not until much later that the meanings of certain syntactic patterns are correctly understood.

3.1.1 Sounds and intonation

Almost from birth infants are attentive to the source of sounds, and within days can distinguish the human voice from other sounds. A recording device contained in a dummy given to 1-month-old children registered an abrupt increase in their sucking rate when a sound being

Figure 3.1
Stages of language acquisition

Age	Linguistic performance
0;3	Babbling begins
0;9	Intonation patterns emerge
1;0	First, single words (holophrases)
1;3	Lexical overgeneralisation
1;8	Two-word utterances
2;0	Inflections; three-word utterances (telegraphic speech)
2;3	First pronouns used
2;6	Questions; negatives; four-word utterances, and longer; vowel system complete
3;6	Consonant system complete
4;0	Correct but limited syntax
5;0	Complex constructions
10;0	Mature speech

SOURCES: Adapted from Aitchison (1976, p. 80) and Cruttenden (1979, p. xii).

played to them was changed from a constant [ba] to [pa]. These two consonantal sounds are significant in English in that they oppose pairs of words, like *pan* and *ban*. That is, they allow contrasts of meaning. When the change did not correspond to a meaningful sound distinction made in adult speech, the sucking rate did not vary. Does this mean that children are 'programmed' to discriminate certain phonetic features and not others? (For an explanation of phonetic features, see Chapter 8.) Within six months the infant responds to differences between male and female voices and variations in emotional quality and intonation. However, it takes children several years before they can correctly interpret many intonation patterns and stress contrasts such as hot dóg and hót-dog. The perception of the language's system of sound oppositions is much more rapid. Research on Russian and English has shown that the order of acquisition of these oppositions is, in the main, constant, though the detail may vary greatly from child to child. While no two languages are identical in sound structure – and thus the acquisition order will differ correspondingly – there seems to be a general rule that vowels are first distinguished from consonants and that the individual vowels are distinguished from each other before the consonantal contrasts are made. By 3½ years of age English-speaking children not only recognise that sequences like [mrul] and [ʃkib] are not permissible but tend to modify them to produce possible sequences, like [skib]. However, these perception experiments used only contrasting word-pairs and 'it is at least doubtful whether discrimination in such a situation means that the child will register the difference as meaningful in on-going speech' (Cruttenden, 1979, p.28).

Production similarly follows an over-all order with individual variations of detail. The child's first reflex at birth is to cry, and by 8 months parents can identify distinct cries of pain, hunger and surprise. In addition to producing these reflex sounds, the child is beginning to gain control over his articulatory apparatus and experiment in producing sounds closer to those of adult speech. The making of sounds for sheer pleasure is known as the 'babbling' stage, and it continues for some time after single words have been uttered. During this period children utter a wide range of sounds, yet the earlier belief that they produce all the sounds of the world's languages has been discounted. Indeed, some children never produce during this stage some of the sounds they hear spoken around them, while other sounds, like [l] and [r], disappear from their repertoire as they utter their first words. Many children do not master [r] in speech until they are 5 or 6 years old. Prior to the first words, '[bdgmn] become the predominating consonants. These same consonants are usually utilised in the first [meaning] distinctions in any language (not just English)' (Cruttenden, 1979, p.3). The precise role of babbling and its relation to speech remains unclear. There are no doubt elements of fun and articulatory exercise and also of direct preparation for speech sounds.

Syllable patterns for first words tend to be mostly CV (consonant + vowel) or CVCV, for example [pa] and [dada]. Longer words are often simplified by the reduction of consonant clusters, so that *squirrel* may be pronounced [ga], and by the omission of final or unstressed sounds, as in [bu] for *boot* and [wei] for *away*. The prominence of the final syllable caused one child to learn [nɪt] for *open* from *open it.*

The sound system is the first to be mastered. Many adults have little or no call to modify it permanently, unless they try to adopt a regional or social accent which they feel to be more desirable.

3.1.2 Words and meanings

The size of a child's active vocabulary expands rapidly from age 1 year onwards, when the phonetic shape of many 'words' may be recognisable only to a loving parent. At 18 months it is about 100–200, at age 2 about 500, at least 2,000 at 5 and some 4,000 at 7 (Cruttenden, 1979, pp. 83–4). The early words refer to objects in children's immediate surroundings and are those commonly used by adults in conversation with them, like *juice*, *milk*, *sock*, *dog*, *car* and *baby*. This is not to say that children do not repeat (sometimes embarrassing) words not addressed directly to them. Initially children create meanings by relating sounds to non-linguistic experience, but soon – as early as 20 months – they are able to guess at the meaning of new words, such as *doll*, from the presence of known words, like *rock* and *feed*. Only later can children learn meanings from exclusively verbal explanations.

The first meanings are one-to-one associations between sounds and a particular object or event. Thus *mummy* refers only to the child's *mother*. But meanings are extended, or *overgeneralised*, and *mummy* may come to refer to all females. A child referring to a pleasure-steamer on the Thames as a *bus* was overgeneralising, presumably because it had a lot of windows and carried passengers, and thereby overcoming the limitations of his vocabulary. As the child adds more words to his vocabulary so the meanings of overgeneralised words are restricted and approach adult norms of differentiation. It is not until age 6 that children begin to express perceived similarities between objects already differentiated, by referring to *apples* and *oranges* as *fruit*, for example. This process continues until as late as 18 years of age.

In the course of the one-word stage it is apparent that children are in fact expressing meanings that are later expressed by a complex utterance, hence the term *holophrase* ('whole sentence') in Figure 3.1, above. *Down* may be interpreted as a request to be put down or as a statement that the child has sat down. *Anna*, uttered on seeing Anna's empty bed, indicates possession, and *garden*, while holding a plant brought indoors from the garden, indicates location. Adults often expand such holophrases in replies like *Yes, that's Anna's bed* or *Yes, it's from the garden.*

The acquisition of new vocabulary continues throughout a speaker's life as new situations are encountered and new words are coined – *quango* (quasi-autonomous non-governmental organisation) was unheard of five years ago and probably will soon be so again.

3.1.3 Syntactic development

It is premature to talk of a child's syntactic development at the two-word utterance stage. Functions like demanding, requesting or expressing ideas can now be more explicitly expressed, though utterances often remain highly ambiguous out of context – the interpretation of *Throw Daddy* as *Throw it to Daddy*, for example. Analogous patterns are to be found in children's speech in other languages, from Finnish and Samoan to German and Russian. Location may be expressed by *there book, buch da, see doggie, gukuk wauwau*; demands by *more milk, mehr milch, bitte apfel;* description by *mail come, sofa sitzen, баба кресло* ('granny armchair'); possession by *mama dress, mein ball, мами чашка* ('mummy's cup'); questions by *where ball, wo Ball;* negation by *allgone milk, no wet, no wash, nicht blasen, kaffee nein, нет спать* ('no sleep') (see Slobin, 1971, p. 44).

Once children have produced their first three-word utterance they progress rapidly and without any discernible interruption to utterances of four and five words and longer. A major threshold has been crossed, marking a qualitative change in their speech. They must now give attention to the order in which they put words together, since order affects meaning (e.g. *John had it done* vs *John had done it*). In short, syntactic development begins. Because linguistic progression correlates only very approximately with chronological age, linguists find it more realistic to compare the syntactic development of children who are producing utterances of the same average length rather than of children of the same age. Young children having the same Mean Length of Utterance (MLU) are found to have roughly equal linguistic abilities. The variations between MLU and age are highlighted by Roger Brown's (1976) study of three children, Eve, Adam and Sarah, who had an MLU of 3.5 at 24, 36 and 41 months respectively.

Certain characteristics of adult speech are conspicuous by their absence from Slobin's data presented above: articles, pronouns, the verbs *be* and *sein*, the third-person singular markers *-s* and *-t* (*comes, bläst*), the possessive *-s* (*mama's*) etc. Longer utterances, like *No want stand head* and *You want eat*?, reveal the absence of the auxiliary *do*, the copula *to* and the preposition *on*. These grammatical markers are known collectively as *functors*. For obvious reasons linguists have been prompted to label child speech of this sort as *telegraphic*. Several studies of the acquisition of functors including those above and the tense markers *-ing* and *-ed* have brought to light a remarkable consistency in the *sequence* of their acquisition. It would appear, then, that not only the major stages but also some of the finer details are universally ordered.

The absence of functors is unlikely to lead to confusion, given their often highly predictable nature, the contribution of situational information and the increasing use made by the child of gesture and distinctive intonation. In languages with a case system, like Russian, the case endings unambiguously mark words as subject, object, etc., and adults may vary word order for purely stylistic reasons. The absence of endings in Russian children's telegraphic speech is compensated by their preference for a fixed order (subject + object + verb) whereas with adults the order SVO is more frequent. Even in non-inflecting languages children tend to stick to a single word-order pattern.

During the mastery of the functors a process of overgeneralisation is apparent, parallel to that of lexical development. In Russian children's acquisition of gender agreement (between noun, adjective and verb) the feminine first predominates, then the masculine, followed by a period of confusion before correct agreements are stabilised. Many English children produce the form *hisself* rather than *himself*, so ironing out the exception to the regular pattern of possessive adjective + *self* manifested by *myself*, *yourself*, *ourselves*. German children will use the auxiliary *haben* with verbs like *gehen* which are accompanied by *sein* in adult speech. The variation of pronouns according to position in the utterance (*I, me; je, moi, me, m'*) is also eliminated in favour of a single form, usually *my* or *mine*, and *moi*. The tendency to regularise is evident in plural formations like *mans*, *foots* and *feets*, *mouses* and *mices*, and in verb forms, *comed*, *goed*, *ringed*. Figure 3.2 presents some French and Spanish examples. The interesting point is that children are very often heard to utter the correct, irregular, adult form prior to their own regularised version.

The gradual conforming of children's syntax to adult patterns is clearly seen in their use of negative and interrogative constructions. Initially, yes/no questions are marked by intonation alone – *Sit chair*?; WH-questions and negatives are formed by tacking the question word (*what*, *where*, *how*, etc.) or the negative (*no, not*; in French simply *pas*) to the front of the utterance – *What boy doing?*; *No the sun shining*; *Why not me drink it?* Later, *no* is inserted into the clause – *There no squirrels*. Finally, the auxiliaries are mastered and used correctly both in the negative – *I didn't did it*; *Paul didn't laugh* – and in the interroga-

Figure 3.2
Overgeneralisations in French and Spanish

Child's utterance	Adult norm	Analogy
tu servis	*tu sers*	servir: fin-ir (infin.) -is
il allera	*il ira*	aller: donner-a (infin.)
j'ai prendu	*j'ai pris*	prendre: vend-re (infin.) -u
j'ai buvé	*j'ai bu*	buvons: donn-ons (1st pl. pres.) -é
ha hacido	*ha hecho*	hacer: vend-er (infin.) -ido
ha rompido	*ha roto*	rompir: viv-ir (infin.) -ido
ha escribido	*ha escrito*	escribir: viv-ir (infin.) -ido

tive, where auxiliary and subject are regularly inverted in yes/no questions – *Can't you get it*? – but less consistently in WH-questions. In this last case wrong word order – e.g. *What I did yesterday?* – persists much longer in the child's transition to correct word order – e.g. *What did you doed?*

Thereafter, children rapidly proceed to the use of relative clauses (*the man who . . .*) and adverbial clauses (*when*, *if*, *'cos*, etc.). Such complex constructions are common by the age of 5, and it was once thought that the language-acquisition process was then complete. However, further research has shown that children are apt to misinterpret certain structures up to the age of 10 or later. A question of the type *Is this dolly easy to see*? often elicited a response to the effect that the doll could not see easily (the dolly in the experiment wore a blindfold). *Dolly* was taken for the logical subject, as in *Dolly is happy to sleep*, whereas in *Dolly is easy to see* it is the logical object (Chomsky, 1971). The complex rules (pronoun agreement and positive–negative polarity) determining the form of *tags* at the end of sentences (1) and (2) –

(1) John's going, isn't he?
(2) Mary isn't going, is she?

– continue to cause difficulties beyond the age of 5, whereas their invariant equivalents (*n'est-ce pas, nicht wahr, verdad, не правда ли*) are quickly mastered.

The acquisition of syntax, although a more protracted process, is still rapid in view of the complexity of the task. It is unlikely that the speaker's knowledge of how the system works is modified after puberty.

3.1.4 Communicative development

We have concentrated until now on the acquisition of a formal *system* (with phonological, lexical and syntactic levels), making only passing reference to the child's growing awareness of the *uses* to which language can be put and the *situations* in which its use is appropriate – in short, the rules of speaking (4.3 and 4.4 look at these questions in the adult context). In one case study Halliday (1975) describes how his son first used language to prompt reactions from those around him – *Give me that*; *Let's do that* – or to express feelings, and only later to request information and then to give it.

Children learn at an early age how to hold a conversation. This experience begins as early as the babbling stage when parents indicate by their intonation, facial expressions and pauses that they are putting a question, even if they themselves supply the verbal response. By the age of 3 children learn learn to co-operate with adults and other children to keep the conversation on track by repeating key words of the partner's utterance and adding to them. Their intonation patterns, too, are in harmony with the rhythm and function of the exchange.

The realisation that different styles of speech are appropriate to different situations also comes early. Before the age of 3 children use a range of voice qualities from whisper when someone is asleep to a high pitch for complaining. By the age of 4 children have distinct styles of talking with adult strangers, their parents, their peers and with babies. Children's speech to infants closely resembles mothers' speech to babies (Cruttenden, 1979, pp. 81–2). Research into this aspect of children's (and adults') verbal behaviour is relatively new, but the art of appropriate conversation often undergoes refinement far into adult life.

The acquisition process is not as effortless as we may wish to assume. The tears and tantrums of children frustrated by their inability to express themselves bear witness to the fact.

3.2 Two explanatory theories

So much for the description of the development of speech in children. But how can we *explain* the process? We now outline, in rather black-and-white terms, two theories put forward in recent years and see to what extent they fit the data.

3.2.1 The 'nurture' viewpoint

In 1957 the psychologist B. F. Skinner published *Verbal Behaviour*, a work which sought to account for the acquisition of language in strictly behaviourist terms. In other words, it rejected any explanation which was founded on unobservable phenomena (mental processes, for example). The phenomena which Skinner chose to observe were experiments in shaping the behaviour of rats and pigeons by a process called *operant conditioning*, the essence of which is the selective rewarding of desired behaviour. For example, pigeons were trained to press a bar in their cage in order to switch on a green light. This was done by rewarding with a food pellet their first, accidental pressure on the bar. Later the task was made more complex by requiring the bar to be pressed more than once before the light was activated and the behaviour rewarded. In time the birds were conditioned into intricate behaviour patterns by this technique of *reinforcement*, which Skinner claims is equally applicable to human behaviour in general, including linguistic behaviour. Thus meaning and learning are seen as a response to a given stimulus. By careful control of stimulus and reward it is possible to reduce the amount of trial and error on the part of the 'guinea-pig' before the desired response is made. Skinner argues, then, that language is no more than a set of habits learnt by imitation and repetition once the child realises that by producing certain sounds he will be rewarded with food, a smile, encouragement, and so on.

But this does not fit the hard facts of children's speech. If they are supposed to learn only from experience and imitation, how do they come to say *mices* and *doed*? How is it that a child who commonly produces seven-word utterances and who knows all the individual words is incapable of repeating correctly *The boy the book hit was crying* and says instead *Boy the book was crying*? Why, despite hearing *held* twice in a short conversation, does a child persist in saying *holded*? Imitation would not appear to be a feasible explanation, nor does explicit instruction have much effect. Treating a child's truncated utterances as a turn in a conversation and responding to them with different words (*Throw Daddy?: Yes, watch him drop it*) appears to aid children's linguistic development *more* than simply expanding them (3.1.2) – that is, essentially repetition.

What of reinforcement? Observation shows that parents tend to reject utterances which are grammatically correct but untrue, while rewarding – by *Yes* or *That's right* – factually correct statements which are ill-formed. For example, *He a girl* referring to the child's mother is approved. Where is the stimulus for the child to 'correct' his usage? Further, since learning is seen as a fortuitous product of experience and since every child's linguistic experience is different, how can we account for the wholesale *similarity* in the speech output of all children, even across languages?

3.2.2 The 'nature' viewpoint

All these objections to the theory that speech is attributable to a general ability nurtured by experience alone were advanced by Noam Chomsky (1959) in a devastating review of Skinner's book. In addition, he pointed out that Skinner's view of language is an impoverished one. Linguistic behaviour is creative, as we saw in 2.4, and human verbal response to a given event is not predictable as are the majority of animal cries (see, however, 4.3 and 4.4.3). Second, language manipulation is a structure-dependent operation. Transforming *Sam shot the sheriff* into *The sheriff was shot by Sam* is not simply a matter of mechanically switching the first word with the last two and then inserting two more words at certain points. It involves knowing where the subject and object of the sentence are.

The speed, invariance and universality of the acquisition process led Chomsky to postulate that every child is born with a specific ability, an intrinsic predisposition for language processing. Hence the labels *mentalist* or *rationalist* which attach to his theories. He argues that far from being a 'blank slate' a child must bring with it into the world a knowledge of structural principles and 'building-blocks' common to all human languages. The speech which he hears serves merely to trigger off the acquisition process by enabling the child 'to determine which of the (humanly) possible languages is that of the community in which he is placed. Language learning would be impossible unless this were the case' (Chomsky, 1965, p. 27). It is as if the child knows in advance the dimensions of a jigsaw puzzle and the possible shape and interlocking capabilities of the pieces, and is simply waiting to receive some pieces in order to create, largely unaided, the over-all picture. The 'pre-planned' nature of the process accounts for the regularity of the stages. The innate language faculty guides the child into making successive, overlapping hypotheses about the rules of his language. Hence the order to gender agreement acquisition and the other syntactic and lexical over-generalisations described in 3.1.2 and 3.1.3. Hence, also, the inability to imitate utterances more complex than those which characterise the child's stage of development at that time.

But how specific can this ability really be? Chomsky suggests that the child's hypotheses must be 'sufficiently rich' to cope with the false starts and hesitations of normal speech (see 1.3.2) and compensate for the relatively small amount of speech he hears. This assertion has prompted investigations of how adults talk to children: they speak slowly and carefully, using short sentences, exaggerated stress and giving frequent repetitions – in short, language lessons. Since most early conversations are about the 'here and now', children exploit many non-linguistic aids to comprehension (Clark and Clark, 1977, p. 331). These facts weaken Chomsky's position.

Neurological research lends only inconclusive support to the specific ability thesis, in that there appears to be a 'critical period' after which the plasticity of the brain declines and language acquisition becomes difficult if not impossible. The critical period is thought by many to end at the age of 13 or 14. From the age of 2 most of the centres which control speech become localised in the left hemisphere of the brain, a process known as *lateralisation*. Its completion was believed to mark the brain's loss of plasticity. This is consistent with evidence from two children who had been cut off from human speech, Isabelle until 6½ and Génie until 14. Isabelle was speaking normally within two years, while Génie is still making only very slow progress (see Cruttenden, 1979). However, recent research points to lateralisation being complete by the age of 5. Is Isabelle a remarkable exception, or has the critical period no neurological basis?

We must conclude that the child's specific 'language-acquisition device' proposed by Chomsky finds little positive support and that the only innate ability which the child contributes is probably a general cognitive, problem-solving capacity. The acquisition of linguistic competence (see 1.3) parallels the development of many other intellectual skills. Nevertheless, even children with an IQ in the 80 range acquire their first language at the normal rate. While Skinner's stimulus–response approach cannot account for all aspects of linguistic behaviour, we must not discount entirely the contribution of the environment nor the importance of the child's desire to speak in order to control the environment and become a member of a community. The further investigation of the child's communicative strategies will undoubtedly lead to important discoveries.

3.3 Bilingualism

3.3.1 The nature of bilingualism

The bilingual individual is able to use two or more languages (no consistent distinction according to the exact number is made here). This definition spans a huge range of competence, from the person who can stammer out a word of thanks in Tibetan to a truly remarkable polyglot like George Steiner:

> I have no recollection whatever of a first language. So far as I am aware, I possess equal currency in English, French and German.

> What I can speak, write, or read of other languages has come later and retains a 'feel' of conscious acquisition. But I experience my first three tongues as perfectly equivalent centres of myself. I speak and I write them with indistinguishable ease (1975, p. 115).

To include the first case or to limit bilingualism to 'perfect equivalence' will serve us no useful purpose. A more serviceable definition is one which stresses the habitual use of two languages to produce meaningful utterances, while admitting a range of proficiency (Christophersen, 1973, p. 63).

Weinreich suggests the following: 'the ideal bilingual switches from one language to the other according to appropriate changes in the speech situation (interlocutors, topics, etc.). but not in an unchanged speech situation, and certainly not within a single sentence' (1963, p. 73). The ability to sense when to switch and then to do so fluently is a target often set for students of modern languages in further and higher education. Yet almost inevitably one language will be more closely associated with certain situations than the other (see 4.3.2 and 4.5). Wine-tasting may have been experienced predominantly 'in French', applying for a job only 'in English'. In other words, at a given time and in a given situation one of the bilingual's two languages is likely to be *dominant*. Weinreich proposes a set of criteria which permits us to describe the degree of dominance (see Figure 3.3).

In passing we can note that the benchmark of 'educated native speech' against which many language students are supposedly measured is itself a fuzzy notion, since even monolinguals – especially, perhaps, educated ones – vary their performance in a way which we can describe only approximately (see 1.3).

Figure 3.3
Dominance criteria

Relative proficiency – judged by 'normal' standards

Modes of use – speech and/or writing?

Order and age of acquisition

Usefulness in communication – in what situations can the language be used? (see also 4.5)

Emotional involvement – loyalty and attachment

Function in social advance – does the language enjoy social esteem?

Literary-cultural value – does the language's social background enjoy prestige?

Steiner uses the adjective 'first' with a certain ambivalence Does it mean 'first acquired', first in terms of proficiency, frequency of use, emotional involvement, or all of these? We will use 'first' and 'second' (L1 and L2) only to refer to the chronology of acquisition. This is a simplification in that many children reared in bilingual environments acquire two languages simultaneously, a fact which shows the term *mother tongue* with its connotations of uniqueness and attachment to be misleading. There are similar problems with the expression *native language*; the discussion of first-language acquisition demonstrated that any linquistic knowledge the child may bring to his task is equally valid for all languages (English is no more innate or 'native' to us than is German). Even *foreign language* is problematic. Is French 'foreign' to a child born in Luxemburg, or German to a child born into a Schwyzertütsch-speaking community in Switzerland and who uses standard German in writing? For multilingual communities such as these we might talk rather of an *alternate* language. For some Welshmen and members of other linguistic or ethnic groups in Britain English may be considered an alternate language. For the overwhelming majority of students in British schools and universities the language they are studying will be foreign rather than alternate. This is less applicable in North America. But is French as an alternate language – for an English Canadian in Montreal, say – any easier to learn than French as a foreign language for an English person in London?

For the purpose of this discussion we assume a student who has acquired English as L1 in childhood and who adds a knowledge of a foreign L2 in the course of formal education. In such circumstances the learner typically becomes what is known as a *compound bilingual*. For example, he learns in class that *Bleistift* means *pencil*, when the two words are used to refer to the same object, or that *frémir* means *shudder*. Thus the words of L1 and L2 are equated by identity of reference; or the association between an L2 word and an event may be indirect, mediated by an L1 word.

At the other extreme is *co-ordinate bilingualism*, which is typically developed when the two languages are used in distinct situations where there is no switching. The two systems of meanings evolve independently.

In practice, speakers can be placed along a continuum between these theoretical extremes, having developed a compound relationship for some experiences and a co-ordinate relationship for others. Experiments, while showing some support for this contrast, have not revealed any significant difference between the two types in their ability to translate or recall from memory words of either language. However, will a relationship of dependency between systems result in their distortion? This outcome appears likely if we accept that no two languages have identical word systems (see 6.1 and 9.4). One may become forced into the mould of the other.

Different languages are not stored in separate parts of the brain. All items pertaining to 'animacy', say, are held in the same memory area and are simply 'tagged' according to language. It is not known if this fact in itself leads to retrieval errors, but there is some indication that co-ordinate bilinguals can more easily shut out the potential distraction of language A while speaking language B (Lambert, 1969, p. 109).

Bilingualism encompasses, therefore, varying levels of proficiency and dominance, and varying relations between the individual's languages. Now we look at the process of becoming a bilingual.

3.3.2 Are first- and second-language acquisition the same?

It is common to talk of *acquiring* a first language and *learning* a second. Does this terminological distinction simply underline a difference in the role of explicit instruction and in circumstantial factors, or does it point to a fundamental contrast between the processes? Does the acquisition of L1 help or hinder the learning of L2? Does the ability to learn a language decline with age?

Let us deal with this last question first. We have already cast doubts on the validity of the 'critical-period' notion (3.2.2). It is further weakened by results from studies of English-speakers learning French and Dutch in Geneva and Holland, in a mixture of both formal and informal contexts. The older children in both surveys learned faster than the younger children. Older learners seemed to have an enormous advantage in mastering Dutch syntax, and although teenagers progressed more rapidly than adults, the latter caught up after longer residence. They also derived greater benefit from classroom teaching. Age had no bearing on the understanding of Dutch speech sounds and only a marginal influence on the learners' pronunciation attainment. However, none of the learners achieved a native-like score on the pronunciation tests. In contrast, this did happen in the grammar tests after some two years' residence (Hatch, 1978, pp. 202, 338–9). So we can dismiss the idea that there is any inherent reason why L2 learning should be more difficult after puberty, except for pronunciation.

As to the first two questions above, there is a deep-rooted belief that the processes are different and that the knowledge of one language intervenes in the learning of a subsequent one. The consequent assumption that all points of difference between two languages will give rise to learning difficulties led linguists to undertake contrastive analyses in order to show up these differences, predict the errors and design teaching exercises accordingly. Unfortunately, learners not only make unpredicted errors but even fail to make those that are forecast. This is not surprising in that what is viewed as a difference or a similarity between two languages will depend on which grammatical framework is used to contrast them. Moreover, the fact that an English learner of French says *malcontent* instead of *mécontent* is not due to the structure of English but to the productive French pattern of *malheureux*, *malhonnête*, etc. When a Spaniard says I *know to do that*, is it attributable to interference from *sé hacer eso* or to the English *I want to do that*? In this case, both explanations are plausible, but it is now accepted that 'even under conditions where interference between languages should be greatest – in classroom learning where children have no contact with native-speaking peers – students develop strategies based on L2 rather than L1' (McLaughlin, 1978, p. 203). These strategies bear a striking resemblance to children's overgeneralisations in first-language acquisition; indeed, the two groups often commit identical errors.

What is more, the strategies may be universal. Japanese, Chinese, Norwegian and Spanish learners of English have been shown to make the same mistakes, which is totally counter to the contrastive assumption. And speakers of eleven different mother tongues were found to master English functors in the same order, though in a different order to the English child (see section 3.1.3). 'There thus seem to be two invariant orderings for functors: one for children learning English as a first language, and the other shared by children [and] adults learning English as a second language' (Bailey *et al.*, in Hatch, 1978, p. 369). We intuitively recognise a style of 'foreigner-talk' and may even be apt to slip into a similar style ourselves when addressing foreigners with a poor command of English. It is virtually identical in form to the telegraphic speech of children: few functors, questions marked only by intonation and negatives indicated by a *no* separate from the verb. These same formal features, or the lack of them, are to be found throughout the world, from Africa to Melanesia and Haiti, in pidgin languages based on languages as different as Swahili, English and French. The widespread nature of these apparently reduced and simplified characteristics of certain varieties of child and adult speech is further persuasive evidence that universal processes – here of *pidginisation* – are at work. We conclude, then, that the processes of L1 acquisition and L2 learning are basically one and the same: 'There is a single language system that forms the basis for acquisition, storage and retrieval of first and second languages' (McLaughlin, 1978, p. 211). In times of stress or uncertainty the learner can revert or resort to this basic language system in order to form an L2 utterance which can be viewed as a simplified, incorrect version of native speech, or alternatively as a revealing guess at what an appropriate native utterance might be.

However, we need to account for the fact that, despite the underlying sameness of the processes, the disparity of achievement in L2 is far greater than that in L1. Age does have some influence on learning efficiency, it is obvious. Interference does occur, of course. And since adults have more extensive linguistic experience to draw on, they are understandably more subject to interference. But we go on now to look for an answer in two general sets of factors which affect L2 learning – the first pedagogical, the second socio-psychological.

3.3.3 Approaches to teaching

Our average language learner gets relatively little exposure to 'real-life' French or Russian, except during periods of travel or residence abroad. He is therefore at the mercy of his teachers and their methods for much of his study time. In the early stages at least, the teacher determines the amount and nature of the L2 input – narrative or dialogue, imperfect subjunctive or not? – the sequence of presentation, the vocabulary, and so on. How are such decisions reached?

Application lags behind research, but not always far enough to save us from taking a wrong turning. So it was with behaviourism and its introduction into language teaching in the guise of the *direct* or *audio-lingual* method. As is to be anticipated from the brief account in 3.2.1 of behaviourist views of language, its objective is the acquisition of habits by repetition rather than attending to explicit rules. It consists typically of language-laboratory pattern drills where 'the relationship between stimulus and response sentences is quite unlike any that might occur in natural language use' (Wilkins, 1972, p. 167). This is because in pre-recorded drills there must be only one possible response – that given after the blank – so that the correct choice can be rewarded and thus reinforced. Rote learning tends to be boring and does not allow a learner to initiate a conversation.

The mentalist revival ushered in the *audio-visual* era – not unlike traditional grammar-translation methods, in fact – despite Chomsky's profound scepticism concerning practical spin-offs from his own theoretcial work. The essential ingredient is adequate exposure to meaningful, natural language to allow development to take its natural course without need for reinforcement. Conscious attention is given to structural relations – between affirmative and interrogative sentences, for example – and visual information accompanies the aural. The goal is to know the L2 grammatical system.

Both methods have something to commend them, as do the viewpoints on which they are founded. But, as Ervin-Tripp says of the recent past, 'we have defined language far too narrowly, omitting just those skills in the social use of language which may have more to do with social acceptability and communicative success than knowledge of school vocabulary' (in Hatch, 1978, p. 190). This approach shifts the emphasis from manipulation to communication. Tucker and Lambert make the further point that communicative competence in a foreign language 'involves the development of an awareness of and sensitivity toward the values and traditions of the people whose language is being studied' (in Oller and Richards, 1973, p. 246). Failure to do so will result in a 'turn off'. This is our next issue.

3.3.4 Attitude and motivation

There are three reasons for learning a language: (1) as a means in itself, because of an interest in languages *per se*; (2) as a means to a cultural end, in that it gives access to another linguistic group having its own values and behaviour; and (3) as a means to a utilitarian end, like passing an examination or negotiating a contract. Each of these three reasons may contribute in varying measure to a student's motivation to learn a second language. In a nation-wide survey conducted in Canadian schools in both mono- and bi-lingual areas, Gardner discovered that the third component of motivation above – *instrumentality* – is a poor indicator of linguistic achievement. It emerges as a 'short-range motivational prop' which does not have 'the staying power or the generality to maintain consistent levels of motivation over prolonged periods of time or diverse opportunities to develop proficiency' (in Giles and St Clair, 1979, p. 206). It is the first two components – *interest* and *integrativeness* – which keep motivation fuelled and correlate highly with linguistic success. These findings hold, in general, for both mono- and bilingual learning contexts.

Of course, motivation, whether instrumental or integrative, is only one of a number of factors which account for individual differences in achievement. We must also consider the learner's aptitude for languages (in so far as this can be distinguished from intelligence – see 3.2.2), his attitude to course and teacher, and the extent of parental encouragement. The finding that the first two factors are more important in monolingual contexts, while the last factor correlates more closely with success in bilingual contexts, indicates that community attitudes are also at play. It is only to be expected that if two groups hold negative attitudes about each other – or themselves – this will filter through to young learners. When one group sees the other as inferior or when there is a wide culture gap which the two groups wish and have the power to preserve, then bilingualism will be felt to subtract from rather than add to personal growth. Thus *in this social context* an integrative motivation is unlikely to be a determinant of achievement (ibid, p. 218). Intensive instruction may improve the 'hostile' learner's performance in the classroom, but it will have virtually no effect on his spontaneous speech in informal situations with native speakers of his second language. In fact, he will probably try to avoid such situations wherever possible.

It is difficult to assess the applicability of these conclusions from the very complex Canadian setting (see 5.3 and 5.4.3) to a predominantly monolingual Britain. As a nation Britons are by their own admission nationalistic, insular and unshaken in their assumption that 'foreigners' should learn English. Such a stereotype offers bleak prospects, but it is being challenged constantly as the number of L2 learners grows.

How can positive social attitudes be fostered? Tucker and Lambert suggest starting instruction by 10 years of age, before adult prejudices – and inhibitions – have taken root (in Oller and Richards, 1973, pp. 248–50). The greatest improvements in proficiency are recorded as a result of 'total immersion' in the foreign community. But any preparatory teaching programme must be designed to minimise culture shock – *How can those continentals eat horse meat?* – and avoid the disappointment which stems from a discovery that the rules learnt in class are of little help in communicating with real native speakers. Being tongue-tied or feeling child-like when speaking L2 are part of a vicious circle.

Immersion by spending a period of residence abroad is an integral part of many university and college courses. One pilot survey of university languages students confirms that it is the 'open-minded' whose linguistic skills improve most (Willis *et al.*, 1977, p. 84). This fits previous findings that an 'authoritarian' personality is a barrier to L2 learning; a flexible outlook on acquiring new behaviour patterns is necessary. Further benefits of living abroad were brought to light: students' self-esteem was enhanced, and their attitude to the French, German *and* British communities improved as a result of a 'considerable reappraisal' of their perceptions of all groups. Most interesting is the fact that students who had office jobs during the year abroad showed a significantly greater all-round benefit than those who followed university courses. This underlines Gardner's insistence on the role of social context, and we can look forward to more insights coming from this area.

3.3.5 Is bilingualism harmful?

Weinreich reports the suggestion that 'bilingual persons may be morally depraved because they do not receive effective religious instruction in their mother-tongue in childhood' (1963, p. 119)! A more common contention concerns the effects of bilingualism on intellectual and emotional development. We can discredit the claim that child bilingualism has any lasting negative effect on intellectual development; in fact, in later childhood bilinguals often perform better on intelligence tests than do their monolingual peers. A detrimental effect on emotional adjustment is by no means an inevitable consequence of becoming bilingual and thereby more or less bicultural. Some learners may experience a loss of identity or a division of loyalties which leaves them in doubt and confusion. Some may feel that their foreignness prompts suspicion and rejection on the part of the L2 group. But where the attitudes of both communities are favourable to each other, bilingualism widens horizons and grants independence.

The question of attitudes is taken up again in Chapter 5.

Further reading

Clear introductions to first-language acquisition are to be found in Cruttenden (1979) and Aitchison (1976), who treats related issues in an entertaining style. Halliday (1975) documents a case study from a functional viewpoint, Brown (1976) in syntactic terms. C. Chomsky (1971) describes later comprehension difficulties. Ferguson and Slobin (1973) provide data from many languages. Piaget (1960) relates linguistic to intellectual development.

A readable introduction to adult second-language learning is given by Christophersen (1973). McLaughlin (1978) is a comprehensive study of childhood learning. Hatch (1978) presents a collection of empirical studies. The major work on attitudes and motivation is Gardner and Lambert (1972). Gardner gives a succinct account in Giles and St Clair (1979). For an emphasis on teaching see Corder (1973) and Wilkins (1972).

Suggestions for inquiry

1 Describe how adults communicate with infants and children of different ages.
2 How do adults succeed in interpreting what infants and children are communicating?
3 What are the implications for second-language learning of the assumption that for children language is sound, for adults sense?
4 If it is impossible to achieve native proficiency in pronunciation, what kind of standard should teachers set?
5 If there is a single process for first- and second-language learning, should teachers tolerate students' grammatical errors?

6 Review all the errors made in L2 written work over a term. Can they be categorised according to their source?
7 How can your contacts with L2 outside of the classroom be supplemented while in the country of your L1?
8 How can integrative motivation be introduced into the *teaching* of a foreign language?
9 In using L2 for what purposes – e.g. counting, reprimanding – do you get tongue-tied, and why?
10 Is there any fundamental difference between switching from formal to informal English and switching from L1 to L2?
11 Was Sweet (opening epigram) right in his statements on linguistic ability and intelligence?
12 Using Weinreich's dominance criteria (Figure 3.3), draw up profiles of the relation between L1 and L2 for (a) yourself; (b) an immigrant child in this country; and (c) an immigrant adult.

4

Language and Situation

> Ordinarily a cultural pattern is to be defined both in terms of function and of form, the two concepts being inseparably intertwined in practice, however convenient it may be to dissociate them in theory.
>
> E. Sapir (Source unknown)

4.1 Sociolinguistic inquiry

The study of the interrelation between language and society comes, as we noted earlier (1.4), under the heading of *sociolinguistics*. In this chapter we shall look at some of the situational factors which influence the linguistic behaviour of individual speakers and also of larger social groups.

Sooner or later every learner realises that L2, whether it is French or Ponapean, Russian or Telugu, is by no means uniform and homogeneous but in fact subject to many variations of form. Just how soon this awareness is achieved depends on the nature and diversity of his contacts with that particular speech community and the linguistic varieties (4.3.6) in use there. The telex operator in England receiving and decoding messages in, say, German, will certainly guess that their truncated form draws on only a few of the options offered within the German grammatical system as a whole. The foreign scientist, quite able to deliver in fluent English a conference paper on his specialism, learns that a variety of English laden with passives and devoid of personal reference is totally inappropriate for the small-talk in the bar afterwards.

The concept of *appropriateness* which we discussed earlier (1.3.4 and 3.3), the 'suiting' of language use to the situation, is a crucial one in improving the efficiency of communication in terms of both impact on the receiver and economy of effort. After all, the listener has certain expectations of how the speaker will behave, and if these are not fulfilled, reception of the message may be impaired in some way. We will return to this idea below (see 4.5). The fact that a speaker, when using his native language, makes these often subtle adjustments almost unconsciously does not speed his realisation that there is equivalent variation in the use of other languages in terms of 'who says or writes what to whom, how, when and where'. This sensitivity to speech variation is essential for anyone concerned either with attaining an active command of a foreign language in more than one situation, or with a language as a key to those who speak it and to their place in a social organisation. Most learners in these categories have at some stage the occasion to go abroad and meet members of the foreign speech-community face to face. This is often an integral part of a formal teaching programme during an undergraduate period of residence abroad, for example, or it may take the form of a business or holiday trip. It is necessary to refine constantly perceptions of appropriateness in the foreign language, because the social norms governing speech not only vary from one group of speakers to another but also change over time. Just as a person during socialisation may have to master for L1 the rules of classroom language, essay writing, presenting a seminar paper and addressing colleagues, so that same person, as a learner abroad, will be called upon to perform new *functions* (giving orders, creating relationships, etc.) in new *roles* (as a receptionist, a washer-up, etc.) in new *situations* (registering at a police station, enrolling with a university administration, etc.). These activities may be entirely new, or novel only in so far as they involve foreign interlocutors and a foreign sociocultural background. Even in this latter respect their range will far exceed anything experienced 'at home' in the classroom, however great an emphasis has been put on role-playing and other simulation techniques.

In this chapter our aim is to indicate the kind of factors which can be held to underlie decisions as to what constitutes an appropriate utterance in a given context. It will be helpful here to view language use as one form of societal behaviour, conditioning and conditioned by other processes, like social mobility, itself related to factors such as age, sex and socio-economic class. Whether language behaviour *or* social structure is seen as primary in shaping the other is a matter of perspective. Without doubt both viewpoints are useful and complementary. During instruction in the country of L1, access to the social characteristics of L2 speakers will often have been through the study of texts, spoken or written, removed from their situation of production. The *contextualisation* of these source materials, the identification of the speaker or writer, the audience and their situation, reconstitutes some of the links with the L2 speech community. There is often parallel instruction focusing explicitly on the social, economic and political institutions of the foreign country, which in its turn provides a framework within which to view groups of speakers. The factors described below are intended to ensure the compatibility of approaches from the two directions – to permit the learner to anticipate the need for a change of language variety as the social situation changes, and conversely to infer a change in situation from a change in language use.

There is, moreover, a further intention, one which is directly related to field-work methods in sociolinguistics. Gumperz expresses it very clearly:

> The most successful investigators are those who can utilise their background knowledge of the culture in elicitation. It is not enough . . . simply to observe performances. The investigator must find ways of testing the speakers' ability to vary their performances. Hence his success depends on his knowledge of sociolinguistic rules (in Gumperz and Hymes, 1972, p. 25).

The learner must discover 'the rules of the game' and learn how to use them. A prior insight into their nature, together with a determination to seek contact with a broad range of speakers and situations may make progress in L2 performance more rapid.

Finally, let us turn to a definition of sociolinguistics as 'the study of the characteristics of language varieties, the characteristics of their functions, and the characteristics of their speakers as these three constantly interact, change, and change one another within a speech community' (Fishman, 1970, p. 4). These are the concerns which will occupy our attention for the remainder of this chapter and in Chapter 5.

4.2 Categories of information

As we noted in Chapter 1, there has been considerable reluctance on the part of some linguists to study and describe *speech*. The emphasis was instead on the construction of an underlying *system* – *langue* or *competence*. However, the language learner is strongly motivated to follow this change of focus from system to use since his chances of ever meeting Chomsky's 'ideal speaker-listener' or finding himself in a 'completely homogeneous speech-community' are nil. Halliday gives clear guidance as to what our preoccupations must be: 'It is only by reference to the various situations and situation types in which language is used that we can understand its functioning and its effectiveness' (in Fishman, 1968, p. 151). We will be taking each of these factors in turn – situation types (4.3), functions (4.4) and effectiveness (4.4.3) – and illustrating how they influence language variation.

But first, if we are to view speech as an instrument of communication, mediating between persons and their situations, it is necessary to ask what *kinds* of information can be communicated verbally.

One possible distinction is in terms of three broad categories. First, *cognitive* information concerns the factual content of an utterance, the communicating of emotions and desires and of ideas about the outside world. It has long been a central topic in linguisitcs, and one of interest to philosophers also. We shall return to this theme elsewhere when we look at how relations between language and 'things' are expressed (6.1 and Chapter 9).

But to maintain that speech conveys only cognitive information is to adopt a narrow view. When an individual talks, he reveals a great deal to a perceptive interlocutor about his own identity and his social, educational, professional and regional background. On meeting a stranger, at a party, say, a listener instinctively attempts to 'place' that person on one or more of the above dimensions, while the other person is going through the same detective process. Accent, the possible use of dialect words or unusual grammatical structures and other, *non-vocal* behaviour like facial expression, gesture, posture and gait all supply clues to identity (see 5.1 and 5.2). This second kind of information is termed *indexical*. Unlike cognitive information to a large extent its control escapes the speaker.

The involuntary nature of the information conveyed also applies, although perhaps to a lesser degree, to *situation management*, our third category. It is not normal in Western societies for both interlocutors in a *dyadic* (two-participant) exchange to speak simultaneously (whereas in certain African communities it is). The norm is to speak in turn (but not 'out of turn') even if the turns are not distributed to the equal satisfaction of both partners. Exchanges are initiated not only by asking *What have you got to say for yourself?* or ordering *Speak up!* Eye contact, smiling, a shrug of the shoulders, a trailing intonation and downward body movements may all signal a willingness to pass over the responsibility for talking. The same kinds of devices ensure that conversation continues without awkward moments and is concluded when appropriate, perhaps with a glance at one's watch and an *Anyway, must dash*.

All three kinds of information will be present in any sequence of utterances, and clearly their relative weight will depend on the particular *situation* and on the *functions* the utterances are intended to serve. It is these two concepts which we will now proceed to explore.

4.3 Components of the speech situation

We are concerned here only with situations in which speech is expected to occur, that is, *speech situations*. Whereas at a concert or in an examination there is normally no talking, a party is a typical example of a speech situation. Several conversations may be in progress simultaneously at the same party, and each may be seen as being constituted by one or more *speech events*. These are 'the largest units for which one can discover linguistic structure' (Coulthard, 1977, p. 39), and are directly governed by rules or norms for the use of speech. Jokes are a good example of a speech event (see 10.4).

What is now needed is a framework which will allow us to distinguish the various elements constituting the situation of a speech event. The first requirement is for a *speaker* or *sender*, who in most cases will be communicating with a *hearer* or *receiver*. People do talk to themselves, of course, both unconsciously and quite deliberately to regulate their own behaviour (*Care-ful, let's not slip up now*), or perhaps in a theatrical soliloquy intended to be overheard. Speaker and hearer are in contact, linked both by some kind of *rapport* which motivates their exchange and by a *channel* through which the message can pass. The message, which is intended to achieve some end, has a *content*, a *form* and a *structure* – paragraphs, verses, groups of ciphers, bursts of speech punctuated by silence, and so on – and is composed of elements chosen from a given *code*. That is, it draws on a system of signs (see 1.2 on the question of system and use), linguistic or other, for its realisation.

Together these elements are termed the *components of the speech situation*. Below we will elaborate on them, basing our presentation on that of Hymes (1972, pp. 58–65).

4.3.1 Participants

Obviously the number of people present at the speech event will have a bearing on its form, and a meeting of six people will not be the same as one of 600. A quorum for a meeting is essentially a minimum required number of potential speakers, even if not all may have the right to vote. Not all may have an equal right to speak. Which individual is cast in which role – speaker, hearer(s) or observer(s) – at any one moment depends, as we have seen, on some form of agreement, and in many instances the allocation of these roles is determined by wider social convention. Children, and in some cultures women, are expected to 'be seen but not heard' or 'speak only when they are spoken to'. Hymes relates an anecdote of a Russian guest's astonishment when the children of his French host did not address him at the dinner table since his own children would have been expected to join in conversation with a visitor to their home (in Fishman, 1968, p. 129).

When two people engage in conversation, they engage in a relationship which can range from the most remote to the most intimate. It is to be expected that the nature of this relationship will be overtly expressed in the course of the speech event, and nowhere more obviously than in the forms of address used by the participants. In French, German, Italian, Russian and Spanish the personal pronoun systems are more developed than in English, offering choices between *tu/vous, du/Sie, tu/lei, ты/вы* and *tu/usted*. Other languages present even more complex systems. However, we shall defer discussion of forms of address until later (5.4), partly because they merit generous attention, but most of all because in the present chapter we are focusing less on individuals than on *social identity*. In addition to having a unique identity as 'Christine Dupont. or 'Hans Schultz', these individuals also have a *status*, a recognised position in a social structure, examples being wife, lover, teacher, worker, doctor. Each status entails certain values, responsibilities, rights and duties, and requires its holder to enact certain *roles*, or behaviour patterns. Every member of society is often called upon to enact a variety of roles within the space of a day or even an hour – husband-wife, father–child, man–woman, employee–employer, witness–magistrate, and so on. These are known as *role relationships*. A simple illustration of how they may affect speech is that of parent–child 'baby talk': *go tatas* for *walk*, *peton* for *pied*, *chicha* for *carne*, *hacer nonon* for *dormir*.

In many role relationships individuality may be suppressed, while one's standing as an actor in a social category is stressed. The relative emphasis can be described on a scale defined at one extreme by the term *private* and at the other by *transactional*, but the existence of only two terms is not meant to imply a necessary polarisation. A vicar addressing his flock at matins may prefer 'the personal approach' to a rigid clergyman–parishioner relationship, but one of the parishioners may still find it hard in the local pub afterwards to forget the vicar's official standing and crack a dubious joke in his presence. That the form of speech varies with the role relationship is immediately felt for L1, and it can be assumed that this is a universal phenomenon.

4.3.2 Setting

Setting encompasses not only the place or *locale*, and the *time*, but also the *scene*, which is a more abstract concept. For example, two acts of a play which take place on the same stage and with the same scenery might be separated in the programme by the indication *Ten days later* or *The next morning*. The scene has changed, though the locale has not. Certain types of activity tend to recur in certain scenes at relatively fixed and predictable times. British Members of Parliament, for instance, tend to gather in the Chamber of the House of Commons or committee rooms between, say 10 a.m. and 6 p.m., yet on occasions a session may last all night. Classes typically are held between 9 a.m. and 4 p.m. in a classroom, sometimes on the grass outside. In both of these examples the presence of certain participants is obligatory, in the first that of MPs and the Speaker, in the second a teacher and pupils with the optional participation of a student-teacher. This provides us with a definition of a *situation* as 'a *cultural form* consisting primarily of understandings concerning the scheduling of, and allocation of space for, the occurrence of *other* cultural forms'; in other words, the teacher is expected to do something, i.e. teach. Departure from the socially recognised situation might introduce confusion in the role relationships. To hold an academic seminar at midnight, or at noon in a public house is an *incongruent* situation which could alter radically the participants' perception of their roles. Of course, this might well have been the desired effect. Since *situation* is culturally defined, cross-cultural differences can be expected. A lecturer at the Sorbonne may not tolerate any questions from his audience. An English woman employed in an office in Madrid might find it strange to have to answer to her boss in the evening and on a Saturday morning. Women might find in certain situations (and in a wider range in France and Spain than in England) that their initiating an exchange is misconstrued.

Situation is, then, a generalisation which enables us to handle interactions between role relationship, time and setting. A further level of abstraction will be presented in our discussion of the next component.

4.3.3 Message

There are two components to be mentioned under this heading. The first is the *message form*, 'the way we say things'. That form co-varies with situation is the main thesis of this chapter, and as the illustrations accumulate, so the possible dimensions of variation should become more apparent.

In the second place we distinguish *message content* or *topic*, 'what we say'. *To change the subject for a moment* is a commonly heard English utterance. An example will suffice to underline the difference between these two components: *Would you mind passing me that book?* and *Give me the book!* differ not in topic but in form, and signal sets of role relationships which contrast in their open expression of authority. The form–content distinction is implicit, too, in the familiar criticism of 'empty rhetoric' so often levelled at politicians. Form itself signals information, either providing indexical clues to the sender's identity, or, to take the case of a warning notice printed in bold red type, deliberately underscoring the verbal content.

That certain topics tend to occur or not to occur in defined situations is evidenced when a speaker is reprimanded for 'straying from the subject', 'talking shop' or even 'dropping a clanger'. Taboos operate in all spheres of human activity, and again vary from culture to culture. Censorship is not only institutional but also conventional. We find that we can group together social situations constrained by a common set of rules of behaviour and where typically a predictable range of topics is voiced. Thus 'the class', 'the lecture' and 'the tutorial' situations can be said to constitute a higher-level grouping which we call the *domain* of Education. Similarly, we can set up domains of Religion, Work, Family, Government, Law. The exact number and their delimitation will be determined by the social structures of the speech-community in question. Which variety of speech (4.3.6) is used in which domain(s) is a question considered later in this chapter (4.5.1).

4.3.4 Norms

All social behaviour, including language behaviour, is patterned. Such patterns are the reflection and expression of normative rules, often unwritten, which exert pressures towards conformity. Speech *norms of interaction* govern when it is appropriate to speak or to be silent, whether to whisper or shout, to use slang or ritual expressions. Different sets of norms will be seen to apply in different domains. Witness *You may act like that at school, but it won't do at home!*

The interpretation put on speech behaviour remains largely consistent within a speech community (see 2.2), but when members of two communities are in contact interpretations may be unpredictable. An Englishman may well ascribe non-existent motives to a Frenchman, Italian or Spaniard who constantly touches his interlocutor's arm, and this again anticipates the question of attitudes to language use (see Chapter 5).

4.3.5 Channel

While we do not intend to look at such media as sculpture, painting, dress and traffic-lights (these are the objects of other branches of semiotics – see 1.4), there are, however, certain 'non-verbal communicating activities which accompany verbal behaviour in conversation' and which are known collectively as *para-language* (Abercrombie, in Laver and Hutcheson, 1972, p. 64). These activities include not only gesture, voice modulation, eye movements and facial expressions but also touch, posture and the relative spatial positioning of the interlocutors. We have noted their function in initiating and sustaining contact (4.2), but of course they may at times replace verbal communication entirely. A nod may be as good as a wink or a shrug of the shoulders, though not over the telephone. Para-language tends to be culture-specific, and in so far as it is indexical of a particular speech community we shall be looking at it again (5.1 and 5.2).

A second channel of interest to us here is *pseudo-language*, which consists of vocal sounds interjected by the speaker in a pause for thought and by the listener to indicate continued attention, agreement, surprise. They occur frequently in face-to-face interaction and especially over the telephone, though it seems that Spaniards are much happier than the English to talk away without this reassuring feedback. An interesting point to note is that, while the actual sound uttered is very similar in many languages, its conventional representation may vary considerably. English *uh-uh*, *mm*, *hm* has the equivalents *aha*, *mm*, *hm* or *mhm* in German and угу (*ugu*) or гм (*gm*) in Russian. Words, too, may be interjected, for instance *claro*, *ya*, *d'accord*, *ach so*, but they are not truly verbal in that they do not constitute structured combinations (cf. 2.4 for the characteristics of animal communication).

Lastly we have (structured) *language* proper. The principal channels are speech and writing, and the corresponding variations in language use can be striking. However, because in L1 we rarely speak as we write or write as we speak, the contrast is not always present in our minds. This is perhaps the area where L2 learners most frequently confuse their styles. While for French it is well known that the preterite tense is reserved for written communication, and perhaps speeches or lectures from dusty notes, learners may be less aware of variations like those shown in Figure 4.1. Obviously the role relationship, the formality of the situation and a desire to impress or otherwise likewise constrain the selection of form.

As the channel is more narrowly defined, so other variations become apparent. Telephoning, which limits participants to the vocal–auditory channel with no recourse to gesture, tends to be verbally more explicit. The EXCARRUTHERS ADVISE UPFOLLOWING STORY ROMEWARDS STOP 'telegrammese' is an example of how far written usage can vary.

4.3.6 Variety

Broadly this refers to the language used in the sense of Arabic, Chinese or Swahili, more narrowly to Australian, American, Indian or 'Oxford' English, for example. A variety may be, then, a language or a regionally

Figure 4.1
Writing and speech contrasted

Writing	**Speech**
Que vous a-t-il dit?	*Il vous a dit quoi?*
Combien avez-vous payé cet appareil?	*Tu l'as payé combien, ce machin?*
Je ne crois pas qu'il vienne	*Je ne crois pas qu'il viendra*

defined dialect (see 2.3), or a concept defined by reference to the class, sex and age of its speakers (5.3). Here we prefer to use *variety* as being a neutral term for any situationally and socially defined form of speech in common use by a group. The components of situation therefore allow us to distinguish different varieties, but at the same time the variety is itself a component in that it furnishes information on the speaker and, at least in part, determines the form of any response.

4.3.7 Genre

Familiar in the literary sense of poem, comedy, short story, etc., *genre* here includes riddle, prayer, sales talk, curse, business letter, proverb, and other functionally defined styles. Genre often coincides with speech events, but not necessarily. For example, a sermon typically occurs at a specified point in a church service, but the properties of the genre may be invoked in a lecture or at a party for some special effect. This effect could well be lost on a foreigner who is unaware of the allusion 'embedding' one situation in another.

4.3.8 Key

Key covers the tone, manner or spirit in which an utterance is produced and incorporates such notions as solemn, serious, perfunctory. To strike an appropriate key is a concern of public speakers and of participants in any kind of ceremony.

4.3.9 Ends

No utterance is produced entirely without constraints, as we are seeing, nor is it gratuitous. An utterance is an act, a *speech act* having a purpose, which might be to inform, to persuade, to advise, to thank, to order, etc. A survey of speech acts is central to our view of language as an instrument, thus more space will be devoted to this topic below (4.4.3).

4.3.10 Feedback

A speaker normally receives a constant flow of information from his interlocutor – via all channels – indicating the latter's reaction to what he is saying and allowing him to modify one or more of the variables given above. For example, he may suggest a change of scene, talk louder, be more polite or agree to give explanations.

This concludes our survey of the components of the speech event. We now move on to some different approaches to the uses or functions which language can fulfil.

4.4 Language functions

We hinted earlier (4.2) at some of the shortcomings of viewing language as 'communicating ideas, emotions and desires' (Sapir, 1921, p. 8) by arguing that language use conveys varied and complex kinds of information relating not only to the speaker's beliefs but also to his identity, group affiliations and relationship with his listener. We can make a corresponding broad distinction, then, between *informational* and *interpersonal* functions. Malinowski wrote that 'to regard [language] as a means for the embodiment or expression of thought is to take a one-sided view of one of its most derivative and specialised functions' (in Laver and Hutcheson, 1972, p. 152). What, then, are its other functions? We will look at the categories of language functions proposed by Hymes, adapting them slightly, and then briefly compare those of Ervin-Tripp (in Fishman, 1968).

If we see language as a system offering to the speaker possibilities which he can use selectively, then the concept of function, closely relevant as it is to language-learning goals, affords some guidance as to where the selections are best made.

4.4.1 Function as focus

The basis of Hymes's taxonomy is that of *focus* on a given component of the speech event. We will isolate nine basic components from among those treated above. It must be remembered that these functions can be realised through other channels, especially para-language, but we will restrict ourselves to their verbal realisation.

(1) **Expressive**. The prime focus is on the sender, his emotions and attitudes. Different languages may have different conventions for the expression of such feelings. On the French stage one might hear *Je t' H'aime* with strong aspiration of [h]. Vowel length can serve the same function: *Qu'elle est beeelle!* We can compare this with English *What a fiiiine boy!*, or with word stress *What a fine bòy!* The modal system of *can*, *may, should, probably, certainly*, etc., enables someone to express judgements on the likelihood or necessity of an event. To use such conventions is a deliberate choice on the part of the speaker, whereas indexical information is conveyed unconsciously. This is not to say that one cannot 'lose' a regional or foreign accent in order to conceal one's origins. It means simply that listeners will assign to such a speaker an identity which is not his real one. An English person who has lived in Munich, for example, and acquired the accent could well be labelled in Hamburg as a Bavarian and be credited with a character to match.

(2) **Directive**. Here the focus is on the receiver, to persuade, influence, command in order to bring about changes in his attitude or behav-

iour. *Prière de faire suivre, Links fahren, This way up, Don't do that* are examples. This is an important function to which we will return at length (4.4.3).

(3) **Contact**. *Hearing you loud and clear, Are you reading me?, The line's bad, Plus fort!, C'est illisible, La communication a été coupée* all stress the physical channel between the two parties.

(4) **Phatic**. For communication to take place effectively some kind of psychological *rapport* must also be created. Whether it is between two strangers meeting for the first time, with or without introduction, or between two friends of long standing meeting for the first time that day, their conversation will very often be prefaced by remarks about the weather. These are probably not motivated by any desire to inform or genuine interest in climatic conditions. They serve as a customary preamble, a decent delay before entering into transactions, a sounding-out period to ensure that the other is willing to talk. Rather than passing comment on 'the dismal day', a Russian might prefer to embark on the topics of work and family, while a German's preoccupation is likely to be with his health. Thus, an English person in Kiev or Kiel could be surprised to find his banal remark on the cold taken as a cue for a lengthy exposition on fluctuations in temperature over the previous five years. Is it only in the English-speaking world that the need for *phatic communion*, as it is termed, is *so* heartfelt? Does this explain the reputed English reserve and diffidence? Does no one else beat about the bush before getting down to brass tacks?

(5) **Referential**. The message content or topic is of prime interest to the scientist and the philosopher concerned with conveying information on phenomena, beliefs and theories. Form is important, but for logical rather than aesthetic reasons. Not so much the beauty of the idea as its consistency. *О чем он говорит?*, *Qu'est-ce qu'il raconte?, What's he on about?*, highlight the referential function, and the answer will invoke vocabulary and terminology related to a particular sphere of activity or interest.

(6) **Aesthetic**. Sometimes termed the *poetic* function, it is of interest not only in the study of Rilke, Pushkin, Lorca or Verlaine. Any use of language where the form itself is intended to be of focal interest serves an aesthetic function. *Une phrase bien tournée* points to this function, which may predominate in an advertisement for beauty products or bath oil, in chanting, babbling or tongue-twisters. Considerable prestige attaches to such forms of eloquence in many societies where the raconteur, the toast-master and the poet, or equivalents, are held in high esteem.

(7) **Situational**. The focus is on the situation – the intersection of setting, time and role relationship (see 4.3.2). *An apartment in Brooklyn in the late twenties* sets the scene, while *This is not the time or place*

for that invokes not only setting but norms, as does *It's your turn to speak now*.

(8) **Contextual**. Attention can be focused on the sequential organisation of the message structure. This serves a 'cross-referencing' function important in any book or lecture: *voir chapitre 2 ci-dessus, wie bereits erwähnt, see below, s.o., más abajo, As I said at the outset.* (Chapter 10 presents a fuller discussion of this function.)

(9) **Meta-linguistic**. Using language to talk about language is to focus on this function. *What does 'gazebo' mean?* It resolves, or attempts to resolve misunderstandings to ensure that the code – that is, the system – is shared and agreed upon by its users. The meta-linguistic function is apparent throughout this book, giving as it does definitions of terms such as *language, situation, consonant* to expand an already familiar meta-language including *noun, adjective* and *sentence.* The importance of speech within a society is reflected in the richness of its meta-language. A glance at the entries for 'speech' in *Roget's Thesaurus* will confirm this for English. In many communities verbal artistry and virtuosity confer prestige, as in Black American English which has a proliferation of meta-linguistic terms, like *rapping, shucking, running it down, gripping, playing the dozens, signifying, marking* (Burling, 1970). The 'conteur' of Quebec and the few remaining reciters of the Yakut 'olonxo', whose telling may last five or six evenings, enjoy privileged status indeed.

Summary

Function is a matter of focus, and it would be a mistake to assume that a speech act performs only a single function. Phatic expressions like *Hi, Hola, Salut* cannot be said to refer to anything. They acknowledge presence. On the other hand, *Nice weather for ducks* does have a manifest topic, but one which is trivial in that situation. *Insert coin when light flashes* is directive, referential and situational, and *Kindly refrain from smoking in the auditorium* has an added function of creating a (limited) *rapport*. Any speech act is likely to serve several functions simultaneously, thus it is their relative importance, the role relationship binding the speakers and the prevailing behavioural norms, all culturally determined, which will mould the speaker's ultimate choice. This is assuming, of course, a mastery of the linguistic means and of the conventions for their appropriate use. A learner wishing to use L2 for communicating scientific information might profitably concentrate on the referential, meta-linguistic, contextual and, possibly, directive functions. For a pilot the contact and referential functions might be of foremost interest. But these are obviously restricted uses of language and generally a learner will wish to exploit all functions. Certainly, any direct contact with L2 speakers will be an incentive to develop subtle means of directing others. And here another complication emerges, namely that there is no one-to-one correspondence between form and function. *It's stuffy in here* and *Open the window* may in appropriate circumstances fulfil the same directive function. Research in this area is in its early stages and patterning is of a tentative and partial nature of little help as yet to language learners.

4.4.2 Function as goal

This system was devised specifically to classify the initiation of two-participant conversations and it is of interest to us in that it sheds some light on *why* people choose to speak to one another.

Requests for goods, services or information – *Tell me a story* but not, of course, *Tell me another*.

Requests for social responses – These reactions may include dominance, recognition, praise, sympathy. *How do I look?, Aren't I clever? Forgive me* are acts in point.

Offering information or instruction – *Let me show you, Can I help you?*

Avoidance conversations – Where the alternative activities are thought unpleasant or silence unbearable, then a person may attempt to strike up a conversation. Phatic communion figures prominently in this category. The coffee-bar next to the university library is a likely setting.

Expressive monologues – The important point with this function is that the speaker is reacting to an external stimulus and expressing joy, sorrow, preoccupation 'without attending to the hearer's comments which may be minimal or absent'. Such obliviousness may or may not be a breach of etiquette. The writer V. S. Pritchett (1954) describes two Spaniards in 'conversation': 'They are aware of nothing but their individual selves, and the very detail of their talk is a method of defeating any awareness of each other. They are lost in the sound of their own humming, monotonous egos and only a bullet could wake them out of it.' The Spanish are not alone in unburdening their souls to 'good listeners'.

Routines – The examples given by Ervin-Tripp are greetings, thanks, apologies, offers of service by waitresses and salespeople. Their predictability serves to underline the normative nature of rules of interaction between actors of different roles in recurrent social situations. To imagine that routines are confined to a narrow range of *transactions* (see 4.3.1) may well be to underestimate their over-all frequency. Some, like *Do you come here often?*, are well-known clichés. Ceremonies are an extreme case of predictability. Two weddings held in the same church on the same day will be identical in sequence, only the names of the couples and, perhaps, the sermon varying. Many everyday exchanges show a similar ritual form. To answer *Yes* to *Have you heard the one about . . .?* is to deflate the would-be joke-teller.

We can describe the speech event as a series of utterances ordered by a set of *sequencing rules*. The opening of a telephone conversation can be broken down into the following sequence:

(1) *summons* → (2) *answer* → (3) *continuation* → (4) *response*

The summons is the ringing of the bell, while the answer provides a greeting and/or number with usually a further identification of the receiver, by name and/or status. Depending on the relationship, the caller may or may not offer greetings and identification before proceeding with the message. The response follows in due course. We have so to speak, a series of 'slots' which can be filled in different ways. Just as the 'fillers' may vary from situation to situation and be more or less stereotyped, so the number, order and nature of the 'slots' may vary from community to community. A Frenchman answering the telephone says *J'écoute* ('I'm listening'), whereas a Spaniard says *! Digame!* ('Speak to me!') and a Norwegian waits for the caller to speak first! The admonition of a young child for not 'saying hello' to a friend of her mother contrasts with Hymes's report that among the Wasco, an Amerindian community, 'practice is *not* to greet someone who joins a group, courtesy requires that one does not call attention to the new-comer until he or she no longer is such' (in Ardener, 1971, pp. 72-3).

The question of ritual use of language leads us to consider next a particular function of language use where not only form but also the precise characteristics of the situation are crucial.

4.4.3 Speaking as doing - performatives

The term *performative* is due to Austin (1962) and it refers to a particular class of speech act (see 4.3.9). In his highly entertaining argument he draws attention to the difference between utterances such as *I apologise* and *The man broke the window*. While the second utterance is verifiable and can be classified as referentially 'true' or 'false', the first is to be judged instead by its sincerity, its acceptance, in short its felicity. We ask whether the speaker achieved his intention, not whether he was right or wrong. Austin labelled the first type of utterance *performative*, the other *constative*.

On closer examination, however, the two examples quoted above reveal themselves to be marginal cases. We have already demonstrated that few, if any, utterances have an exclusively referential function (4.4.1). Furthermore, if the utterance *The man broke the window* is reported to a third party, the reporter may well use any verb of speech other than *say*: *He claimed/declared/boasted/swore that the man broke the window*. The speaker himself, if wishing to emphasise his statement, may say *I maintain* . . . or even *I testify that the man broke the window.* Such verbs are intuitively closely allied in this use to *I apologise*. Already the constantive–performative distinction is becoming blurred, the constative being a concealed' performative.

We can pick out many utterances on the same *I + first person singular, present simple, active* model: *I name this ship 'Happy Days', I find you guilty, I bet you £5, I challenge you to a duel, I resign, I promise to go.* They all have in common that they cannot be literally false and that their utterance is an essential part of the performance of the act. You cannot make a promise without saying so. We can term this class *explicit performatives.*

However, we do not have to look far to find other utterances which satisfy these same conditions, yet which have a different syntactic form: *Notice is given that* . . ., *Dogs must be kept on a lead, Check, Snap, Out, Guilty* are a few examples. Going beyond these well-defined situations, we realise that acts of 'promising', 'warning', 'advising' and 'directing' can be realised by many different forms of utterance. *Thin ice* and *The ice isn't as safe as it might be* can both serve the same purpose. *I'll see you tomorrow* – a threat, a promise, or a simple declaration? Only a knowledge of the context of utterance can allow us to decide which interpretation to favour.

If we look for a consistent relationship between the syntactic classes of interrogative and imperative and the situational functions of 'requesting information' and 'ordering', we soon stumble on such sentences as *Will you close that door* and *Don't tell me you don't know*. Do we end them with a question-mark or an exclamation-mark?

We come, therefore, to three conclusions: that the constative–performative distinction is misleading, in that *to say anything is to perform an act of some kind*; that form is no necessary indication of function; that the components of situation are an essential factor. Let us explore the implications of these conclusions further to arrive at a better understanding of the notion of 'performative'.

First, if a variety of forms can be used in a performative function and simultaneously in other functions, it is necessary to distinguish between the different kinds of act performed. At one level the production of an utterance can be considered a *locutionary act* (the act *of* saying) which conveys *meaning*. At another level it is an *illocutionary act* (an act performed *in* saying), perhaps of stating, perhaps of ordering or requesting. We call the communicative purpose which motivates the illocutionary act – the intention to advise, oblige, permit, etc. – its *illocutionary force*. At a third level we distinguish a *perlocutionary act* (an act performed as a result of saying), which may be non-linguistic (the closing of a door) or linguistic (the uttering of a refusal).

Whereas the illocutionary force of explicit performatives is not open to doubt, there may be considerable uncertainty over the force of the other utterances given above, which we will call *indirect performatives*. Both require the presence of certain conditions. We will first ask in general terms what these conditions are and then go on to consider performatives produced in public and private situations (see 4.3.2).

First, the speaker must be able to perform the act in question – only a monarch can dub a knight; only a 'superior' can give an order. Second, the speaker must want to perform the act – it must be *sincere*. Third, the act must be recognised by all concerned to be what it is intended to be. If one party declares *I didn't realise you meant it*, then the act has *misfired*. Finally, the content of the utterance must be in keeping with its illocutionary force. One cannot, for example, genuinely promise to do something one has already done.

In a public situation, where status and pertaining rights and responsibilities are stressed, it is rare that the above conditions are not satisfied. Occasionally a marriage is invalidated because one partner is a bigamist, or a drunk who turns the breathalyser crystals green goes free because he was not properly cautioned. We can therefore expect performatives to be an interesting indicator of social structure in that their effective use is the prerogative of certain officers in defined situations. Conversely, the foreigner must beware in case a condition is not fulfilled which might invalidate a commitment made to him. A few examples will be helpful to illustrate some cross-cultural differences.

In English we *name* a ship and *christen* a child, whereas in German both acts use the same verb: *Ich taufe dich* . . . and *Ich taufe das Schiff auf den Namen* . . .

In French and Spanish a chairman can use only an indirect performative to open or close a meeting: *La séance est levée, Se levanta la sesión.* In Russian the performative is explicit – *Обьявляю заседание открытым*. In German it may be either *Ich erkläre die Sitzung für beendet* or *Die Sitzung ist aufgehoben*.

Cross-cultural differences in the interaction of setting, participants and speech act are found in the marriage ceremony. In England a marriage ceremony can be conducted either by a minister, typically in a church, or by an official at the Registry Office. In France the only legally required and binding ceremony is that performed at the *Mairie*, while in Spain civil ceremonies are discouraged, even since the death of Franco. A registry official is in attendance at the church, however.

Very often in writing, when the *I* is not used, an indication of status accompanies the pronouncement, together with a signature in some cases. *No cycling. Signed (A. Brown) Town Clerk* is a typical example. Comparing the performative acts printed on some European bank-notes (Figure 4.2) we find that the English note is the only one to use *I* (*For the Govr. and Compa. of the Bank of England*). The Russians and Spaniards prefer the corporate (or collective) image: *Государственное Казначейство* ('state treasury'), and *El Banco de España*. The Spanish *pagará* may be indirect, but it is backed by the signatures of *El Gobernador, El Interventor* and *El Cajero*. The German signatures are unattributed, while the French are content with anonymous threats of fines and imprisonment (evidence which would appear to show the social unacceptability of being explicitly threatening).

As the situation becomes more private or less ritual, so the possibility of using alternative forms increases. So, too, does the possibility of misinterpretation. A study of eight Edinburgh firms reported wide discrepancies between management and staff in their understanding of whether messages were intended on the one hand to be 'instructions and decisions' or on the other 'information and advice'. It does seem, however, that in an English speech-community there is a tendency for persons of inferior status to address superiors indirectly – *Would you mind doing . . .?* for *Do . . . !*, *Could I . . . ?* for *Let me . . .* – while equals and superiors use direct and indirect formulations with more or less the same frequency. The latter offer the great advantage of allowing the speaker to be non-committal.

Across speech-communities such misinterpretations may be considerable. A literal translation into Russian of *Can you open the window?* may well be taken as impugning the hearer's ability, certainly not as a

Figure 4.2
Performatives used on bank-notes

	Performative				**Performer**			**Mark**	
	Promise		*Threat*						
	Explicit	*Indirect*	*Explicit*	*Indirect*	*I*	*The bank*	*Unspecified (passive)*	*Signature*	*Status*
English	+				+			+	+
Spanish		–				+		+(3)	+(3)
Russian	+					+			+
French				+			+		
German				+			+	+(2)	

request. And a polite comment passed in admiration of some item of a Russian's personal possessions may result in its being pressed upon you as a gift.

A recent classification of speech acts is that proposed by Katz (1977). Only the main classes are given, by way of example:

Requestives	request, order, beg, urge, etc.
Advisives	advise, warn, recommend, etc.
Expressives	thank, congratulate, apologise, etc.
Permissives	permit, authorise, grant, etc.
Obligatives	vow, resolve, guarantee, etc.
Expositives	claim, insist, concede, etc.
Stipulatives	name, dub, call, etc.

4.4.4 Summary

'One must begin from speaking as a mode of action, not from language as an unmotivated mechanism' (Hymes, in Ardener, 1971, p. 67). It is from this viewpoint that we began the chapter by outlining a simple model of communication (4.1), and making an initial assumption that language use and situation co-vary. We elaborated on a possible set of *components of the speech event*, one of which is speech itself, and illustrated how these interact in a patterned way. That society functions at all stably and that its members co-operate successfully is evidence of rule-governed, normative behaviour. So, too, are the occasions when the rules are not respected, as when jokes fall flat or admonitions like *You shouldn't speak to me like that in front of other people* need to be issued. The components of the speech event provided an initial definition of *speech function* on which we elaborated in the discussion of *performatives*. Much work remains to be done before we can account for the relation between functions and the form of their realisation, or explain systematically just what meanings can be expressed in what situations.

4.5 Repertoire, switching, diglossia

Each individual can be seen as possessing a *repertoire* of varieties whose range will be a reflection of the range of social roles the person is called upon to enact. If his communicative competence is sufficient (see 3.3), the individual can alternate, or *switch* varieties as appropriate from situation to situation. The fact of switching can in itself signal a change in situation.

Blom and Gumperz make a distinction between *metaphorical switching*, which occurs without any accompanying change in roles or situation, and *situational switching*, where there clearly is (in Gumperz and Hymes,

1972, pp. 425–6). They cite in illustration of this distinction the constant switching between the local dialect and the regional standard by citizens and officials in the setting of the local government offices of a small town in northern Norway. The role relationship remained constant throughout, and the excursions into the local dialect served simply to allude to a shared background. When, however, an official and a citizen agreed to talk on a private matter, they literally stepped aside – a change of scene within a fixed locale – and their conversation continued entirely in local dialect, a clear instance of situational switching. Students from family backgrounds with a marked regional dialect often report adopting a more standard variety of English during term and reverting to their local variety when at home.

So far in this chapter we have been concerned primarily with the individual speaker-listener. If we now widen our perspective to encompass groups of speakers, we can imagine a *community linguistic repertoire*. In some instances we find that a community consistently allocates to specific domains (4.3.3) of activity the varieties which collectively it controls, such that in one set of situations only variety A is appropriate and in another only variety B. *Domain* therefore emerges as a concept which bridges the distance between small- and large-scale interactions.

This 'societal allocation of functions to different languages or varieties' (Fishman, 1970, p. 83) is known as *diglossia*. It is very rare for such a 'division of labour' to exist without certain values attaching to the varieties in question, usually on a scale of relative prestige ranging from 'high' (H) to 'low' (L) with perhaps a variety occupying a 'middle' position (M). This is the case, for example, in the Arab world with Classical Arabic (H) and local vernaculars (L), in Greece with Katharevusa (H) and Dhimotiki (L) and in German-speaking Switzerland with Hochdeutsch (H) and Schwyzertütsch (L). The stigma of the 'low' variety may be so great that some L speakers deny using it or even that it exists. This is in spite of the great differences – grammatical, phonological and lexical – which are always found between the two. Speakers acquire L in the home, H being *superposed* in that it is usually added later, beginning from early socialisation at school. This private–public split can be seen throughout the range of domains, with L normally preferred in the family, folk literature, radio 'soap operas' and the shop floor, while H is reserved for government, education, religion, and the media.

Fishman's definition of diglossia includes not only different varieties but 'different languages' (2.3), so relating this essentially social phenomenon to *bilingualism*, which is essentially a characterisation of *individual* linguistic versatility. Bi- and even pluri-lingualism are widespread within the frontiers of European nations like Belgium, France, Luxemburg,

Switzerland and the Soviet Union (which has over 100 nationalities). Some countries, like West Germany and France, have sizeable groups of transient *Gastarbeiter* in addition to what are considered indigenous populations.

The relationship between bilingualism and diglossia admits four theoretical possibilities. Communities displaying *neither bilingualism nor diglossia*, if they exist, will be small and isolated, certainly not the case in Europe. *Bilingualism with diglossia* is the case in German-speaking cantons of Switzerland where the majority of speakers have control of both Hochdeutsch and Schwyzertütsch, which is commonly used with great pride in the cantonal assemblies. In Luxemburg the child first acquires Letzeburgesch, adding at primary school Letzeburgesch–German and later German and French. Religion is conducted in German, government in French. In Sauris, a German linguistic enclave in north-eastern Italy, three varieties are in common usage, Italian (H), Friulan (M) and German (L), which is losing ground.

Diglossia without bilingualism obtains among older speakers in rural Alsace, thus the German dialect (L) survives. If we look to England following the Norman Conquest, pre-revolutionary Russia and Finland until 1939, we see French and Swedish being used by a ruling elite, with a class of interpreters acting as go-betweens. A similar dislocation was apparent in the 1960s in Montreal businesses, with English monolingual managers and French monolingual workers. The government promotion of bilingualism in Canada is now altering the picture. *Bilingualism without diglossia* characterises communities in the process of rapid social change where there is no widely accepted social consensus on values attaching to varieties. Thus all survive, at least temporarily. This was the case in the last 1960s in East Belgium where the majority of persons are German–French bilinguals, yet no functional pattern had been established.

'Who speaks what and when' is further influenced by government policy as to the status accorded to the language of the community. French is the sole national official language of France, but Breton, Occitan, Basque and Alsatian are tolerated and are taught – except for Alsatian – in some schools. Switzerland has four joint official languages – French, German, Italian and Romansch. Belgium is divided into French and Dutch linguistic zones, with Brussels having bilingual status. In the Soviet Union regional languages are recognised in eduation and administration, while everyone is expected to learn Russian, the national official language. In Spain Catalan is on the verge of regaining the official status lost during Franco's rule.

More and more the fact of plurilingualism seems to result, in Western Europe, in violent conflict. Open clashes opposing Flemings against

Walloons, Basques and Bretons against French, Welsh against English, highlight the overlap of linguistic and political-economic factors. A language is an obvious and powerful symbol of cultural unity, easily invoked when a cultural heritage is threatened with disappearance. But the mainspring of reaction by linguistic groups appears to be a belief that their lack of control of the prestige variety bars their social mobility, their access to status and power. In rural societies the cleavage may be less acutely felt, but awareness is hastened by urbanisation and industrialisation. A clear demarcation of functions and stable, established, close-knit groups favour language *maintenance*. Communities in flux are more open to shift; in parts of the Soviet Union, for example, the planned migration of Russian-speakers has taken place. Whether one variety will erode the domains of use of the other or whether both will enjoy equal status is a question answerable only case by case.

Language change instigated by the individual and by groups would seem to be conditioned by three sets of factors: attitudes to use; contact between varieties, including contact between languages; and the intrinsic properties of the language system. These three threads will be taken up in Chapters 5, 6 and 9 respectively (5.3; 6.2 and 9.6).

Further reading

Lively and accessible introductions to sociolinguistics which deal with issues raised in this chapter are to be found in Fishman (1970), Robinson (1972) and Trudgill (1974). Bell (1976) is slightly more advanced, and Dittmar (1976) presupposes familiarity with linguistic and sociolinguistic theories. Collections of readings, which are the source of much of the information in this chapter, are available in Fishman (1968; 1971–2) Giglioli (1972), Gumperz and Hymes (1972), Hymes (1964) and Pride and Holmes (1972). Halliday (1978) shows how language can and must be interpreted within a socio-cultural context. Joos (1961) isolates different styles of speech. Crystal and Davy (1969) present a framework of components of the speech event and some sample analyses of English. Kostomarov (1967) provides a list of politeness routines in Russian.

Suggestions for inquiry

It will be especially valuable to pursue these questions during a period of residence abroad:

1 Determine how many varieties you have in your own L1 speech repertoire.
2 Trace the network of contacts you have with L2 speakers and classify them in terms of role relationships.
3 Establish the normal sequence of acts and forms of speech at the initiation of conversation (a) at a party, (b) at an official information office, and (c) by telephone, bearing in mind the role relationship and the function of the interaction.
4 Establish a list of greetings used in face-to-face and telephone encounters and in letters, and classify them according to situation and role relationship. Do the same for leave-taking.
5 Try to discern how turns are distributed in conversations and why they are broken off.
6 Devise rules for restricted varieties like the weather forecast and the language used by waiters to transmit orders.
7 Note how the contextual and meta-linguistic functions are realised in a lecture and in a textbook.
8 Note the status of the participants and the exact form of the utterances produced during any ceremonial occasion you may attend.
9 Note the form of notices and instructions, and try to classify them according to role relationship and function.
10 In the presence of bilinguals – e.g. foreign language assistants – establish if, why and when they switch languages.
11 In a plurilingual community, establish the domains of use of each variety.

5

Language Users: Identity and Attitude

> Language unifies and divides. It symbolises a common bond. It ties people together and it marks them off as distinct from others. At all levels and in all communities, language is a symbol of group and individual identity.
>
> Open University (1973) *Language Variation and English*

In the preceding chapters we have seen the great variety with which the human faculty for speech expresses itself. Over a mere 500 kilometres, from Dover to Saarbrücken via Brussels and Luxemburg, we can hear five different languages - English, Flemish-Dutch, French, Letzeburgesch and German - each with greater or lesser dialectal variation from region to region. Moreover, if we were to stop over in the two capitals *en route*, we might notice individuals switching between three languages in the course of a day. A Luxemburg lawyer, for example, could well use German to speak to a farmer or factory-worker client, French in court and to his colleagues, and Letzeburgesch to his family and friends. Regional variation and switching conditioned by changes in social situation and domain (see 4.5) are not neutral. People hold attitudes, favourable or unfavourable, concerning groups of speakers and their speech styles, including their own. A Fleming in Brussels may regard the increasing shift towards French as a target for which he too must aim in order to achieve social advancement or, on the contrary, as an obstacle to the continuation of a culture and a network of relationships expressed through the medium of Flemish. Accordingly he may seek to identify linguistically with or dissociate himself from the Walloon population. Views like this may be highly personal, in the nature of connotations (9.2), or widely held and a defining characteristic of a speech-community bound together by allegiance to a common set of norms for language behaviour and beliefs concerning its values. The riots in Brussels in protest at the 'linguistic situation' show how high such feelings can run. The choice of a particular variety is in itself a message.

In the present chapter we are going to look more closely at the different attitudes which language use can indicate and provoke. Beginning with the individual, we will see what speakers reveal about their social identity, personality and state of mind, giving some emphasis to non-verbal cues. These again may be characteristic of a group. Then we will consider how groups of individuals, clustered according to inherent or acquired social characteristics like age, sex and class, evaluate the speech styles of their own and other groups, and how their reactions can motivate linguistic change. Finally, we will examine how speakers perceive and mould interpersonal relations by the use of personal pronouns like *tu* and *vous* and other forms of address.

5.1 Non-vocal clues to individual attitude and identity

We judge the internal characteristics of others from all manner of cues, from their eating habits to their clothes, from their build and complexion to their gestures and smell. Of the information available to us the most consistent is speech behaviour. We have already alluded to *para-language* (4.3.5), and many of the activities we discuss in this and the next section are para-linguistic. But some, escaping conscious control, cannot be said to be an intentional component of communication; they are simply informative rather than communicative. Para-language is closely synchronised with speech, serving as it does to emphasise and illustrate, to punctuate, to take or give up the floor and to indicate the key of the utterance (4.3.9).

In the words of Abercrombie, 'We speak with our vocal organs, but we converse with our entire bodies' (in Laver and Hutcheson, 1972, p. 64). Visible behaviour such as facial expression, gaze, gesture, body movement and posture conveys many messages. Emotion is signalled primarily through facial expression, especially in the areas surrounding the eyes and mouth. Gestures like touching the hair or covering the face, together with a closed posture, often indicate anxiety, and a clenched fist can accompany anger. Facial expressions of emotions show great similarity across cultures and the basic signals at least are thought to be innate. They have even been observed in blind and deaf children (Argyle, 1975, p. 73). Not all cultures permit equal intensity in the expression of emotion – the 'inscrutability' of the Japanese is one example, the discreetness of tears at an English funeral is another.

Interpersonal attitudes – what one speaker feels towards his interlocutor – are also conveyed principally by facial expression. The main attitudes can be classed under the headings of affiliation (demonstrating friendliness, warmth and 'belonging'), sexual attraction, aggression, dominance and submission. Of course, standing with arms akimbo, looking away from the speaker, or leaning over someone also reflect and shape interpersonal relations. Shifts in posture function chiefly to structure a conversation by marking turns to speak, a willingness to listen, a readiness to respond or a desire to interrupt or terminate the interaction. They also serve to include participants in a conversation, or to exclude unwanted outsiders. The very fact of a circle of people at a party or a ring of chairs can be enough to deter someone from entering a conversation, and the traditional disposition of desks in a class is calculated to reduce talking between pupils.

As we said earlier, personality judgements are prompted more by vocal than by visual cues, though in every case all components of the performance contribute to an evaluation. Judgements tend to be favourable as long as speakers behave as expected, but when they do not this can result in misunderstanding and negative attitudes. Such norm violation is especially likely in cross-cultural contact and it is worth while giving closer attention to two areas where such behaviour is often seen – eye contact, and proximity.

Eye contact can fulfil several major functions: it obtains feedback on the interlocutor's reactions to what is being communicated and it indicates a willingness or confers an obligation to talk, besides establishing an interpersonal relationship along the dimensions we have just outlined. In normal circumstances when two speakers are trying to establish a *rapport* – that is to say, some degree of affiliation – an equilibrium is reached within the set of factors which contribute to intimacy: eye contact, physical proximity, intimacy of topic, amount of smiling, voice quality, etc. (Argyle and Dean, in Laver and Hutcheson, 1972, p. 304). If one component changes in emphasis, compensatory adjustments will be made in the others. For example, people tend to avoid direct eye contact in order to contain embarrassment when discussing very personal topics. A negative shift along one of the dimensions without the concomitant reinforcement of another will give a person the impression of being kept at a distance and elicit judgements of 'coldness' or 'aloofness'. Greeks and Arabs, who hold their gaze and expect it to be returned, often have such reactions when conversing with Englishmen and North Americans.

We can imagine a speaker as being in the middle of a series of concentric circles, each ring representing a zone which correlates with the degree of intimacy or distance in his relationship with another speaker. The most remote zone is that of public interaction, far beyond the range of bodily contact, and all the features of the public speaker are highlighted – gesture, posture, loudness and facial expression. The distance may be accentuated by speaking from a platform, or from behind a lectern or a desk. The innermost circle is that of intimacy, where touch and contact are easily possible. Most business is transacted within the intermediate zones, with work colleagues and social acquaintances tending to closer proximity than speakers in a more formal relationship. Hall reports that in this range Americans talk louder than the English upper class but not as loud as Spaniards or Russians (in Laver and Hutcheson, 1972, p. 278). Members of the same speech-community tacitly agree in recognising the transition points between zones, and as a new zone is entered, so the relationship crosses a threshold. North Europeans tend to set somewhat greater distances than Mediterranean peoples in this mid-range. That is why an English person often feels that a Frenchman or Spaniard is encroaching on his space or being over-friendly. When he retreats to attenuate his feeling of discomfort in the face of the 'pushy' foreigner, he may in his turn be labelled 'cold' or 'standoffish'. American males misconstrued the failure of a female from a Mediterranean country to react immediately (e.g. by stepping back) when they crossed into what they regarded as a close personal zone. To their minds she had consented to being touched; to her mind she had entered no such agreement (ibid, p. 282).

The Englishman's distaste for public physical contact explains his reluctance to travel on a Russian bus or in the Paris metro at rush hour, and also the success enjoyed by deodorant and toothpaste manufacturers.

Many greeting and leave-taking ceremonies involve varying degrees of contact, depending on the culture and the 'publicness' of the situation. Again, an Englishman may be made ill at ease by a Frenchman's lingering, double-handed handshake and positively shun a welcoming hug from a Spanish or Russian male.

We now turn to gesture. It can serve the general functions of paralanguage, already outlined. For example, a blow with the fist on the table, together with a raising of the voice, may emphasise a verbal remark, and a shrug of the shoulders with upturned palms, a trailing intonation and an appealing gaze will invite response. Gesture is particularly useful for illustrating objects, like a bed-spring, which are difficult to describe verbally. Experiments have shown that hand movements make the description of shapes more effective and that the improvement is much more significant for Italian than for British subjects. Experiments with French speakers could well produce similar findings.

Some gestures are conventional, varying in form or interpretation from one culture to another and often replacing speech entirely. The language learner must therefore try to incorporate them in his repertoire of communicative skills. Germans will drum on the table rather than clap to indicate approval or congratulation. In Germany a tap with the hand on the table by a newcomer will serve to greet those already seated, whereas in France a round of handshakes and *bises* is called for. Germans, Spaniards and French understand the kissing of one's own fingertips to communicate praise more readily than do the British. The thumbs-up sign is a sexual insult in Greece. The British 'V-sign' is not taken as obscene or offensive by a Frenchman, who has instead the more emphatic *bras d'honneur* and who might therefore be surprised at the hostile reaction when he waves two fingers at a London barman in request for two pints.

One of the advantages of visual signals for expressing interpersonal attitudes is that in the tentative stages of negotiating a relationship they can be used very discreetly and, if necessary, withdrawn. There is an obvious parallel with the use of indirect performatives, where requests and orders may be expressed in an interrogative form (see 4.4.3).

5.2 Vocal clues to individual attitude and identity

As Sapir pointed out as early as 1927, 'Some of us are more intuitive than others, it is true, but none is entirely lacking in the ability to gather and be guided by speech impressions in the intuitive exploration of personality' (quoted in Laver and Hutcheson, 1972, p. 71). It is worth asking what is the basis for evaluating not only the personality, but also the emotional state and social identity of a speaker. And to what extent are any such judgements valid, either when they concern speakers of the same language as the judge or when speakers of a different language are being assessed?

First of all, it seems well established that the content of a speaker's utterance – while obviously carrying some information relevant to making judgements on the three attributes above – is less influential than the manner of speaking. It has been estimated that content cues are five times less significant than vocal non-content cues in judging attitudes, and eight times less significant than facial expression. For personality judgements vocal non-content is more revealing than visual clues, and is a primary indicator of 'social attractiveness'. Verbal content is seen as an important pointer to 'benevolence' (Giles and Powesland, 1975, pp. 1–4). Thus we leave aside here what is stated verbally and overtly – in the way of opinions or an idiosyncratic preference for certain words – in order to focus on the more or less covert vocal cues, which we can group under the four main headings of *vocalisations, voice quality, voice dynamics* and *pronunciation*.

Vocalisations include such behaviour as coughing, laughing, crying, whining, moaning, belching and yawning. They may be involuntary or voluntary and their occurence encouraged or frowned upon in different situations – for example, there is no such thing as a 'polite yawn' in

Spanish society, while in some communities to belch after a meal is the done thing.

Contributing to each speaker's unique 'voice-print', which can be visually recorded on a spectrogramme, there is, first, *voice quality*, which refers to such characteristics as hoarseness, breathiness, flatness, resonance and high pitch. From such qualities we might judge a speaker to be boring, sexy, friendly, excited, etc. In England a 'thin' voice is generally held to be a sign of immaturity and nasality is considered unattractive, but we cannot assume that the interpretation will necessarily be the same in another society. The pharyngealisation characteristic of working-class Norwich speech and thought unpleasant by middle-class Norwich people is to be found, however, in some high-status German accents (Trudgill and Giles, 1976, p. 9). Voice quality will normally identify the speaker as to age and sex.

Second, intonation, rhythm, speed and continuity of speech are all aspects of *voice dynamics* and may affect our perceptions of the speaker's self-assurance, calmness or sobriety. A fluent speaker is usually considered to be more competent and authoritative. Although it is very difficult for speakers to disguise their emotional state and personality by controlling voice quality and dynamics and although listeners use these features as a basis for personal evaluations, the answer to our earlier question as to the objective validity of these personality judgements must be negative, especially where cross-cultural differences are involved.

The third category of vocal cues, *pronunciation*, must be regarded as only indirectly indicative of personality. Accent allows a listener to assign someone to a particular social group, and it is then that he may be inclined to attribute to the individual speaker those personality traits which he regards as belonging to the group stereotype. There is strong evidence to suggest that no one accent is inherently more pleasant than another. For example, when French Canadian and British listeners were asked to evaluate the relative pleasantness of educated European French, educated Canadian French and working-class Canadian French, the judgements of the two groups of listeners were in complete conflict. While the French Canadians rated the varieties in the order just given, the British accorded them virtually identical aesthetic appeal. It is reasonable to suppose from this evidence that aesthetic judgements are tied to the *social connotations* which accents evoke and which are very often unknown to outsiders. In Britain non-prestige accents are consistently ranked (by Britons) for unpleasantness on a continuum with rural accents at the top, followed by the accents of urban centres like Bristol, and those of heavy industrialised conurbations like Liverpool and Birmingham at the bottom. In fact, those accents which are generally perceived as being the most unattractive coincide with those parts of the country established independently by geographers as being the most undesirable areas in which to live (Trudgill and Giles, 1976, p. 13). In Italy, however, it appears that the prestige accent is that of industrial Milan rather than that of the seats of 'high culture' in Florence or Rome.

The conclusions are neatly summed up for the language learner by Trudgill and Giles (1976, p. 17): 'not to abandon . . . aesthetic judgements – but to recognise them for what they are: the result of a complex of social, cultural, regional, political and personal associations and prejudices'. It would be wrong to adopt unthinkingly the prevalent attitudes and prejudices of any foreign community one lived in as to the relative beauty of the varieties spoken there, but the learner cannot afford to neglect these attitudes.

5.3 Group identity and attitude

In order to highlight the diversity of speech styles within a society we will concentrate on *dialects* (that is, regional varieties distinct in pronunciation, vocabulary and syntax) within a single ethnic group, forgoing consideration of such varieties as Black English Vernacular or Jewish English. We can now isolate more clearly speech variation related to age, sex and socio-economic class rather than to situation and function (see 4.3 and 4.4). As an initial illustration, research has shown that in the Soviet Union regional origin has the greatest effect on pronunciation, followed closely by social position, with age, family environment and education considerably less significant (Krysin, 1974, p. 117).

We have already established that a regional accent (since pronunciation seems to make a more immediate impact on the listener than vocabulary or syntax) is subject to aesthetic judgements which tally closely with the perceived pleasantness of the region itself. In addition, British informants consistently rate accents on a scale of perceived *status*. It may be salutary to note the order in which South Welsh and Somerset schoolchildren rated thirteen accents: (1) Received Pronunciation – RP, (2) Affected RP, (3) North American and French, (5) German, (6) South Welsh, (7) Irish, (8) Italian, (9) Northern English, (10) Somerset, (11) Cockney and Indian, (13) Birmingham (Giles and Powesland, 1975, p. 28). This lends further support to the notion of 'prestige accent', which we invoked above. The prestige of an accent is a reflection of the status of its users, who are regarded as possessing desirable attributes. In Britain the prestige accent is *Received Pronunciation,* – or RP; it is spoken by an estimated 3 per cent of the population, essentially those who have passed through the public schools, and is the accent of most BBC newsreaders (Hughes and Trudgill, 1979, p. 3). Originally the accent of the London area, it was used by the Court and for some four centuries has been considered the most acceptable – that is, the best received – manner of speaking. What was a dialectal feature has evolved into a class-related accent, with the result that RP gives no clues to a speaker's regional origin, only to his social status.

This does not mean that the upper-class speech style is completely homogeneous. In each region there are speakers who are considered to use an educated and acceptable variety – standard English. This is subject to small internal variations both in pronunciation and in syntax. For example, educated speakers in the south of England will normally say *She won't go* and *She gave it to the man*, whereas in the north *She'll not go* and *She gave it the man* are very common (Hughes and Trudgill, 1979, pp. 20–1). In general, the further down the social scale a speaker is, the more dialectal features he will exhibit; and the broader his accent, the lower his perceived prestige. There are some features, like the tendency to multiply negatives (*I haven't seen no pen*) or 'regularise' irregular verbs (*I done it yesterday*), which are widespread in non-standard English dialects. A clear correlation between multiple negation and social class is shown by a survey in Detroit: lower-working-class (LWC) informants used multiple negation on 70 per cent of possible occasions, the upper-middle-class (UMC) informants on only 2 per cent. The dropping of 'aitches' shows a similar pattern. Such class-related variations are not independent of situation. In an informal setting, a UMC and a LWC speaker may both say something like *Et ensuite y avait des . . . un genre de crochet dans un p'tit . . . café, où ils faisaient un crochet radiophonique*, while in a formal situation only UMC subjects have in their repertoire the ability to produce utterances like *Quand on vous donnera une dissertation littéraire à écrire, comment l'entend-on*? (Lindenfeld, in Gumperz and Hymes, 1972).

Thus we are able to pick out linguistic *indicators* of group membership – features which are characteristic of a group but beyond the awareness and therefore the control of the individual.

Attributes other than status are ascribed to groups of speakers. For example, English voices are rated favourably by both Scottish and English listeners for self-confidence, intelligence, ambition, leadership, prestige and wealth, good looks and height, occupational status and cleanliness; Scottish voices are rated more favourably by both nationalities for friendliness only. However, Scottish listeners also evaluated Scottish voices favourably for sense of humour, generosity, good-naturedness, likeability and nervousness. In short, their degree of self-esteem and accent loyalty is high, despite the low opinion the English have of them (Giles and Powesland, 1975, p. 67).

A survey conducted in Montreal in which speakers were again asked to judge their own accent and that of a neighbouring group produced some striking results. English Canadians, males and females, judged English male voices more favourably than French male voices, but French female voices more favourably than English female voices. French Canadian males regarded English voices more favourably for both sexes. French Canadian females downgraded their own voices compared with those of their English counterparts, but felt that French male voices were superior to English male voices. English Canadian emerges as the more prestigious variety, which is that of a more powerful, higher-achieving socio-economic group. Their relative under-achievement may explain the French males' low self-evaluation. Since women tend to be more sensitive to prestige features, as we shall see again, this is a plausible explanation for the French females' low self-evaluation. Yet they found French Canadian men more competent and socially attractive than English males, possibly because they saw the accent as symbolising traditional French Canadian values which should be preserved.

When men and women in Norwich were asked to judge their own pronunciation, women generally claimed to use more prestige forms than they actually did use, while men reported themselves as using *fewer* higher-class forms than had actually been recorded. Trudgill concludes that for Norwich men working-class speech is statusful and prestigious (1974, pp. 96–8). Their accent confers *covert prestige*, as does the French Canadian accent in the eyes of French Canadian women, but not in the eyes of French men.

In the Soviet Union *age* and *profession* have significantly more effect than education on the use of different verb classes. Workers use fewer traditional forms than intellectuals, but it is not clear if this is a spreading trend. Workers are also quicker to innovate in pronunciation. Unfortunately, a breakdown of results according to sex is not given (Krysin, 1974).

If we consider more closely the relationship between female stereotypes and accent in England, we find that RP-accented females are considered very feminine, more so than northern-accented females. This may be partly because women are expected to be more status-conscious, and so when their accent confirms expectations their femininity is enhanced. On the other hand, RP-accented females also score high on male-like traits of independence and adventurousness, while their northern counterparts are thought more sincere and likeable. The researchers conclude: 'Speculatively, one could label the female RP accent as the voice of perceived androgyny' (Elyan *et al.*, in Trudgill, 1978, p. 130).

Great Britain appears to be almost alone in Europe in having a class-related rather than a region-related prestige standard accent. A French deputy is more likely to retain a strong regional accent than is a British MP, and without being downgraded in professional competence. But there are none the less regional stereotypes – from a Swabian accent a German infers traits of thrift, industry, cleanliness and conservatism. The *pied noir* accent of former French settlers in North Africa prompts conflicting sets of judgements.

It is thus clear that the attitudes to prestige and personality which underlie sex- and class-related variation in speech are very important in motivating linguistic change.

At an individual level one speaker will often adjust his speech style to converge with that of his interlocutor. This *linguistic accommodation* may be subconscious, as in the case of an RP-accented student who would adopt a Scots accent when addressing a Scottish lecturer. She was switching to a less prestigious accent because of the lecturer's superior status within the university or, perhaps, there was some other motive for 'closing the gap'. Convergence of speech behaviour may be well received or considered as cheeky mimicry. It is interesting to note that speakers are perceived most favourably when they converge speech rate and content but *not* pronunciation. When they converge on all three dimensions their rating is lower (Giles and Smith, in Giles and St Clair, 1979, p. 60). It would be premature for language learners to throw away their pronunciation manuals! These results were obtained for English accents and cannot automatically be assumed valid for foreign-accent evaluation in other situations. Moreover, examiners expect accents to converge towards a native standard. The impression that the speaker, despite limited ability, is making an *effort* to accommodate is favourably perceived by the listener and is the most important factor in prompting the listener to adjust his own speech so that their repertoires overlap more. The moral is clear.

We can view switching between languages in plurilingual societies (see 4.5) as simply another case of accommodation, or refusal to accommodate (see Lambert, in Giles and St Clair, 1979). This concept is also useful in understanding personal pronoun usage (see 5.4).

At a societal level we see linguistic change in progress through a phenomenon called *hypercorrection*. For example, a Bradfordian pronounces *put* and *putt* identically /pʊt/, while RP distinguishes /pʊt/ and /pʌt/ respectively (see 8.3.2 for the specification of vowels). If he were to aspire to an RP accent, he might well introduce /ʌ/ into a word like *push*, which is normally pronounced /pʊʃ/ in both accents, so giving /pʌʃ/. Similarly, in South Germany an initial *s* as in *Seide* is pronounced variably as /s/ or /z/ while in North Germany it is invariably pronounced /z/. On going to the north and trying to conform to local norms, the southerner may hypercorrect and pronounce *hassen* – always /asan/in the north – as /hazan/. In Spain there is a widespread tendency to pronounce the past-participle ending *-ado* as /au/ rather than /aðo/. Feeling this to be 'incorrect', a Spaniard may even pronounce the last syllable of *Bilbao* and *bacalao* as /aðo/ rather than /au/.

In New York the pronunciation of /r/ at the end of a word – /ka:r/ rather than /ka:/ for *car* – is an indicator of upper-class usage. It was found that New Yorkers of all social classes used /r/ with increasing frequency as they progressed from conversation to reading passages and finally to reading word lists. In formal situations, therefore, speakers monitored their performance more carefully and tended, subconsciously or consciously, towards an upper-class norm. The striking fact is that while the amount of /r/ usage strictly paralleled social-class membership in conversation and reading passages, in the reading of word lists lower-middle-class speakers showed a dramatic, hypercorrect increase in (r/ usage to the point where they left their upper-middle-class 'target speakers' far behind (Labov, 1978, p. 124).

We can briefly sum up the process of change. One group adopts another as its *reference group*, viewing its behaviour patterns as a model, and exaggerates a certain feature as an indicator of group identity. With hypercorrection a new norm is established which may serve as a reference for succeeding groups. An indicator which is *recognised* by a speech-community as constituting one of its norms is called a *marker*. Markers display the kind of variation from one style of speech to another that we have seen in the New York example. The uniformity of reaction to markers is a defining characteristic of a speech-community (see 2.3).

Markers are seized upon by outsiders in comic portrayals of regional and national stereotypes. An Asturian can be imitated by pronouncing the masculine ending *-o* as /u/ and final *-as* /es/, and by introducing the diminutive *-in* and the 'filler' word *o*. Swabians are stereotyped by the diminutive *-le* which matches their ascribed 'home-loving' traits. 'Irish jokes' are a vivid reminder that sterotypes are often very remote from reality.

What conclusions of interest to the language learner can we draw from this discussion of attitude and identity? First, these factors are of consequence for the variety he chooses to adopt. Even if the sensitivity to accents and their prestige rating *may* be less evident abroad than in Britain, it is in the interests of a learner who intends to use his L2 in an international environment to adopt a reasonably standard pronunciation, both to facilitate wider comprehension among an audience for whom the language in question may also be an L2 and to minimise possible adverse value judgements. Interpreters are well advised to have a standard pronunciation for their L1. An interpretation in a Cockney accent of a French presidential speech may cause blank looks of incomprehension from Scandinavian or Indian observers tuned in to the English interpreter's booth, and bring inappropriate laughter from the British contingent.

Second, even if it is arguably preferable, when addressing a Fleming in French, to speak with an English rather than a Belgian accent, a foreign accent classes speakers in an 'out-group' and can hinder adoption by the 'in-group'.

Also, we see a striking parallel between the role of attitudes in motivating linguistic change within a community and their role in supporting the language learner's motivation to increase competence in L2 (see 3.3.4).

Finally, patterns of speech change in the pursuit of *dynamic* norms. What is appropriate today may no longer be so tomorrow. The foreign learner, like the native speaker, is under constant pressure to update his awareness and his performance.

5.4 Forms of address

So far in this chapter we have used the word 'distance' in two senses: to indicate on one hand a *physical* distance (proximity - non-proximity), and on the other a *psychological* distance (intimacy - formality). One is a reflection of the other and both are related to a third type of distance involving status differences and which we can call *social* distance. In this section we examine how an equilibrium between psychological and social distance is achieved and expressed through forms of address in face-to-face *dyadic* (two-participant) conversation.

5.4.1 The choices available

From his very first formal contact with a foreign language a learner is made aware of a distinction not widely made in England between second-person pronoun forms and which, he is told, relates not only to the number of addressees (*singular* vs *plural*) but also to the 'politeness' or 'formality' of the exchange. The contrast between *thou* and *you* survives only in some northern English and Scottish dialects. However, French and Russian present a two-element system with *tu–vous* and *ты–вы*, while German offers a three-way choice between *du, Sie* and *Ihr* and Spanish four possibilities in *tu/vosotros* - *usted/ustedes* (originally *vuestra Merced*, 'your grace'). If we look to Romanian we find a still more complex situation with *tu, dumneata* and *dumneavoastră* all available for singular reference and *voi* and *dumneavoastră* for more than one addressee; there is also a choice of third-person pronouns, in both singular and plural. In general discussion we can designate by T pronouns of the *tu* and *du* category and by V pronouns of the *vous* and *Sie* type.

Historically speaking, the Latin *vos* was originally used only for plurality, but was later employed to address the emperor and then other holders of high office. Usage in old French and Spanish followed no apparent pattern until around the twelfth to fourteenth centuries, when the V of reverence became established.

The options at pronoun level are fewer than at the level of titles and names, like *Sir, Doctor, Mrs, Auntie, Jennifer* or *Jenny*. We can again group them into broad categories. First there is TITLE, which may be social (*Sir, Madam*), professional (*Professor*) or functional (*Minister, Colonel*). Russians employ two social titles, *товарищ* ('comrade') which as a form of address is never differentiated according to sex, and *гражданин* (feminine *гражданка*, 'citizen'). A further title, *господин* (feminine *госпожа* , 'Mr', 'Mrs') never occurs independently, but only in conjunction with a foreign function title, as in *господин президент* ('President'), or with the surname of a non-Soviet citizen. While *Monsieur* is found on its own, French function titles are usually not, thus we have *Monsieur* or *Madame le Ministre* (the *le* appears invariable at the present time) but we may have simply *Docteur*. Similarly, German requires *mein* before *Herr* and *Dame* but not before *Fräulein*. Kin titles (KT - *Uncle, Mum*) are yet another category involving quite special usage rules which may mark social-class differences. In many cultures, of course, they are also used as generalised, non-kinship, forms of address, again with quite specific connotations.

Title with last name (TLN) is a frequent combination (*Mr Jones, la Señora de Perez*). In Russian both 'comrade' and 'citizen' are available for combination with LN, the former indicating shared group membership. LN (*Jones*) seems less widespread in England than it is in North America, where it is extended to females, and in the four European communities with which we are chiefly concerned. First name (FN) is very common, but again Russian offers a further choice of patronymic (P - *Ivanovich*) or patronymic and first name (PFN - *Ivan Ivanovich*) which is widespread among work colleagues. We find also KTFN (*Auntie Una*), but some combinations are very restricted in use - *Grandad Smith* is heard, *Uncle Jones* is not. Likewise TFN (*Mister Peter*) is relatively rare in English usage. The last major category is that of multiple name (MN), which includes nicknames, pet-names, diminutives, and the like. It is, of course, possible to select zero (ϕ) if the addressee's name and title are unknown or if the speaker is uncertain which form to use, for reasons which will soon be made clear below.

The selection of a title or name will normally determine whether T or V is to be used. It would be incongruous for an office junior to ask the director *Tu vas bien, M. le. Président?* (T + TITLE) or a friend *Comment allez-vous, Nini?* (V + MN). Associated greeting and leave-taking expressions show congruity: *Hi, Ciao,* and *Cheers* are unlikely to be selected with TLN nor *Enchanté* with T. *Dupont* (LN) may co-occur with either T or V, as may *товарищ* + LN, and so it is now time to look beyond the forms themselves to the factors which guide their global selection.

5.4.2 The determinants of choice

Every person has certain attributes, both inherent sex, age, family membership, nationality, strength, and acquired wealth, profession, rank. We can view each of these attributes as contributory in conferring status on their possessor. The relative weight carried by each attribute can vary from one social group to another. The participants in any dyadic exchange can be compared along any and all of these dimensions, and indeed they do compare themselves, as we have seen in previous sections of this chapter. They may perceive themselves as occupying equal or unequal positions on each dimension and draw an over-all conclusion as to their equality or inequality of status. Such asymmetrical relations as *older than, senior to,* and *parent of* can be generalised on a scale *superior–inferior*. Superiors have power over inferiors in that they can control the latter's behaviour, which is why the linguistic expression of an asymmetrical power relationship by a corresponding non-reciprocal use of T and V is known as the *power semantic* (Brown and Gilman, 1960). In such cases the superior addresses the other as T and receives V in return. With titles, the power semantic may be expressed by a non-reciprocal use of FN and TLN. Thus we might hear an employer say *Jean, apporte-moi le dossier* and her employee reply *Si vous voulez, Mme Dupont.*

However, one member of a dyad may wish to minimise any power differential; for example, a production manager may use T or FN to his workers in order to harmonise relations and meet targets. Where speakers consider themselves to be on an equal footing, usage favours reciprocity in address: T–T, V–V and, similarly, reciprocal titles. This symmetrical relationship is termed *solidarity* and its linguistic expression is termed the *solidarity semantic*. The more intimate two solidary speakers are, the more likely they are to use reciprocal T, co-selecting reciprocal FN and even MN. As the example just quoted reveals, solidarity is not a relationship confined to people of equal status. The solidarity semantic is potentially dynamic, allowing speakers to span objective social distance by reducing psychological distance. The instigator of such a move will be the superior member of the dyad. For the inferior to initiate an advance to reciprocity or intimacy is generally considered presumptuous. It is the static view of these two relationships that has given us the now outdated labels of 'familiar' or 'patronising' for T and 'polite' or 'respectful' for V.

Brown and Gilman (1960) demonstrate that address patterns in Europe have changed significantly over the last 100 years. Their surveys revealed for France, West Germany and (less so) Italy a strong shift in customer–waiter, officer–soldier and employer–employee relationships from power-coded, non-reciprocal address to reciprocal V. Parent–child and elder-brother–younger-brother relationships overwhelmingly favour mutual T, and master–faithful servant is also shifting that way. This is paralleled in the Russian context by the banning in 1917 of the use of *ны* to lower ranks. Reciprocal V with new acquaintances, an exclusively upper-class pattern in the nineteenth century, is now widely used in all ranks of Soviet society until some intimacy is established. In France there are married couples who continue to address one another with V, yet the general trend is definitely towards not only solidarity but also mutual *Тыкать, tutoiement, tuteo* and *Duzen.* This is especially true of likeminded young people within political, professional or interest groups.

A gradual shift in usage within a society as a whole is the product of more rapid changes in attitude and behaviour on the part of its members in daily exchanges. Let us imagine a management trainee starting a new job. It is likely that he will at first address his boss as *Sir* or TLN, perhaps receiving TLN or LN in return. This state of affairs will continue until the superior advances to a reciprocal relationship, say TLN, or even towards greater intimacy, with FN. If there is a large difference in age and rank, the trainee may think it prudent to maintain TLN to his boss, or nevertheless interpret it as a cue to mutual FN. They may progress eventually to mutual MN. *If* changes in address pattern do occur within a dyad, it is always in the direction just outlined. Reverting from T to V to re-establish distance was a common stylistic device of European literature in the nineteenth century and earlier, but is no longer done in spontaneous conversation. Once T always T, even if neither solidarity nor intimacy underlie its use. Two final points on progression: not all dyads start from reciprocal TITLE nor do they necessarily reach reciprocal MN. Two young people introduced at a party will probably adopt mutual FN from the outset; in many cases they won't know each other's LN. Two Frenchmen who become acquainted late in life may never progress beyond *Monsieur* + LN.

5.4.3 Cross-cultural comparisons

The first influential factor we will examine is not a personal attribute but the external component of *setting* (see 4.3.2). In a situation where official role is emphasised over individuality, such as the high court, a Senate meeting and a parliamentary debate, rigid speech norms operate which extend to address, and status is marked by *My Lord, Mr Chairman* and *My Right Hon. Friend* or *The Hon. Gentleman.* A glance through

Debrett's Correct Form or *Hansard* will reveal a bewildering array of forms for the uninitiated. The greater the number of distinctions, the greater the opportunity subtly to flatter or insult. Nevertheless, in status-marked situations in those communities which directly concern us, TITLE will be used even between people who in an informal setting employ mutual FN.

Lambert and Tucker (1976) discovered that in French Canada a change from rural to urban setting also affected address patterns. For example, interactions between children and parents, grandparents, uncles and aunts, godparents and priests showed more non-reciprocal contacts in the country than in the city.

Now we will consider to what extent sex, age, class and role differences can act as barriers to the expression of solidarity and intimacy. From their comparison of French, German and Italian, Brown and Gilman (1960, pp. 263-4) concluded:

> In general it may be said that the solidarity coded by German T is an ascribed solidarity of family relationships. The French T, in greater degree, codes an acquired solidarity not founded on family relationship but developing out of some sort of shared fate. As for the Italian T, it very nearly equals the German in family solidarity and it surpasses the French in camaraderie. The camaraderie of the Italian male, incidentally, is extended to the Italian female; unlike the French or German student the Italian says T to the co-ed almost as readily as to the male fellow student.

Modern Russian usage also shows a generalisation of T within the family, even to older kin. France's move towards mutual T in the family is confirmed by Lambert and Tucker, in contrast to French Canada, where T-T and T-V are in competition. The former family is judged as more, perhaps too, tolerant, the latter as more religious. In France, outside the family girls receive V from a much earlier age than do boys, and social class has little impact. Social class and sex have a very pervasive influence in French Canada: 'With *male service personnel* . . . city boys from upper-class backgrounds have fewer RT contacts and more NR, T-V than those from lower-class backgrounds . . . This trend is reversed, however, for contacts with *female service persons*' (Lambert and Tucker, 1976, p. 147).

Thus address patterns signal that the speaker is treating his interlocutors with the respect due to their age, sex, class and status or associating them with a privileged in-group. The shock reaction of a middle-aged French-Canadian saleslady - *Le garçon qui vient de passer m'a tutoyée!* - and her colleague's reply - *Oui, bah, c'est pas bien grave* -

show that attitudes are never fully predictable. All we have been able to do here is see the factors at play. Exactly how they shape patterns of address in a particular community is for the language learner to discover by trial and error using vocal, bodily and verbal feedback.

Do pronoun semantics offer insights into social structure? Obviously they do, but the valuable surveys conducted so far provide only a few pieces in the social jigsaw puzzle. Pointing to the static, asymmetrical pronoun usage of Afrikaans speakers in South Africa and of Indians, which they see as consistent with two static, even feudal societies, Brown and Gilman regard the European shift to symmetry as a sign of a more developed egalitarian, democratic ethic. Language unifies, but unless it is to unify all it will continue also to divide.

Further reading

The introductory textbooks and collections of readings listed for Chapter 4 all contain relevant sections. Argyle (1975) provides a comprehensive introduction to non-verbal communication, while Laver and Hutcheson (1972) and Hinde (1972) offer a range of readings. Morris *et al.* (1979) is very readable, but Birdwhistle (1971) and Scheflen (1972) are more specialised. Harper, Wiens and Matarazzo (1979) give a detailed assessment of current research. Hughes and Trudgill (1979) is excellent on English dialects, and Giles and Powesland (1975) and Trudgill and Giles (1976) discuss the evaluation of speech style. Giles and St Clair (1979) and Shuy and Fasold (1973) are more advanced collections of articles. Scherer and Giles (1979) develop a coherent basis for considering speech cues and social characteristics, but assume a knowledge of the other works by Giles just listed. Edwards (1976) is a good introduction to class-related varieties and linguistic change. Labov (1978) revises and brings together a number of the author's classic articles on these same topics. The pioneering studies on address forms are Brown and Gilman (1960) and Brown and Ford (1961), both widely reprinted, including in Laver and Hutcheson. Comparative analyses by Ervin-Tripp are found in Pride and Holmes (1972) and Gumperz and Hymes (1972), which also contains an article on Russian by Friedrich, complemented by Corbett (1976). For German, see Ammon (1972) and Augst (1977). Lambert and Tucker (1976) contains a mass of information on France, French Canada, Columbia and Puerto Rico.

Suggestions for inquiry

1 Devise a questionnaire to investigate the forms of address used by your foreign-language assistants according to situation and interlocutor.
2 What are the rules of adjective and verb agreement for the V pronouns of your foreign language?
3 In Russian and Spanish what is the significance of omitting or inserting the second-person pronoun subject?
4 What factors determine the form of address (TITLE, T + LN, FN, etc.) used in reference to a *third* person?
5 During a television film turn the sound fully down. To what extent can you continue to follow the plot?
6 Using foreign informants find ten gestures commonly used to replace speech.
7 Listening to a radio play, make notes on the social origins and personality of each character. Compare notes with a friend.
8 Compare your evaluation of your fellow students' accents with their own judgements.
9 Find out from foreign informants what they consider to be the main regional accents of their country and what characteristics they attribute to regional-accented speakers.
10 What is your reaction when a speaker's para-linguistic behaviour appears to contradict the verbal content of his utterance?

6

Languages, Cultures, Contacts

> Those who may be alarmed about the spread of English, or of any other language, may be reassured that there is insufficient evidence for thinking that such a language has within itself, like a Trojan horse, a particular view of the world.
>
> John B. Carroll (1963) 'Linguistic Relativity, Contrastive Linguistics and Language Learning', *International Review of Applied Linguistics*, 1, p. 19

Language and culture are linked. If we take culture to be a set of beliefs and practices which govern the life of society, then language is, on one hand, a vehicle for the expression of those beliefs, for their transmission from generation to generation, and an instrument for finding out about the world. Being itself a social practice it is, on the other hand, a part of culture.

Languages and cultures are also linked. It would be hasty to assume that there is a one-to-one relationship between them any more than there is between languages and nations (see 2.2 and 2.3). We must look to anthropology for guidance on what constitutes a change of culture, but it would seem reasonable to admit the notion of a culture continuum, analogous to that of a dialect continuum, which is divided variably according to the observer's viewpoint. What may be perceived by the outsider as a culturally unified community may be felt by its members to embrace several different cultures. Such attitudinal factors, we have seen, are important in defining a speech-community. They influence, too, indirectly or directly, whether an individual becomes a bilingual. Personal convictions of this kind, then, are not to be dismissed lightly. One such conviction is that a linguistic frontier *is* at the same time a cultural frontier; a common language is a symbol of a common culture, at once a flag and a shield against outside intervention. A hostile attitude towards another culture will often lead to a rejection of the language which is seen to express it, as is demonstrated by the insistence in Quebec on marking roadsigns *Arrêt* in addition to *Stop,* despite the fact that the latter alone is to be seen throughout France. A favourable attitude will often result in the adoption and assimilation of foreign expressions, shown by the entry into German of *Punk, Freak, Coolness* and *ausgeflippt*. Having seen in previous chapters the impact of these different attitudes on inter-group relations and individual motivation, we shall discuss here their varying repercussions on the linguistic system, especially the lexis (9.4.1). But first we must look more closely at the nature of the relation between language and culture.

6.1 Linguistic determinism and relativity

At one extreme we can adopt the opinion that thinking and the perception of the world are independent of language, which serves simply to express them. It is an idea voiced by the Greeks some 2,500 years ago. At the other extreme there is the view that language is an inescapable 'shaper of ideas, the program and guide for the individual's mental activity' (Whorf, 1956, p. 212). This is the viewpoint of *linguistic determinism*. Since, moreover, no two languages are the same, it follows that each language will mould its speakers' world-view differently. This is the thesis of *linguistic relativity*, and in recent times it has been supported most forcefully by the linguist-anthropologist Edward Sapir and his one-time pupil, Benjamin Whorf. Hence it is generally known as the *Sapir–Whorf hypothesis*. Whorf's standpoint, which is rather more extreme than Sapir's, is encapsulated in the following quotation:

> The world is presented as a kaleidoscopic flux of impressions which has to be organized by our minds – and this means largely by the linguistic systems in our minds. We cut nature up, organize it into concepts, and ascribe significances as we do, largely because we are parties to an agreement to organize it in this way – an agreement which holds throughout our speech community and is codified in the pattern of our language. The agreement is, of course, an implicit and unstated one, *but its terms are absolutely obligatory*; we cannot talk at all except by subscribing to the organization and classification of data which the agreement decrees.
> (Whorf, 1956, pp. 212–13)

Man's perceptions are bound in a linguistic straitjacket, and each society lives in a world of its own. To subscribe to this extreme view is to admit to the existence of insurmountable obstacles to bilingualism and translation.

One of the aims of these two men was to refute the belief that the cultures of some remote societies, such as the Eskimo and the Bantu, can legitimately be labelled as 'primitive'. If language determines culture and it can be demonstrated that the language of a remote society is in no way inferior to that of an 'advanced civilisation', then its culture also is by definition of no less value. Although we will be outlining some of the most serious objections to the extreme determinist viewpoint, it is still wrong and absurd to consider any one language as less adequate in its own setting than another: 'When it comes to linguistic form, Plato walks with the Macedonian swineherd, Confucius with the head-hunting savage of Assam' (Sapir, 1921, p. 219). In a study of American Indian and African languages, Whorf concludes: 'By comparison with many American languages, the formal systematization of ideas in English, German, French, or Italian seems poor and jejeune . . . English compared to Hopi is like a bludgeon compared to a rapier' (p. 85). In his zeal to redress the balance in favour of 'primitive' societies Whorf has returned to the conception of superior and inferior languages dismissed by Sapir as 'rubbish', simply reversing the Western order of precedence.

Let us now return to our main issue of linguistic relativity and review some of the linguistic data adduced by Whorf in its support.

6.1.1 Syntactic data

In sentences (1)- (4) English uses a single conjunction, *that*:

(1) I see that it is red
(2) I see that it is new
(3) I hear that it is red
(4) I hear that it is new

In Hopi, however, different connectors are used in (1) and (2) to indicate, according to Whorf, that in the first case 'seeing' presents a direct sensation, while in the second it presents unspecified evidence of newness. Yet a third connector is used in both (3) and (4), where it is a matter of verbal report. He further claims that Hopi is a 'timeless' language because its verb system is not akin to that of 'temporal' English, where tense indicates anteriority and futurity. Let us take as an example a situation where both speaker and hearer witness the event of a person running. The English speaker will say *He is running* or *He ran* according to the relative time of the event and the utterance. Hopi, on the other hand, uses a single form *Wari* whatever the relative time, since in both cases it is a 'statement of fact' shared by the interlocutors, both present at the time of the event. But whereas an English speaker again uses *He ran* to describe an anterior event not witnessed by the hearer, Hopi requires a different form *Era wari* because it is a statement not of mutually recognised fact but of the speaker's memory. We can immediately object to the implication that English verb forms convey only temporal information by pointing out that the form *He ran* is not necessarily a marker of anteriority; it occurs also in *If only he ran well*. Whorf has been misled by the traditional label 'past tense' into equating a single form with a single function. The validity of Whorf's reasoning rests entirely on the labels which he has proposed; his argument is a tautology. He fails to offer any evidence independent of the linguistic data to substantiate the assertion of differing world-views.

Comparison of more widely spoken languages yields many similar examples. French, German and Russian speakers use a single verb form to indicate both present and habitual action. *Il lit, Er liest, Он читает* are rendered by *He reads* or *He is reading* according to the circumstances. Spanish has *Él lee* and *Él está leyendo*, though the distribution of these forms does not coincide directly with that in English. Are we to conclude that the English and the Spanish have a world-view which differs from that of their neighbours? Spanish has two verbs *ser* and *estar*, the former indicating an essential, permanent characteristic, the latter an accidental, variable attribute. Thus the sentences *Él es muy alegro* and *Él está muy alegre* are to be interpreted as indicating a cheerful disposition and a cheerful mood respectively. In this respect the Spanish view seems in harmony with Russian, where the permanency or transiency of a state are expressed by using the full or the short form of a given adjective: *она больная* ('She is ill/an invalid'), *она больна* ('She is – temporarily – ill'). In English and German adjective precedes noun, in French and Spanish the order is reversed, and in Russian both orders are possible. Is this evidence of three differing conceptions of the relation between things or events and their attributes, allocating our five languages to yet new groupings? We can multiply the examples but it is highly unlikely that the differences will be systematic enough to add up to a coherent and definable *Weltanschauung* imposed by a given language. Moreover, it is perfectly possible for the English speaker to perceive and express the relational differences illustrated by sentences (1)–(4) or by the European examples. In the very exposition of his argument Whorf provides conclusive grounds for denying its validity: he enabled us to share, in English, the Hopi 'world-view'.

The strong view of determinism and relativity appears untenable; nor does there seem to be much weight to Sapir's weaker claim that languages 'predispose' their speakers to an awareness of certain aspects of their environment rather than others.

6.1.2 Lexical data

To describe in Shilluk the 'breaking' of an egg, a string or a stick requires in each case a different verb. Hopi has one word which refers to 'water in a natural environment' and another for 'water from a domestic supply'. Eskimos are reputed to have many words for 'snow', including distinctions for 'falling snow', 'fallen snow' and 'igloo snow', while Aztecs use but a single lexical root to refer to 'cold', 'ice' and 'snow'. It does not mean that Aztecs are unaware of any difference between these three states. To suggest this would be to reach a conclusion parallel to maintaining that Greeks are colour-blind because they lack elementary terms for certain of the English primary colours. The fact that English has only one word to describe 'fish in the sea' and 'fish on the quay' while Spanish has *pez* and *pescado* does not mean that an English speaker is unaware of the difference. French has no one-word equivalent to *in-laws*. What contrast in attitudes to the family can this betray? The French and German week is eight days long (*dans huit jours*; *über acht Tage*), the French fortnight fifteen, the German only fourteen. Are our conceptions of time incompatible? Russian has specific words for 'one and a half' – *полтора* – and even 'one hundred and fifty' – *полтораста* – but no real equivalent to the English 'dozen'.

The above anecdotal examples are instances of differences between languages in respect of single words. They say nothing of the range of expressive possibilities offered through combinations of words. Having a single, more specific word may sometimes be more economical: *Er fuhr dahin, он поехал туда* ('He went there, and not on foot' – this is an explanation rather than a translation). But in some circumstances the speaker may be glad to use *go* or *se promener*, which do not specify any particular mode of locomotion, just as *fahren* and *ехать* do not specify whether it is by bus, car or train. No language precludes the expression of an idea; it is simply that some things are more elegantly or easily said (or avoided) in one language than in another.

If language does determine mental processes or predispose certain awareness rather than others, then this relative ease of encoding certain concepts in one or another language – that is, their *codability* – should influence non-linguistic behaviour patterns. Now, in Navaho important sub-classes of verbs can be defined according to the shape of the object of the verb. The theory would lead us to expect, therefore, that shape would enjoy precedence over, say, colour in classificatory tasks. Yet in an experiment which required Navaho children and both black and white English-speaking children to sort objects of various shapes and colours, it was found that environmental factors – a slum, suburban or reservation background – were as important as linguistic factors in predicting whether a child preferred shape or colour as the basis for sorting the objects.

We must agree, then, with Fishman that 'languages primarily reflect rather than create sociocultural regularities in values and orientation' (1970, p. 91). Differences in social and physical environment result in a difference in *cultural focus* which is reflected in the language. One example is the difference in titles used in Russian to address 'in-group' and 'out-group' members (see 5.4.1); another is the plethora of words for varieties of camel in Arabic. Such variations in focus of interest are found even within what is normally thought of as a single cultural group. A Frenchman who never ventures near the ski slopes may be unaware of the many qualities of snow recognised by his sporting fellow countryman: *la poudreuse, la fraîche, la farineuse, la neige à Mix*, etc. When the need arises to communicate in new situations, the language can be 'stretched' to accommodate that need. Speakers and hearers come to agreement on new meanings of existing forms and on the creation and interpretation of new words.

The language learner must be able to recognise on what basis speakers of L2 codify a given realm of experience (see 9.4) and use that same basis himself. In formal terms this task is no different to coping with communication problems within our own language.

One way of increasing the expressive and descriptive resources of a language is to 'import' words from other languages. This is our next topic.

6.2 Lexical borrowing

'Borrowing' is a process whereby one language adopts a meaningful unit from another. The analogy with borrowing coin is not to be taken too far. First of all, the lender is often unaware of his generosity, and in the second place the borrower is apt to keep his new acquisition and adapt it to suit his own convenience. That is not to say that borrowings are 'non-returnable', but they are rarely the same again for their time in another linguistic system. English *budget* came from the French *bougette* ('small bag'); it has now been 'borrowed back' by French with its current English spelling and meaning. *Nuisance*, too, has come from French only to be reclaimed with a narrowed meaning, since it now refers only to forms of pollution. We must also remember that to say 'English has borrowed *cuisine* from French' is a shortened way of saying that English *speakers* have adopted the word. In so doing they may go some way towards reducing the 'culture gap' between two speech-communities by codifying in a single unit a concept which previously required a whole phrase for its expression.

6.2.1 Contacts

The first prerequisite of borrowing is the presence in the community of bilingual speakers, however imperfect their knowledge of the 'donor' language. Much depends on the borrower's status and influence. A borrowing which is used in the media reaches a large audience and may soon become common usage. Almost overnight *machismo* found wide currency in English, which possibly indicates that the idea behind it had long been wanting adequate expression. Of course, some sectors of the community are quick to react against the use of foreign words in the 'respectable' press. An important factor is the esteem in which the two groups hold each other (see 5.3). A low opinion of the other community provides little motivation for borrowing, unless it is to give the borrowed words a pejorative meaning, as is the case with French *palabres* ('empty words') and *hâblerie* ('tall story') from the Spanish *palabras* ('words') and *hablar* ('to talk'). The direction of borrowing between French and English in Canada is almost entirely one way, as American English is the language of social advance in an economy which is overwhelmingly controlled by American-speaking managers.

Relative prestige is not the only factor to affect borrowing. The duration and proximity of contact between the two cultures, the relative utility of the two languages and the number of bilinguals are also determinant. In other words, those variables which have an incidence on bilingualism (see Figure 3.3, above) are directly or indirectly relevant to borrowing. Invasion can lead to a massive influx of borrowings – Gaul after the Roman conquest, England after 1066. Many African countries retain elements of the vocabularies of their European colonisers and some words have emigrated in the opposite direction, mostly from Arabic.

To trace the entry of borrowings into a given language is to trace the chronology and nature of the cultural and trading links of that community with other nations. English is reckoned to count some 5,000 words of French origin, many dating back to Norman times when specialisations like *mutton:sheep, pork:pig* were introduced. Spanish still bears the traces of the Moorish occupation which lasted from the eighth to the fifteenth century: *algodón* ('cotton'), *arroz* ('rice'), *alcuzcuz* ('couscous'). Russian saw a large influx of 'cultural' words from English literary sources when Dickens, Scott and Shakespeare were translated into Russian in the first half of the nineteenth century: *денди* ('dandy'), *кипсек* ('keepsake'). The pre-eminence of German technology is reflected in the presence of words like *шахта* ('mine') from *Schacht*, and the French favour with the court of St Petersburg has likewise left its mark. The military and cultural prestige of Renaissance Italy led to massive importations into French of military, architectural and fashion words, such as *escalade, vedette, estafette, esplanade, façade, rotonde, moustache, pommade*. In the seventeenth century contacts favoured artistic and musical borrowings – *fresque, gouache, cantate, solfège* – but then anglomania took over from italomania, prompting loans of railway and sports vocabulary – *tunnel, express, handicap, turf*. An exhaustive survey carried out in 1939 put the number of anglicisms in French at 3,000 a significant number but representing nevertheless a positive balance of exports over imports in France's commerce with England. But the terms of trade have swung dramatically and the trend to borrowings from American is accelerating rapidly to a point where some Frenchmen fear that *franglais* is a threat to the integrity of their language. Similar concerns have been expressed about *Spanglish* and *Deutschlisch,* or *Engleutsch.* Two reasons for the fast growth of the latter are the widespread knowledge of English among Germans and the prestige of the American pop-culture. Since the war American English has replaced British English as the major source of borrowings: *Jet-Setterin, Hard-Core-Porno, Punk-rocker, Underdog-Songs.* In the pre-war period English assimilated *schadenfreude, cartel, bakelite* and *U-boat,* then came *ersatz* and *blitzkrieg* or simply *blitz,* which is now in common use with a non-military meaning. The post-war era has seen very few borrowings from German, with the notable exception of Brandt's *Ostpolitik.*

These examples have allowed a brief sketch of some results of direct cultural contact. If we adopt the approach of following one word through successive contacts, we uncover some amazing vagaries. 'Apricot' originated in China and was brought eventually to Italy under the name *praecoquum*. Thence, passing through Greek *praekókkion*, Arabic *al barquq* and Catalan *albercoc/abercoc* it became French *abricot*. It is to French that English owes *apricot*, German *Aprikose* and Russian *абрикос.*

6.2.2 Motivations for borrowing

We can distinguish two major categories of borrowings according to their motivation, though some words may fall simultaneously into both. The first are *denotative*, the second *connotative* (see 9.3). *Denotative* borrowings fill a gap in the system. Their purpose is entirely functional. When a discovery or advance is made by one speech-community, its designation is frequently taken up, at least initially, by other groups. Thus *nylon* has been widely borrowed; it was coined with a view to facilitating its widespread acceptance, as are many trade-names. *Hovercraft* has entered French and Russian intact. Economic and scientific dominance are the major underlying reasons, as is witnessed by the large numbers of American computing and marketing terms borrowed by European languages. In addition to making a new distinction of meaning it may be necessary to borrow a word to maintain a distinction which is threatened. In the dialects of south-west France the words for 'cat' and 'rooster' both developed, as a result of sound change, from Latin *cattus* and *gallus* into [gat]. The clash was overcome by using the local variants of *faisan* and also *poul* from Latin *pullus* for 'rooster'. Another functional consideration is regularity of patterning. *Lift* is making headway in French because it allows the formation of *liftier*, which is more succinct than *garçon d'ascenseur.*

Connotative borrowings seize on the symbolic nature of the word as a token of another civilisation. This is true of *panache* and *je ne sais quoi* in English, which occupy no clearly definable semantic space of their own. The Arab borrowing *chouïa* denotes no more than *un peu*, but it is full of eastern promise. Such borrowings may be less integrated into the structure of the borrowing language – in contrast to *huguenot* from *Eidgenosse* or *quichenotte* from *kiss-me-not* – since their foreignness is intended to be a salient feature.

6.2.3 What forms are borrowed?

It is rare for syntactic features to pass from one language to another, though it may happen as a consequence of prolonged contact. French Canadian has the construction *Il n'a pas été permis d'y aller* by analogy with *He wasn't allowed to go* and in contrast to European French *On ne lui a pas permis d'y aller*. The resistance to change of a language's syntactic structure is understandable in that it is the framework which shows, by word order or case endings, the relationships of the words to each other and thereby makes an essential contribution to meaning. Any modification of the syntactic rules will have far-reaching repercussions. Some 80 per cent of the lexis of Basque, for example, is of Latin or Romance origin, yet the syntax is most definitely not of Indo-European descent.

Similarly, the borrowing of prepositions and conjunctions is very exceptional, again because of their 'logical' rather than referential nature. The French do use *because*, but for humorous effect rather than to express a relation, and often with the meaning 'because of'. Interjections tend to be used only connotatively, as with *Ach so!*, rather than being integrated.

Of the meaningful elements of the lexis, adjectives and adverbs account for, yet again, only a tiny percentage of borrowings. Verbs are more prominent, but it is nouns which represent three-quarters of borrowed words. This is because nouns enjoy a greater range of grammatical freedom, their unity of form may be more easily perceived than that of verbs which change according to person and tense, and some meaning can usually be assigned by the borrower without difficulty, even if it is not identical to its common acceptance in the donor language. For example, *un training* is 'a tracksuit'. When the word has several meanings in its own language, usually only one is retained. For example, *спутник* ('sputnik') means both 'fellow-traveller' and 'satellite', but only the latter meaning was apparent in the context of the space-shots. The relationship between the word's spelling or pronunciation and its perceived meaning is totally arbitrary. The average Russian will be completely unaware of the motivation underlying the composition of *ховеркрафт* ('hovercraft'). German *Keks* is singular despite its derivation from *cakes*. This arbitrariness is graphically illustrated by the unanalytical borrowing into Italian American of complete phrases like *azzoraiti* 'That's all right') and *vazzumara* ('What's the matter? ') and the Catalan borrowing of Arabic *al baquq* as *albercoc* ('apricot'), integrating the article with the noun in the process. The Spanish say *un elepé* for 'LP' without necessarily realising that the original model is an acronym rather than a noun.

From French, English has borrowed affixes such as *-ess, -ment, -ance, -age* and *-ty*. From the same source German has more recently borrowed *-abel* (*blamabel, akzeptabel)* and transformed the French verbal affix *-er* into *-ieren* (*egalisieren, buchstabieren)*. French owes *-asque* and *-esque* (*rocambolesque*) to Italian, and *-ade* to a number of Romance sources. The affix *-ing* is gaining ground in French, but is found only in combination with English roots such as *foot-ing*, even if the resultant composition is unknown in English in the French sense of 'a jog'. The French have borrowed *jogging* also, but the two words are not interchangeable, as one says *faire un footing* but *faire du jogging*.

6.2.4 A typology of borrowings

A convenient method of classifying lexical borrowings is according to what has been borrowed: whether it is both the physical form of the word and its meaning, or the meaning alone.

The adoption of *Teenager* and *Bestseller* into German and of *hit-parade* and *hold-up* into French are examples of borrowings of form and meaning together. Furthermore, their reference has remained unchanged, though this is not true of all cases. Once in the 'host' system, the borrowing becomes subject to its many pressures. *Le lobby* has acquired pejorative overtones, with the result that 'neutral' lobbying is done by *groupes de pression. Le meeting* has been similarly narrowed, to 'political gathering'. In the opposite direction, English contrasts *cuisine* with *kitchen,* reserving the former, along with *chef,* for gastronomic creations. In its denotation *джинсы* ('jeans') remains unchanged, though its connotation for fashion-conscious Soviet young people is strong. *Sputnik* seems restricted to reference to Soviet space-craft, perhaps even to the earlier flights. The word for (any) 'railway station', *вокзал* – /vokzal/, was inspired by the name of a single London station, *Vauxhall!* In the nineteenth century *увлечение* spanned a broad semantic area which included 'distraction', 'pastime' and 'enthusiasm'. It overlapped to some extent with *спорт* ('sport') until the latter lost its meaning of 'gaming' and was confined to physical activities. When *хобби* ('hobby') was borrowed it took over the area of 'pastime' and 'interest', leaving *увлечение* to express 'passionate interest'. Such shifts of meaning are a commonplace result of borrowing. *Película* was used for both 'roll of film' and 'movies' until Spanish borrowed *filme* and even *films* for the latter, despite the very un-Spanish shape of the words. *Tenis* is both 'game of tennis' and 'tennis court'.

Sometimes we meet *pseudo-borrowings*, which are in fact inventions of the borrower having no equivalent in the 'source' language, such as *footing*, and German *Twen* ('person in his twenties') and *Know-what.*

The third class of borrowings involves the adoption of meaning only. In this group we can first distinguish *sense borrowings*, in which the meaning of a foreign word is 'grafted' on to a word of similar form already existing in the host language. Thus, under the influence of English, *réaliser* has come to mean 'realise' as well as 'achieve' and *adoptieren* now applies not only to 'children' but also to 'measures'. French *dada*, originally a 'hobby-horse' of the wooden type, is now more frequently used as 'passion' or 'hobby'. Portuguese American has added to *grosería* ('rudeness') the meaning 'grocery store'.

Finally, a *calque* is a translation of the constituent parts of a foreign word into the corresponding units of the host language. It has the advantage of ensuring the word's transparency. In addition to *ховеркрафт* Russian has *судно на воздушной подушке* ('craft on an air cushion') and French offers *aéroglisseur. Skyscraper* has the loan translation equivalents *gratte-ciel, Wolkenkratzer, rascacielos* and *небоскрёб* German also favours this process: *Flaschenhals* ('bottleneck'), *Schnappschuss* ('snapshot'), *Lautsprecher* ('loudspeaker'). In many instances a borrowed word exists alongside a home-grown version: *кооперация. сотрудничество* ('co-operation'). However, *piebalón* and *balompié,* proposed as replacements for *futból,* have not caught on at all.

6.2.5 Integration

Unless it is intended as a connotation-charged allusion to a different culture, a borrowing will be assimilated more or less rapidly into the phonological, semantic and syntactic systems of the host language.

If word stress in the borrowing language is fixed, as in French, where it falls on the last fully sounded vowel, then borrowings will usually be fitted into this pattern. Thus French has *le leadér*. In Spanish, a two-syllable word ending in *r* normally carries the stress on the final syllable, yet in the case of *el líder* the English pattern has been retained and the exceptional stress indicated in writing by an accent. The spelling has also been changed to reflect the English pronunciation. The transfer of stress from last to first syllable on the borrowing of German *Bakelit* into English seems entirely random, however.

Sounds which are definitely outside the host phonological system are also subject to change, but again this is unsystematic. French has contained words ending in *-ing* for many years, but in comparatively recent times the number of borrowed words incorporating this affix has increased dramatically. Pronunciations fluctuate among [iŋ, iɲ, in], the speaker's choice possibly being swayed by a knowledge of English. There is similarly a hesitation between [tʃ] and [ʃ] in French *charter.* Since many borrowings are imported from written sources, spelling undoubtedly influences pronunciation. The spelling of *bulldozer* favours [y] as the French pronunciation of the first vowel; but with an oral source [u] is more likely, as it is closer to the English pronunciation. In the event, usage varies. On the other hand, *le pull(-over)* is invariably pronounced [pyl] since [u] would result in confusion with *poule*. Another common area of fluctuation among French speakers is the English suffix *-er*, as in *starter* or *container,* which is pronounced either [er], or [œr] by analogy with the French suffix *-eur* which has a similar function. A change in pronunciation may be accompanied by an altered spelling – *paquebot* ('packet boat'), *boulingrin* 'bowling green').

It should not be inferred from a 'deviant' pronunciation – like the initial [ʃ] rather than [tʃ] in English *chagrin* – that a word has not been integrated into the language. It is semantic and syntactic integration which are more important.

We have already made many passing references to the readjustments which take place in the semantic system as a consequence of borrowing. The eventual fate of pairs or even series of competing words – *Fallout, Ausfall, Ausschüttung, Niederschlag* – is a valuable indicator of possible drift in favour of calque or the borrowing of both form and meaning. The extension of a borrowing beyond its single meaning on entry into the language is strong evidence that it has been assimilated semantically. For example, French *challenger* is now employed in reference to economic and political competition as well as to sport.

The use of a borrowing as a base for the formation of new words – *sprinteur, sprinter* (verb) – demonstrates that the 'foreign' element has become an integral part of its new system. The productivity (see 9.6) of borrowed words can be prodigious, either as bases (*gadget, gadgétiser, gadgétisation, gadgetière, gadgétophile),* or as members of new compounds (*appareil-gadget, avion-gadget, cadeau-gadget*). The popular interpretation of *hamburger* as *ham* plus *burger* (rather than *Hamburger*) has elevated *burger* to the status of an independent word and given us *beef-, cheese-, egg-* and *fish-burgers.* No doubt this is only a foretaste of things to come. *Self* has become integrated into French to the point where the words *self-étreinte* and *self-recyclage* have appeared, compounds of the patterns *self-service* and *auto-recyclage.* This trend seems further advanced in German, with such coinings as *Top-Verdiener, Non-stop-Flüge, Gag-Schreiber* and *Live-Sendung.* It is quite conceivable that in time the 'foreignness' of these words of English origin will be no more felt than is that of *tele* or *vision.*

6.2.6 Reaction to borrowing

'Bastardised', polluted', 'corrupt', are epithets not infrequently applied to borrowings in general by defenders of the purity of a given language. In some critics it is little short of a xenophobic reaction to an invasion by an alien culture, in others a lament that the community lacks the imagination to use its own linguistic resources. But borrowing has taken place ever since different linguistic communities came into contact, and the 'pure' vocabulary which such enemies of borrowing wish to protect is itself a mixture of words from many different sources, shaped to meet changing communicative needs.

If the intolerance of borrowings becomes widespread - at least, among those who have the authority to lay down the law - then official action may be taken. This frequently involves mandating a body to propose 'home-grown' words to substitute for the borrowed forms. It is not usually the concept which is rejected, merely the physical form. Therefore, the procedure adopted is the calque or translation. When the body involved is empowered only to make suggestions, these may fall on barren ground. The Spanish Royal Academy has included *güiski* in its dictionary and invented *cinta fonóptica*, yet it is *whiskey* and *video* which figure in everyday communication. The *Académie Française* was founded in 1635 to establish the norms of good usage, but the deliberations of academicians have had little effect on the linguistic habits of the French people at large. Since 1973 the use by radio and television announcers and civil servants of foreign terms in all official texts has been banned by ministerial decree. They are required to use instead substitutes put forward by special commissions. While *logiciel* and *matériel* ('software', 'hardware') seem to enjoy some currency even outside the government sphere, *gros-porteur* ('jumbo-jet') has had less success and the long-winded *projecteur ponctuel* ('spot') would appear to have a difficult future in store.

In Germany there is at present no organisation mandated to prevent borrowing. During the Third Reich, however, there was considerable resistance to the import of foreign words; yet even then some borrowings were officially adopted for the expedient purpose of disguising or attenuating their full significance. Initially, at least, *Sterilisation* must have been totally obscure to most Germans, and *Konzentrationslager* remains euphemistic even if the foreign element in the word is understood.

In the various branches of science and technology, at both national and international levels, there are many organisations with a brief to formulate and recommend standard terms. One task is to make fully explicit the relationship between the meaning of any new term and that of existing terms. If it is a borrowing, it is preferable that its meaning in both languages should be the same. In other words, the creation of 'faux-amis' is to be avoided. The other tasks concern the borrowed term's form: the spelling must be fixed, a gender assigned if the language requires, and the plural specified where there is doubt (*phenomenons* or *phenomena, corpora* or *corpuses?*).

The interpreter and translator are important agents in the borrowing process. Working under pressure, lacking time and information, one may retain a foreign word, while others translate it, but in various ways. The published translations can reach a wide public which is left confused by the unnecessary multiplication of terms. Hence the standardisation of terms and the updating of specialised dictionaries which can be made available to scientists and translators alike is an urgent task which is being accomplished on a European scale with the aid of computerised data banks and desk-top terminals.

Further reading

Whorf (1956) contains an interesting collection of articles on lesser-known languages and analyses of their lexical and syntactic structure compared with English. Sapir (1921) is a thought-provoking book which deals with languages in contact, and language change and classification. Allen and Corder (1973) introduce two critiques of the Sapir–Whorf hypothesis, one of which deals with its implications for language learning. For a well-illustrated discussion of borrowing, see Weinreich (1963). Foster (1970) gives an entertaining review of the influences of foreign languages and social change on contemporary English.

Suggestions for inquiry

1 Compare the specialised vocabulary of articles in English and a foreign language taken from equivalent sources (e.g. newspapers aimed at a similar readership) on the topics of fashion, architecture,

science and technology. Note differences and similarities. Using comprehensive dictionaries of both languages, trace the origin of the words.

2 Find ten widely used English words which were originally specialised scientific terms.

3 Find ten borrowings from English used in the following foreign-language publications: advertising copy, pop-magazines, business reviews. Look them up in a foreign and an English dictionary. Try to establish when they entered the foreign language. Compare their 'original' and 'borrowed' meanings.

4 Compare the list of words beginning with *auto* and *mini* in the latest edition of a large foreign-language dictionary with the list given in the previous edition.

7

Grammars

> In speaking or comprehending a language, people implicity conform to a system that relates sound to meanings. This has traditionally been called the *grammar* of the language.
>
> H. H. Clark and E. V. Clark (1977) *Psychology and Language*, p. 5

We have already used the term *grammar* in referring to the system of a language as a whole (1.3.1). In the preceding chapters it has been shown that different languages and varieties of a language have a symbolic value which accompanies their other functions. Moreover, we have seen to what extent situation conditions the way in which people speak or write. It will be helpful at this point to outline a grammar model which relates social setting to linguistic system (7.1) in order to pave the way for more detailed consideration of specific aspects of the system (Chapters 8–10). No one grammatical viewpoint has as yet been proven to be 'the best', and so we look briefly at three models which have inspired interest in recent years (7.2), before discussing at greater length an approach which seems particularly well-suited to the task of syntactic analysis for language learners (7.3).

First, however, we must make a basic distinction between types of grammar. Modern linguistics is characterisd by a *descriptive* rather than a *prescriptive* goal; that is, it seeks to circumscribe and interpret actual linguistic behaviour rather than to influence this behaviour by setting up one way of speaking as 'correct' or 'elegant' usage. The emphasis in this chapter is on descriptive grammars. As was pointed out in 1.4, school grammars, whether of a native or a foreign language, tend to be prescriptive. In the first case they attempt to make explicit those rules which speakers already follow subconsciously, and may in addition make prescriptive statements about such things as split infinitives or ending a sentence with a preposition. Grammars devised for foreign-language learners are by nature prescriptive, since they do not make subconscious knowledge explicit but provide new information on a new language. Ideally, the advanced learner should be able to produce his own description of the varieties of his native and foreign languages in order to contrast them. By then assigning to each structurally described variety a social value, the learner is in a position to make appropriate use of the varieties he commands.

7.1 A grammar model

Figure 7.1 summarises a model of language proposed by a school of linguistic inquiry known as *systemic linguistics*. (Some of the labels have been changed in order to maintain a consistent use of terms in this book.)

The different levels within the model are linked by a relationship of *realisation*. That is to say, each level is realised by the level or interlevel immediately below it; conversely, moving up the scale we make statements of ever greater generalisation or abstraction. Let us start from the interlevel of *context* by way of illustration. Here are situated particular instances of situation types (4.3.2); for example, a class held in Bradford on the morning of Wednesday, 3 October 1979 is a realisation, or actualisation, of the situation type 'the lecture'. The partici-

Figure 7.1
Language: the systemic model

level: **SITUATION**	Social structures Access to varieties Varieties Situation types
interlevel:	*Context*
level: **FORM**	Syntax Lexis
interlevel:	*Phonology* (*graphology*)
level: **SUBSTANCE**	Sounds (writing)

pants in that situation draw on certain of the choices open to them at the level of *form* - structures and words - and these choices are themselves realised by sound waves in the air and by chalk marks on the blackboard.

Each level represents a *potential* available to speakers. Working upwards from the lowest level, we can distinguish potentials defined by: the range of audible sounds which the human voice can produce; those sounds used in a given language; the words of a given language - its lexis - and the rules for their combination in sentences; the situations which occur in a community; and the behaviour, linguistic or otherwise, permitted by that same community. At this upper level not all individuals have equal access to all the varieties spoken within the community (see 4.5, for example) and there are social constraints governing 'who speaks when, to whom, about what'. These various potentials interact in the production of speech and writing in situation, or - to use a term proposed by Halliday to subsume both of these modes of expression - *text* (Chapter 10).

We have already argued at length (Chapter 4) that situation is the level which ultimately determines linguistic form. There are obvious parallels between this view and the concepts of appropriateness and rules for use introduced in 1.3.4. At the other end of the scale, the description of sound substance is covered in Chapter 8.

Occupying a central position is the level of *form*. To this extent we are respecting de Saussure's thesis that language is form, not substance (1.3.2). At the interface between form and substance we have phonology (8.4), which is concerned with establishing sound systems. At the interface between form and situation, where the system articulates with the outside world, we are confronted by questions of semantics and pragmatics, as these notions were defined in 1.3.1. At the core of language, then, we are left with syntax (1.3.1) and lexis. They are not separate but merge together along a continuum. The set of words available to speakers of a language is potentially unlimited, which militates against the economic statement of general rules, as we shall see in Chapter 9. On the other hand, it is more reasonable to claim that it is possible to formulate a relatively small number of rules to account for word patterning within the sentence. This last question is at the focus of the present chapter.

7.2 Grammatical perspectives

Not all linguists would subscribe to the model of language just sketched out. We stressed in 1.4 that it is the viewpoint that creates the object, and we now present three such differing vantage-points.

7.2.1 Transformational-generative grammar (TGG)

The initial development of TGG was by Noam Chomsky, whose goal was a better understanding of linguistic knowledge, or *competence*. His concern was with *ideal* speakers with a uniform set of speech habits and living in a perfectly uniform community (1.3.4). Thus, for him,

> A grammar of a language purports to be a description of the ideal speaker-hearer's intrinsic competence. If the grammar is, furthermore, perfectly explicit – in other words, if it does not rely on the intelligence of the understanding reader but rather provides an explicit analysis of his contribution – we may (somewhat redundantly) call it a *generative grammar* (1965, p. 4).

In addition to its meaning 'explicit', the label 'generative' refers to a grammar's capacity for *predicting*, from the basis of the small set of sentences on which its rules are founded, every possible sentence of that language. At the same time, the grammar must not predict (generate) any sentence which is not accepted as belonging to the language in question. This capacity is necessary if the grammar is to reflect adequately the human ability to create an infinite number of new messages (2.4).

Chomsky's grammatical model has a *syntactic* base – that is, sentences are first specified as a configuration of syntactic categories (noun, verb, adverb, etc.) and only later are lexical items inserted into the syntactic frame. Below we give a set of instructions known as *phrase structure* rules, similar to those proposed by Chomsky, which will generate a small number of *underlying strings*. These strings, the output of the phrase structure rules, are not sentences, but sequences of abstract elements which are later transformed – hence the label *transformational grammar* – into sentences having a phonetic or graphic shape.

(1) Sentence → NP + VP
(2) VP → Verb + NP
(3) NP → { NP sing / NP pl }
(4) NP sing → T + N
(5) NP pl → T + N + s
(6) T → the
(7) N → {mechanic, car, television . . .}
(8) Verb → Aux + V
(9) V → {drive, watch, repair, kick . . .}
(10) Aux → Tense (+ M) (+ have + ed) (+ be + ing)

(11) Tense → { Present / Past }

(12) M → {will, can, may, shall, must}

The arrow indicates 'is to be rewritten as'. Thus rule (1) requires that any sentence be constituted by a noun phrase (NP) plus a verb phrase (VP). The other symbols stand for: definite article (T), noun (N), auxiliary (Aux) and modal (M). The brackets of rules (3), (7), (9) and (11) require the choice of one of the items enclosed in the brackets, while the bracketed items of rule (10) are optional.

These phrase structure rules will produce a large number of strings, one of which is *the + mechanic + Present + must + have + ed + repair + the + television + s* underlying the sentence *The mechanic must have repaired the televisions*. As we increase the number of lexical items at (7) and (10), so we extend the set of potential sentences. We must ensure, of course, that the transformation of the string *the + mechanic + Present + drive + the + car* eventually produces *drives* and not *drive*. Some of the transformations which operate on the underlying strings in order to generate actual sentences are therefore obligatory. Others, however, are optional.

One such optional transformation is that by which passive sentences are derived from underlying strings. The rule can be stated as follows:

(13) NP1 + Aux + V + NP2 → NP2 + Aux + be + ed + V + by + NP1

This can be interpreted as indicating that any string with the description NP1 + Aux + V + NP2 can be transformed into the string NP2 + Aux + be + ed + V + by + NP1. Since the string above fits this description, we can derive from it the transform *the + car + Present + be + ed + drive + by + the + mechanic* underlying the passive sentence *The car is driven by the mechanic*. Further optional transformations outlined by Chomsky include *negative, interrogative* and *imperative*. Several transformations may be applied in an ordered sequence to derive, for example, the sentence *The car can't be repaired by the mechanic, can it?* from the same basic underlying string as above.

This vastly simplified account of Chomsky's early grammatical model (which has evolved considerably since then in his writings and those of other generative grammarians) can only hint at the ways in which he attempted to capture the economy of description considered so valuable in 1.1 (see there, sentences 17–23). The considerable impact of the notion of transformation is immediately obvious to those readers who recall the 'pattern drills' of some audio-lingual language teaching methods (3.3.3). Yet the formulation of a single set of rules is in conflict with the inherently variable nature of a speaker's knowledge of his language, and any effort to integrate Chomsky's model into a framework of the kind suggested in 7.1 appears to meet insurmountable difficulties.

7.2.2 Case grammar

Anyone familiar with Latin, Russian or German is familiar with the traditional notion of *case* as the inflexional categories of the noun. Latin and Russian are generally said to have six cases (although labelled differently) and German four (see Figure 7.2). By extension we sometimes talk of case in English, even though nouns are not inflexionally marked except in the genitive – *the boy's book*; we might describe *girl* as nominative and *mirror* as accusative in (1):

(1) The girl designed the mirror

For English, at least, it is perhaps more usual to offer a description in terms of syntactic function; from this viewpoint *girl* is subject and *mirror* direct object. Let us now examine sentences (2)–(6), all of which 'mean the same':

(2) женщина предложила подруге фото
(3) Die Frau schenkte ihrer Freundin ein Photo
(4) La dame offrit une photo à son amie
(5) The woman offered a photo to her friend
(6) The woman offered her friend a photo

The Russian and German sentences offer clear examples of case in the narrow sense of the term. In the Russian example it is the case endings which carry all the information concerning the syntactic functions of the three nouns as *subject, direct object* and *indirect object*. The four

Figure 7.2
Case in Latin, German and Russian

	'wolf'	'blow'	'table'
nominative	*lupus*	*der Schlag*	*стол*
vocative	*lupe*		
accusative	*lupum*	*den Schlag*	*стол*
genitive	*lupi*	*des Schlag(e)s*	*стола*
dative	*lupo*	*dem Schlag(e)*	*столу*
ablative	*lupo*		
instrumental			*столом*
prepositional			*столе*

words could, in fact, be arranged in any order without this affecting the meaning of the sentence. In the German example the syntactic functions are again specified by case, though the rigid word order points to an identical analysis. In (4) and (5) syntactic function is determined by a combination of word order and preposition (à and *to*), and in (6) by word order only.

Thus, even within one language a single function – here that of indirect object in English – can be realised by more than one means. Moreover, a single case can be used to realise more than one function, as is shown by the use of the dative in (7):

(7) Er brach den Stein mit einem Schlag ('He broke the stone with one blow')

It signals not an indirect objective but an *instrumental*, after the preposition *mit*.

The cases of 'case grammar', developed initially by Fillmore, categorise not nouns but verbs. It is claimed, moreover, that each case is related to a *consistent* semantic function and that these functions are valid across languages, even if their realisation may take different forms. Let us again look at some examples. A traditional analysis of (1) and (8) would describe *mirror* as direct object in both:

(1) The girl designed the mirror
(8) The girl shattered the mirror
(1a) *What the girl did to the mirror was design it
(8a) What the girl did to the mirror was shatter it

Yet an underlying semantic difference between the two verbs becomes apparent when we attempt the transformations (1a) and (8a) – unsuccessfully for *design* but acceptably for *shatter*. This justifies the setting up of two distinct cases: factitive (F) – associated with verbs like *design, create, make;* and objective (O).

Furthermore, a traditional, surface analysis of (8)–(11) yields four different words in the slot 'subject':

(8) The girl shattered the mirror
(9) The mirror shattered
(10) The hammer shattered the mirror
(11) The girl shattered the mirror with a hammer

This is obviously counter to our intuition, which recognises that *girl, mirror* and *hammer* each plays a single semantic role. A more elegant analysis, then, is to consider *mirror* as (O), *girl* as *agentive* (A) and *hammer* as *instrumental* (I) at their every occurrence in (8)–(11). Extending our data to (12) and (13), we may decide to distinguish a *benefactive* case (B) realised here by Larry:

(12) Lucy (A) gave Larry (B) the loot (O)
(13) Larry (B) received the loot (O) from Lucy (A)

We might also add *locative* (L) to cope with (14) and (15):

(14) Four (A) can sleep in this tent (L)
(15) This tent (L) sleeps four (A)

How many cases should be distinguished, and on what criteria exactly? These questions are still a matter of debate. In the meantime, we can tentatively classify verbs according to the number of cases associated with them:

flow (O)	*The water flows*
catch (A, O)	*The man caught the ball*
give (A, B, O)	*The woman gave her money to the needy*

Even with this *ad hoc* framework we can discern some marked differences between English verbs and those of other languages:

(16) In this chapter the author describes language
(17) This chapter describes language
(18) *Dieses Kapitel beschreibt die Sprache
(19) In diesem Kapitel wird die Sprache beschreibt

It is obvious from (16) that *chapter* is (L) and not (A) in (17). In English (A) may be suppressed by moving (L) to the position of 'surface subject'. This is not possible in German (18), where (L) cannot be 'disguised'. Sentences (20)–(24) illustrate how common it is in English for (I), (L) and (B) to appear as 'surface subject':

(20) The table (L) seats eight
(21) She (B) was promised a gift
(22) This gun (I) killed the man
(23) One tin of paint (I) covered the wall
(24) £50 (I) will buy you a bike

None of these sentences can be translated 'word for word' into French, Spanish, German, or Russian. In every case the 'deep case' has to be realised explicitly, as in (19).

7.2.3 Systemic linguistics

The *systemic* approach to language has developed out of the research of the English linguist Halliday, whose model of the levels of language and their interrelationship was outlined in 7.1. We saw there that each level defines a *potential*; the level of situation represents a behavioural potential (what we can do), whereas grammar represents the linguistic resources available. At the interface between the two we must recognise a *semantic potential* – 'what we can mean', as Halliday puts it. This consists of three functional components – *ideational, interpersonal* and *textual.*

The ideational function is equivalent to what we called earlier the *informational* function (4.4). Language serves to express our experience of the world and also, to some extent, shapes our perceptions of it (6.1). This component enables the speaker to play the role of *observer*, and tends to be activated by the situational feature *topic* (4.3.3).

The interpersonal function of language is manifest in its use to establish and maintain social relations (4.4). We interact with other speakers, asking questions, making requests, issuing orders, and so on. In addition, we assess the likelihood of actions and events, expressing doubts, assumptions, convictions – *Surely this won't happen! Maybe it could?* In other words, we act as *intruders* into the world. This component tends to be activated by the situational feature *role-re lationship* (4.3.1).

The textual function is similar to what was described in section 4.4.1 as the contextual function. In speaking and writing we construct texts (as defined in 7.1), the constituent sentences of which are bound together by a web of cohesive relations. These links may be realised by intonation patterns, unity of topic, pronouns like *the former* or *this*, and conjunctions like *however*. In this way, successive utterances are linked together to form a whole. These same devices further relate the text to the situation of its production. In short, the textual component allows the speaker to be *relevant*. It tends to be activated by the situational feature *channel* (4.3.4), whether this is the spoken or the written word.

Each of these three semantic components is realised by certain lexical and syntactic options. The language system offers choices to the speaker – one word, intonation pattern or construction in preference to another. The task of a grammar is to clarify these choices and the factors which constrain them. The systemic model postulates that within each component the available choices can be organised into networks which are relatively independent of one another. That is, the choice within the ideational network to use an active rather than a passive verb and a present rather than a past tense, say, does not affect, and is unaffected by, the choice within the interpersonal component to agree with rather than to contradict one's interlocutor. Within a given network, of course, a choice made at one point automatically closes some options while leaving others open. Figure 7.3, which shows a simplified

Figure 7.3
Interpersonal network: a simplified example

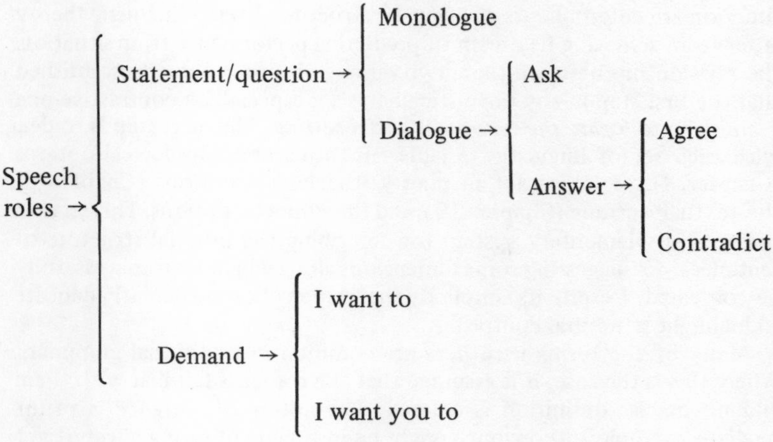

SOURCE: Halliday (1978, p. 119).

fragment of the interpersonal network, illustrates this point. In a dialogue one is forced to ask or answer, while demand and contradiction are seen as mutually exclusive.

The speaker's choices from within the networks are reflected in the structure of the text, where all three functions are realised simultaneously (4.4.1). In (25) the ideational component is represented by certain actors (*you, her photo*), processes (*take*) and circumstances (*yesterday*):

(25) Was it yesterday that you took her photo?

The interpersonal role adopted is that of questioner. Textually, *her* relates to a female previously specified in the situation; the strong focus on *yesterday* leaves that part of the question open, while presupposing that 'the taking of her photo' has been already established as fact.

It is not possible to elaborate here beyond the basic principles and components of systemic linguistics. Rooted in social reality, this approach appears to offer more insights of interest to the language learner than does transformational generative grammar, which was conceived in a social vacuum.

7.3 Sentence structure

We return now to the 'core' area of general descriptive linguistics – the level of *form*. We have seen above and in Chapter 4 that situation and function are determinants of linguistic structure. Even if linguistic theory is far from achieving its dream of predicting performance from situation, the relationship between these two variables is firmly enough established that the first step in any linguistic analysis – especially a contrastive one – must be to *locate the text in its social setting*. The next step is to deal with each set of linguistic variables in turn: the phonological options (Chapter 8), so important in poetry; the lexical options (Chapter 9); the textual options (Chapter 10); and the syntactic options. This section presents an elementary system for describing the internal structure of sentences, so suggesting some dimensions along which texts may usefully be compared. Despite its simplicity the framework is sufficiently delicate to highlight structural contrasts.

Many of the terms used here are common in traditional grammars. Where this is the case, it is assumed that the reader is familiar with them and no precise definition is offered. The notion of *sentence* is an immediate example; although we might be incapable of giving a watertight definition of it, we rarely have difficulty in, or disagreements about, recognising a given stretch of text as a sentence. This is certainly true of written prose, where full stops and capital letters provide unambiguous indications. In listening to conversation, too, where we are trying to impose order on the continuous flow of speech, we are seldom unable to decide where sentence boundaries lie. We do recognise, of course, that some sentences remain incomplete for a variety of reasons. A high incidence of incompleteness or uncertainty over placing sentence boundaries is in itself an indication of a particular kind of text – impromptu speech.

Taking the complete *sentence* as the primary analytical unit, we view it as being composed of one or more *clauses*, and each clause as being constituted by one or more *groups*. Below this level we have that of *word*. The most convenient approach is first to describe the clause before moving up and then down the scale to deal with the levels of sentence and group.

7.3.1 Clause types

There are five possible elements of the clause: *subject* (S), *predicator* (P), *complement* (C), *adjunct* (A) and *vocative* (VOC). The predicator is always a verbal group and the adjunct an adverbial group. Both subject and complement may be realised by a nominal group, a personal, interrogative or indefinite pronoun, or a noun clause:

(26) S P A C
He/had guessed/full well/what they meant

(27) S P C
What they meant/didn't matter/ to him

(28) S P C C A
The lion in the cage/will give/you/a shock/soon

The vocative is a nominal group, very often a proper name:

(29) P A VOC
Go/away/Percy!

(30) P S P VOC
Can/you/hear /comrades?

At clause level it is possible to contrast texts according to the number of elements present and their relative order. The number of adjuncts and their position are especially revealing features.

In addition to exhibiting distinctive internal structures, clauses can be classified as *free* (f) or *dependent* (d). A free clause has a SPCA-type structure and is syntactically autonomous, whereas a dependent clause – also a SPCA-type structure – can occur only it if is attached to a free clause:

(31) f d
They will go + and they will return

(32) f d
He'll love you + or leave you

(33) f d
He'll come / / if you invite him soon

(34) f d
They arrived / / holding a bunch of flowers

Naturally, we can cumulate the two analyses suggested so far:

(35) f d
S P S P C
The toast/will burn/ / if/you/don't remove/it

7.3.2 Sentence types

It is obvious that the combinations of clauses in each of the examples (31)–(35) constitute sentences. Moreover, each of the free clauses could, in isolation, constitute a sentence. The distinction we have made between free and dependent clauses provides the basis for a recognition of different sentence types.

A *simple* sentence consists of a single, free SPCA-type structure, as in (28).

A *compound* sentence consists either of a simple free clause plus a co-ordinate dependent clause – as in (31) and (32) – or of a simple main clause plus a parenthetic clause (p):

(36) f p
I can't sleep (, you see)

A *complex* sentence consists of a simple free clause whose adjunct is realised by one or more dependent clauses, as in (33) and (34). The 'two-tier' nature of the complex sentence can be illustrated as follows:

(37) f d
S P C A
S P A
They/rebuilt/the pier / / after/it/collapsed/in a storm

Finally we can distinguish a *mixed* sentence. This is a compound sentence in which one or more of the clauses has a subordinate dependent clause:

(38) f d d
Go to bed + and sleep / / before deciding

We must also take account of units which have the graphic or intonational features of normal 'full' sentences, but which do not contain a free clause. Some typical examples are *Never!, Because I said so* and *Reduced to clear*. As with incomplete sentences, the very presence in a text of 'minor constructions' such as these may immediately characterise it as belonging to a certain genre. Minor constructions are certainly very frequent in conversation.

The study of sentence patterning in terms of free and dependent clauses can bring to light striking differences between texts, some of which make preferential use of one sentence type to the exclusion of others.

7.3.3 Group types

Two classes of group contribute to clause structure: *verbal* groups and *nominal* groups. The former may be finite, in which case they consist of an optional *auxiliary* (aux) and a *verb* (vb), or *non-finite* (n-f); in this case they consist of an infinitive or a participial:

(39) I (*aux*) do (*vb*) want (*n-f*) to go
(40) (*n-f*) Having finished, he (*vb*) slept

The pivot of the nominal groups is the *head* (h) word, which may be *premodified* (pre) and *postmodified* (post). The possible structures are exemplified in (41):

(41) (*pre*) Only the three best (*h*) candidates . . .
(*post*) . . . available (*adjective*)
(*post*) . . . going/selected (*non-finite clause*)
(*post*) . . . who come forward (*dependent clause*)
(*post*) . . . for the job (*prepositional phrase*)
. . . will be interviewed

Noteworthy features of verbal groups to look for when analysing texts are the tenses used, the frequency of passives and the presence of contracted verb forms. As for the nominal group, scientific texts are characterised by complex premodification, legal texts by complex postmodification.

7.3.4 Contrastive analysis

The 'rules' which have been given above concerning sentence, clause and group types are valid only for English. Adjectival premodification, for example, is very limited in French but prevalent in German technical texts. This is not to say that the notions of free and dependent clause, subject, predicator, complement, adjunct and vocative are irrelevant to an analysis of sentence structure in French, Spanish, German or Russian. Indeed, if the learner applies this single set of descriptive categories to similar text types in different languages, most interesting contrasts may emerge.

Further reading

Two excellent introductions to the grammatical model of Noam Chomsky are to be found in Lyons (1977) and Aitchison (1976). More recent developments of his theories are described by Smith and Wilson (1979). Matthews (1979) presents an entertaining argument to demonstrate the inadequacy of TGG in coping with linguistic variety. Allerton (1979) offers a detailed exposition of the core areas of grammatical theory, and includes a brief section on case grammar. Halliday has developed a case-type approach to the description of verbs which is discussed in Kress (1976). The most comprehensive account of Halliday's social approach to language is Halliday (1978). Berry (1975–7) describes at length the systems and structures of the systemic model. Crystal and

Davy (1969) present an analytical framework for considering texts, part of which was adopted in this chapter; they also provide specimen analyses.

Suggestions for inquiry

1. Using the approach outlined in 7.3 contrast the four texts A–D below according to: (1) number of sentences; (2) ratio of free clauses to dependent clauses; (3) ratio of co-ordinate dependent clauses to subordinate independent clauses; (4) clause structure in terms of S, P, C, A, VOC; (5) number of clauses per sentence; (6) number of groups; (7) type of groups; and (8) number of words per group.

A. HOW TO USE YOUR NEW LIQUIDISER
Assembly: Place the sealing ring in the base. Screw the goblet into the base in a clockwise direction. Fit lid and filler cap on the goblet.
Fitting: Remove the high-speed outlet cover from your Mixer by pushing the cover catch away from you. Lift the cover clear and place the Liquidiser on the power outlet engaging the lugs in the base in the slots provided. Turn the Liquidiser clockwise until it locks.
Cleaning: Fill with hot water and switch to top speed for 20–30 seconds. Alternatively, dismantle the Liquidiser and rinse the parts other than the base in warm water (not boiling), and dry. Assemble again ready for use. Do not leave the base to soak in water and do not leave the Liquidiser soaking with water in goblet.

B. WHOLE WHEAT-SESAME CRÊPES
Fry crêpes in a lightly oiled heavy frying pan – a heavy iron omelette pan is best. Make one crêpe at a time, using approximately ¼ cup of batter each. After pouring the batter into a hot pan, tilt the pan to spread the batter into a thin, round layer. Wait until the crêpe is fully solidified and browned on one side before turning it. (With a spatula I loosen all edges before turning.) Cook on the other side until browned. Once you have started frying the crêpes, you may need to add more oil to the pan. If you do, add only a little, enough to barely cover. Also, the batter will tend to separate, so merely stir and scoop from the bottom each time.

C. ECO-MANAGEMENT
We had to look back from the moon, before we fully realized that we have only one Earth. The satellite pictures confirm many of our painfully achieved mapping efforts, but they also give us a greater feeling of authenticity, since it is now physically possible to see whole continents

at a glance. The power of dreams is till with us, however, not only to devise new means of reaching farther out into space but in the interpretation of the sea around us, the restless atmosphere, and the earth between our toes. For instance, we do not directly see how our planet is at once sparsely populated, with immense areas of wild landscape, and overstressed by an alarmingly high rate of human multiplication and a pressing demand for raw materials, industrial products, and cultural amenities.

D. NOTICE: RIGHT OF HIRER TO TERMINATE AGREEMENT

(a) The Hirer may put an end to this Agreement by giving notice of termination in writing to any person who is entitled to collect or receive the hire rent.

(b) He must then pay any instalments which are in arrear at the time when he gives notice. If, when he has paid those instalments the total amount which he has paid under the Agreement is less than one-half the Hire-Purchase Price, he must also pay enough to make up that sum, unless the Court determines that a smaller sum would be equal to the Owner's loss.

(c) If the goods have been damaged owing to the Hirer having failed to take reasonable care of them, the Owner may sue him for the amount of the damage unless that amount can be agreed between the Hirer and the Owner.

2. Find four short foreign texts associated with different situations and contrast their sentence, clause and group structures as with the English texts above.

8

Sounds and Sound Systems

> The accent of the country where one is born remains in one's heart and mind and in one's speech.
>
> La Rochefoucauld, *Maxims*, no. 342

We have already observed, when discussing pronunciation and individual identity (5.2)., the truth in La Rochefoucauld's remark that accent is an emotional issue. It is important to have a good accent if one wants to be integrated into a foreign community rather than marking oneself as an outsider from the very first word uttered. Even if the foreign listener is favourably disposed towards the British or North American communities, he may still become irritated at constant mispronunciations of his own language, or simply distracted by this source of interference. Poor pronunciation can have effects other than psychological ones, of course. It makes understanding hard and can lead to serious misinterpretations: *She cut off her hair* and *She cut off her heir* are distinguished by a single sound.

We have also seen (3.3.2) that there is some foundation for the common belief that it is very hard to achieve native-like pronunciation in a foreign language unless one starts to learn the second language very early. This is due in part to the fact that understanding and planning speech involve only mental processes, whereas actually producing utterances requires the physical articulation of sounds. Now, the organs we use to produce speech sounds become 'set in their ways', as it were. Because the sounds of two different languages are rarely identical to each other, and may often bear little mutual resemblance at all, it is therefore necessary to break out of the articulatory routine of one's first language. In children who still enjoy the sheer pleasure of playing with sounds, this change of routine may not pose any problems. Yet in adults it is usually a matter of conscious effort. This means knowing something of how speech sounds are produced and something of their characteristics. More particularly, it requires a knowledge of the sound system of one's first language and also of that of one's second language since some pronunciation errors are attributable to interference between the two. The mispronunciations by English-speaking learners of a given foreign language tend to follow fairly predictable patterns. In the present chapter, then, we look at the description of speech sounds – a branch of linguistics known as *phonetics* – as a guide to avoiding errors and improving performance in pronunciation.

Speech sounds can be described in terms of the impression they make on the listener's ear (an *auditory* description), their physical properties as sound waves (an *acoustic* description), or their production by the organs of speech (an *articulatory* description). Here we adopt an articulatory approach, which is of the greatest practical use to the learner.

8.1 The organs of speech

It is clear from Figure 8.1 that the organs of speech serve other purposes as well. We can nevertheless say that this apparatus is specialised to the extent that primates are incapable of producing such a wide and finely contrasted range of sounds as human beings. There is no specialisation, however, from race to race. That is to say, there is no physiological reason why a person cannot articulate any sound of any language, however 'exotic' it may seem.

In order to produce a speech sound we first need an *airstream*. In the languages which concern us here, this airstream originates from the lungs and it is expelled through the mouth, the nose or both – that is, it is *pulmonic* and *egressive*. Some languages, like the African 'click' languages, incorporate sounds which originate from higher up the vocal tract. It is worth pointing out, too, that some French speakers draw air in through the mouth to pronounce *oui* – that is, the airstream is *in*gressive.

This egressive flow of air must then be modulated in some way. The first point where this can occur is at the vocal cords, or *glottis*. These are not like strings at all, but are two bands of muscle which stretch across the air-passage and which can be relaxed to allow the air to pass unimpeded, or, on the contrary, brought loosely together so that the air has to force them apart, causing them to vibrate and producing a sound. A sound which involves the vibration of the vocal cords is said to be *voiced*; a sound produced while the vocal cords are relaxed is said to be *unvoiced*. There is a third possibility; the vocal cords may be held tightly together so that the airflow builds up behind them without any vibration. This is known as a *glottal stop*, symbolised [ʔ]. In some English speech, especially popular London speech, a glottal stop is heard as the final sound in words like *cut* or *cup*.

Next, the shape of the *pharyngeal cavity* can be modified by general

Figure 8.1

Organs of speech: physiological diagram

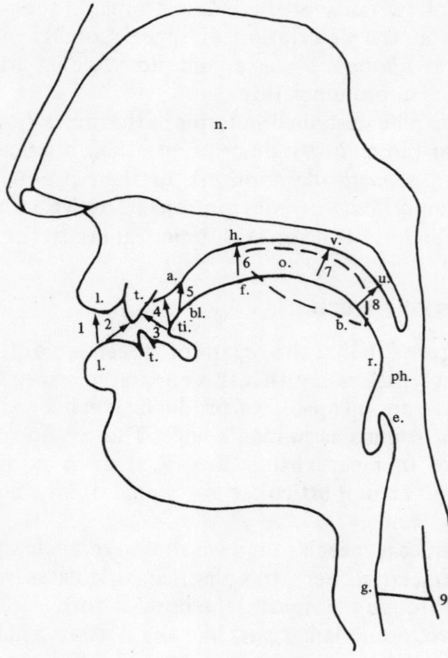

g.	glottis (vocal cords)	r.	root of tongue	1	bilabial
e.	epiglottis	b.	back	2	labio-dental
ph.	pharynx	f.	front	3	dental
n.	nasal cavity	bl.	blade	4	alveolar
o.	oral cavity	ti.	tip	5	palato-alveolar
u.	uvula	t.	teeth	6	palatal
v.	velum (soft palate)	l.	lips	7	velar
h.	hard palate			8	uvular
a.	alveoles (teeth ridge)			9	glottal

constriction or a backward movement of the root of the tongue. At the top of this cavity is the *uvula*, which can be lowered to the position shown in Figure 8.1 to allow the airstream to enter the *nasal cavity* and the *oral cavity* simultaneously. If the air is allowed to escape only through the nasal cavity, because the oral cavity is closed at some point, we talk of a *nasal* sound. If the air is released through both nasal and oral cavities at the same time, we have a *nasalised* sound. By raising the uvula, all the airstream can be diverted into the mouth and expelled through the lips. Sounds produced in this manner are *oral* sounds.

The shape of the oral cavity can be altered in order to allow different possibilities for resonation. Although the teeth, the alveolar ridge just behind them and the hard palate (the roof of the mouth) are fixed, the soft palate and the uvula at its extremity can move, as we have just seen. The *tongue* is the most flexible of the speech organs and can considerably modify the shape of the oral resonating chamber. Just as we divide the palate into sections for convenience of reference, so we recognise the tip, the blade, the front, the back and the root of the tongue. By raising, lowering, advancing or retracting parts of the tongue a wide range of sound qualities can be produced. Finally, the *lips* can adopt several different positions: they may be shut tightly so that the airstream is pent up behind them; they may be held just slightly open so that friction occurs as the air is released; they may be held far enough apart that there is no friction and then either rounded, spread or relaxed. The rounding and spreading may be more or less vigorous.

8.1.1 Consonant and vowel

Before proceeding to the detailed description of speech sounds we must distinguish two broad categories of sounds: those whose articulation involves some easily felt obstruction of the airstream by the movable speech organs, and those whose production depends not on any contact of speech organs but on slight variations in the position of the tongue and lips. The former category we call *consonants*, the latter *vowels*. In addition to this classification on phonetic grounds, we can note that from a functional point of view vowels occupy a central position in the syllable while consonants typically occupy a marginal position.

8.1.2 Phonetic symbols

No language has a one-to-one correspondence between the letters of the alphabet and its speech sounds. Two different combinations of letters may be pronounced in the same way (th*eir*, th*ere*), the same letter may have several pronunciations (*g*ara*g*e, *s*ea*s*) and some letters are not pronounced at all (han*d*kerchief; French ba*s*). Therefore, it is necessary to adopt symbols to note both consonantal and vowel sounds. There is an agreed set of symbols which constitute the *international phonetic alphabet*. This alphabet has the advantage of being independent of any one language and it can be used equally well to describe the sounds of English, Russian, Arabic and Punjabi (all of which have different scripts), or of a language which has no written form. Many of the symbols coincide in shape with the letters of the Roman alphabet, as this is convenient for typographical purposes. In order to distinguish phonetic symbols from alphabetical letters we enclose the former in square brackets, thus [ʃip] *sheep.*

8.2 The description of consonants

To provide an adequate description of a consonantal sound, and assuming an egressive, pulmonic airstream, we need to specify four items of information:

(a) whether it is voiced or unvoiced;
(b) whether it is oral, nasal or nasalised;
(c) the point of obstruction and the organs involved – the *place* of articulation; and
(d) the type of obstruction – the *manner* of articulation.

We have already dealt with (a) and (b), and we now turn to the other two variables.

Figure 8.1 illustrates nine places of articulation, showing which movable articulator enters into contact with which fixed articulator:

1 *bilabial* – lower and upper lips (*b*at)
2 *labio-dental* – lower lip and upper teeth (*f*it)
3 *dental* – tongue tip and upper teeth (French *t*on)
4 *alveolar* – blade, or tip and blade, and teeth ridge (*t*op)
5 *palato-alveolar* – blade, or tip and blade, and teeth ridge, with raising of front of tongue (*g*in)
6 *palatal* – front of the tongue and hard palate (*y*ou)
7 *velar* – back of the tongue and soft palate (*k*in)
8 *uvular* – back of the tongue and uvula (French *r*ouge)
9 *glottal* – vocal cords (Cockney fee*t*)

In addition, we distinguish eight manners of articulation:

1 *plosive* – a complete closure is made at some place of articulation and there is a sudden, explosive release of the air pressure which has built up (*p*it).
2 *affricate* – a complete closure is made at some place of articulation and there is a less sudden release of the air pressure with friction (*ch*ip).
3 *nasal* – a complete closure is made at some place of articulation but the soft palate is lowered and the air escapes through the nose (*m*a*n*).
4 *roll* – there is a series of intermittent taps by the tip of the tongue

against the teeth ridge or by the uvula against the back of the tongue (Scottish *r*un).

5 *flap* – there is a single tap (Spanish pe*r*o).

6 *lateral* – a partial closure is made and the airstream escapes around the obstruction (*l*u*ll*).

7 *fricative* – two articulators are brought close together so that there is friction as the airstream escapes (*sh*in).

8 *frictionless continuant* – phonetically speaking these sounds should be included among the vowel sounds as no closure is involved in their articulation, but functionally they are consonantal, appearing at syllable margins (*w*ill, *y*ellow).

These two series of distinctions of place and manner of articulation constitute the parameters of Figure 8.2. Thus all symbols in the same row represent sounds having the same place of articulation, and all symbols in the same column represent sounds having the same manner of articulation. Furthermore, wherever there is a pair of symbols at an intersection, the one on the left represents an unvoiced sound and the one on the right represents the corresponding voiced sound. To take some examples, the symbol [ŋ] represents a *voiced velar nasal*, [t] represents an *unvoiced alveolar plosive,* [w] represents a *voiced bilabial frictionless continuant,* and so on. To expand even further, we can say that in the articulation of the *voiced bilabial plosive* [b] the vocal cords are vibrating, the uvula is raised, and the airstream, having been held back behind a complete closure formed by the lips, is suddenly released. The symbols are no more than a conventional shorthand notation.

The chart displaying the consonant symbols (Figure 8.2) has been simplified by the omission of symbols representing sounds not found in the five languages we are considering. Some symbols – [p, b, t, d, k, m, n, l, f] – do not require illustration since they correspond in value to the letters of the alphabet of the same shape, but it will be helpful to provide examples for the remainder:

[t̪]	Fr Sp *t*, Ru *т*	[d̪]	Fr Sp *d*, Ru *д*
[g]	Eng *g*et	[ʔ]	Gn Ver'ein
[tʃ]	Eng *ch*ur*ch*	[dʒ]	Eng *j*u*dg*e
[ɱ]	Sp a*n*fora	[n̪]	Fr Sp *n*, Ru *н*
[ɲ]	Fr ba*gn*e, Sp a*ñ*o	[ŋ]	Eng Gn *ng*, Sp ci*n*co
[r]	Fr *r*ouge, Sp pe*rr*o	[ʀ]	Fr *r*ouge
[ɾ]	Sp pe*r*o	[ɫ]	Eng ba*ll*, Ru *л*
[ʎ]	Sp ca*ll*e	[ɸ]	Gn Sch*w*ester
[β]	Sp sa*b*er	[v]	Eng *v*ery
[θ]	Eng *th*in, Sp pla*z*a	[ð]	Eng *th*is, Sp na*d*a

Figure 8.2
Consonant symbols

		MANNER							
		Complete closure			**Intermittent**		**Partial**	**Narrowing**	**No closure**
	PLACE	*Plosive*	*Affricate*	*Nasal*	*Roll*	*Flap*	*Lateral*	*Fricative*	*Frictionless Continuant*
1	bilabial	p b		ɱ				ɸ β	/wɥ
2	labio-dental							f v	
3	dental	t̪ d̪		n̪				θ ð	
4	alveolar	t d		n	r	ɾ	l̥ / lɬ	s z	ɹ
5	palato-alveolar		tʃ dʒ					ʃ ʒ	
6	palatal			ɲ			ʎ	ç	j
7	velar	k g		ŋ				x ɤ	
8	uvular				ʀ			ʁ	
9	glottal	ʔ						h ɦ	

[s]	Eng *s*in, Ru *c*	[z]	Eng *z*one, Ru *з*
[ʃ]	Eng *sh*ip, Gn *sch*, Ru *ш*	[ʒ]	Eng lei*s*ure, Fr *g*ens, Ru *ж*
[ç]	Gn i*ch*	[x]	Gn a*ch*, Sp *g*ente, Ru *x*
[ɣ]	Gn Wa*g*en, Sp lue*g*o	[ʁ]	Fr *r*ouge
[h]	Eng *h*ave, Gn *h*aben	[ɦ]	Eng be*h*ave
[w]	Eng *w*in, Fr *ou*est, Sp *hu*elo	[ɥ]	Fr l*ui*
[ɹ]	Eng *r*ut	[j]	Eng *y*es, Gn *J*ahr, Sp *h*ielo

8.2.1 Lip-rounding and palatalisation

In some instances a secondary distinction is required in addition to the prime axes of voice, place and manner. For example, in the articulation of [b] in French *beau* there is considerable *lip-rounding* in anticipation of the vowel sound where lip-rounding is also a prominent feature. In Russian the articulation of some sounds like [p, b, m, f, v] may be accompanied by the raising of the front of the tongue close to the hard palate, an effect known as *palatalisation*. Palatalisation is also a feature of [ʃ, ʒ, j] in the English words *she, measure* and *yet.*

8.3 The description of vowels

Given the absence of any closure or contact in the production of vowel sounds, a separate descriptive framework is required. The speech organ primarily responsible for the changes in quality of vowel sounds is the tongue, but the position of the lips is also an influential factor. For an adequate description of a vowel, we need to specify, therefore, four items of information:

(a) whether it is voiced or unvoiced;
(b) whether it is oral or nasalised;
(c) the position of the tongue; and
(d) the position of the lips.

We can assume that all vowels are voiced. Since nasalised vowels are important (among our five languages) only in French (see 8.5.1), we will concentrate for the time being on oral vowels.

For (c) we adopt the procedure of noting the highest raised point of the tongue. This point may be towards the tip or towards the back of the tongue, and so we have two relevant axes, high–low and front–back. If the front of the tongue is raised too far or the back of the tongue lowered too far, friction will result and the vowel-like quality of the sound will be lost. The limits of the tongue's possible movement for articulating vowel sounds is shown by the dashed line in Figure 8.1 which marks the *vowel area*.

8.3.1 The cardinal vowels

For convenience the oval shape of the vowel area is stylised in the form of the vowel diagram of Figure 8.3. For ease of reference it is divided into areas in much the same way as a grid divides a map. A vowel produced with the tongue raised to the upper limit of the vowel area is said to be *close*; where the tongue is lowered to the limit the vowel is *open*. Intermediate levels are also marked. Similarly, we distinguish between *front* vowels where the tongue is *advanced* and *back* vowels where the tongue is *retracted*, with an intermediate *central* area.

A set of vowels, known as the *cardinal vowels*, has been established to serve as standard points of reference. These mark positions around the periphery of the vowel area. It is very difficult to feel the position of the tongue within the mouth, and so the classification is based more on auditory impression than on articulatory sensation. Position 1/I (Figure 8.3) marks the front–close limit, position 5/V marks the back–open limit, and position 8/VIII marks the back–close limit. Between 1/I and 5/V we distinguish three positions which correspond to vowels which *sound equally different* from those on either side. The 'sound gaps' between 5/V and 8/VIII and between 8/VIII and 1/I are divided into three and two equal distances respectively.

We distinguish two series of cardinal vowels. In the primary series vowels 1–5 are produced with spread or neutrally relaxed lips and vowels 6–8 are produced with increasing degrees of lip-rounding; in the secondary series I–VIII the lip positions are simply reversed. In addition we include a pair of central–close vowels 9 (unrounded) and IX (rounded). The symbols assigned to these vowel values are given in Figure 8.3.

The cardinal vowel system stands independent of any one language, and we can describe the vowels of a particular language relative to the cardinals. Thus, the RP English vowel (iii) – g*e*t – is describable as a spread, front vowel somewhat more close than cardinal [ɛ] (for an explanation of RP, see 5.3). The English RP vowel (ix) is rounded and slightly more advanced and open than cardinal [u].

French, German, Spanish and Russian have a number of sounds which either coincide with or approximate closely to cardinal values. We illustrate here some of those sounds which differ considerably from the sounds of English:

[i]	Fr s*i*, Gn w*ie*, Ru т*и*п	[u]	Fr t*ou*t, Gn g*u*t, Ru т*у*т
[e]	Fr th*é*, Gn m*e*hr	[y]	Fr l*u*ne, Gn B*ü*hne
[ɛ]	Fr m*è*re, Gn B*e*tt, Ru *э*то	[ø]	Fr c*eu*x, Gn M*ö*hre
[a]	Fr p*a*tte	[œ]	Fr s*eu*l, Gn H*ö*lle
[ɑ]	Fr p*â*te, Sp *a*rm*a*, Gn St*aa*t (advanced)	[ɨ]	Ru с*ы*н

Figure 8.3
Cardinal vowels, with English vowel comparison

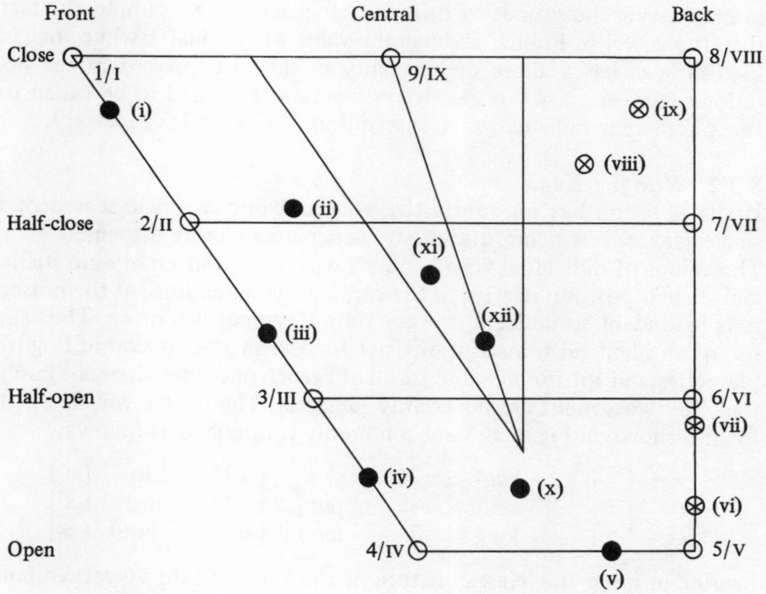

	Cardinal vowels				English vowels	
		○ Primary		○ Secondary	● Spread/open	⊕ Rounded
Spread/open	1	i	I	y	(i)	b*ea*t
	2	e	II	ø	(ii)	s*i*t
	3	ɛ	III	œ	(iii)	s*e*t
	4	a	IV	ɶ	(iv)	b*a*g
	5	ɑ	V	ɒ	(v)	c*a*lm
Rounded	6	ɔ	VI	ʌ	(vi)	l*o*ng
	7	o	VII	ɤ	(vii)	s*aw*
	8	u	VIII	ɯ	(viii)	p*u*t
Open	9	ɨ	IX	ʉ	(ix)	m*oo*n
					(x)	c*u*p
					(xi)	b*ir*d
					(xii)	*a*bout

[ɔ]	Fr h*o*mme, Gn S*o*nne	[Y]	Gn f*ü*nf – rounded version of English (ii)
[o]	Fr t*ô*t, Gn w*o*hl		

Rather than spelling out lengthy verbal explanations it is possible to qualify the basic cardinal vowel symbols using a set of marks standing for 'advanced', 'retracted', 'close', 'open', and so on. This is of interest in contrasting the sounds of different languages. For example, the fact that the vowel in French *site* has the value of cardinal 1 while that in English *seat* has a more open quality could be expressed in the notations [sit] and [si̞t] respectively. Where attention is to be called to fine phonetic detail a *narrow* transcription of this kind is necessary.

8.3.2 Vowel systems

If the notation has no contrastive goal and only a single accent of a single language is being discussed, such marks can be dispensed with. The values of individual vowel sounds within a given variety are stable, and if their position relative to the cardinals is stated once at the outset, it is redundant to indicate it every time a symbol is written. Thus the use of an identical transcription [sit] for *seat* in a discussion of English phonetics and for *site* in a discussion of French phonetics does not imply that the two sounds are necessarily identical. The twelve vowels of RP English shown in Figure 8.3 are commonly transcribed as follows:

b*ea*t	[i]	b*a*g	[a]	s*aw*	[ɔ]	c*u*p	[ʌ]
s*i*t	[ɪ]	c*a*lm	[ɑ]	p*u*t	[ʊ]	b*i*rd	[ɜ]
s*e*t	[e]	l*o*ng	[ɒ]	m*oo*n	[u]	*a*bout	[ə]

Bearing in mind the 'elastic' nature of the values of the vowel symbols we can schematise the vowel systems of the five languages. They are contrasted in Figure 8.4. The values of the symbols are not the absolute values of the cardinal vowels, but simply an indication of relative difference.

8.3.3 Dipthongs and nasalised vowels

So far we have considered only vowels whose quality remains constant throughout their articulation, i.e. *monopthongs*. When there is an audible change of vowel quality within the syllable we talk of a *dipthong*. There are eight dipthongs in RP English:

[bei]	*bay*	[ləʊ]	*low*	[pɪə]	*peer*
[bai]	*buy*	[kɑʊ]	*cow*	[pɛə]	*pair*
[bɔi]	*boy*			[pʊə]	*poor*

In each case the highest raised point of the tongue moves from approximately the position indicated by the first part of the diphthong symbol

Figure 8.4
Basic vowel systems

English

i		u
ɪ	ɜ	ʊ
e	ə	ɔ
a	ʌ	ɒ
	ɑ	

German

i	y		u
ɪ	Y		ʊ
e	ϕ	ə	o
ɛ	œ		ɔ
		a	
		ɑ	

Russian

i	ɨ	u
e		
ɛ	ə	o
a	ɑ	

French

i	y	u
e	ϕ	o
ɛ	œ	ɔ
a		ɑ

Spanish

i		u
e		o
	a	

towards the position indicated by the second part of the symbol, that is, from [e] towards [i], and so on. German has three diphthongs, [ai, ɔi, ɑʊ] – *bei, Heu, Bau.* Every Russian vowel other than [ɛ] forms a diphthong rising towards [i].

French is the only one of the languages under consideration to have nasalised vowels. The tongue positions are approximately the same as for the equivalent oral vowels, but the simultaneous release of air through the nose gives them a distinctive quality. They are [ɛ̃, ɑ̃, ɔ̃, œ̃] – *vin, banc, bon, brun.* Some French speakers do not pronounce [œ̃] but use instead a sound much closer to [ɛ̃].

8.4 Phonemes

Our attention has been focused until now on questions of phonetics, the description of the substance of speech sounds. Obviously, it is very important for the learner to be able to produce the correct absolute values of the sounds of the foreign language. But it is equally important to know the values of the sounds *relative* to each other as members of a *system*. We intuitively recognise that some of the differences in the sounds of our L1 are not significant, in so far as they do not distinguish one word of the language from another. That is, they are not *distinctive*. A certain latitude can be tolerated in the pronunciation of a sound provided it never overlaps with another sound in the same system. Thus we could pronounce the first sound in *run* with any one of the values [r, ɹ, ɾ, ʀ , ʁ] without fear of being misunderstood. On the other hand, if we were to pronounce the initial sound of *coat* with a voiced rather than an unvoiced velar plosive, we would in fact utter *goat*. Those units of sound which serve to distinguish between meanings are called *phonemes*, and their definition is part of phonology (7.1).

Let us take two examples to illustrate the point. A phonetic transcription of the words *play, peel* and *leap* reveals a marked difference in the quality of the consonantal sounds [pʰl̥ei, pʰiɫ, lip]. We see that in the initial position [p] is strongly aspirated, and that [l] has a 'dark' quality in final position in contrast to its 'clear' realisation at the beginning of a word. After [pʰ] it is unvoiced. If we multiplied the examples, we would find that this pattern is a perfectly regular one. The exact quality of sounds is determined by their context; [pʰ] never occurs at the same point in a string of sounds as [p], and similarly [l], [ɫ] and [l̥] occur always in distinct environments. We say that these sounds are in *complementary distribution*. Since aspiration and 'darkness' are merely contextually conditioned and not distinctive features, we can choose to disregard them and assign [p] and [pʰ] to a single phoneme, and [l], [ɫ] and [l̥] to another single phoneme. Phonemes are therefore largely abstract units, and to distinguish phonemic from phonetic transcriptions we enclose the former in angle brackets. We say that [pʰ] and [p] are *allophones* of /p/; likewise, [l]. [l̥] and [ɫ] are allophones of /l/. It is important to remember that to establish phonemes is to make statements about the sound system of *one particular language*.

8.5 Systems compared

Any difference between the phonemic systems of the learner's L1 and L2 is a potential source of error. The first task is to discover which features are distinctive within the L2 system. A failure to realise these distinctive features in speech will result in confusions of meanings. The second task is to know the allophones of each phoneme and the contexts in which they occur. Failure to do this will result in the perception of 'a foreign accent' on the part of L2 native speakers. These two tasks will involve the learner in adding new sounds to his repertoire rather than simply reorganising the stock of sounds he uses in L1 speech. In the next sections we will look at some of the problems facing the English-speaking learner of French, Spanish, German and Russian.

8.5.1 Vowels

The first general difficulty experienced is that of *lip-rounding* (see 8.2.1). The three English back rounded vowels (see Figure 8.4) are only weakly rounded, whereas their counterparts in the other four languages are produced with much stronger rounding of the lips, requiring far greater facial movement in general. This characteristic is most pronounced in French, where it is necessary to 'pout' in order to obtain the correct vowel quality. A failure to round the lips sufficiently can lead to phonemic confusion in French and German. Both of these languages have two series of front vowels, one unrounded, the other rounded. Rounding is therefore the only feature to distinguish pairs of words such as *pure* : *pire* / pyr : pir/. In this case misunderstanding could have unfortunate consequences. The situation in German in the close (high) region of the vowel area is complicated by the presence of yet another dimension of distinctiveness, that of long–short. Thus we have three sets of contrasts: long /i, y, u/–short /ɪ, ʏ, ʊ /; from /i, ɪ, y, ʏ /–back /u, ʊ/; unrounded /i, ɪ/– rounded /y, ʏ, u, ʊ/. It is within this last series that the English speaker finds the distinctions hardest to make: *fühle* /y/, *fülle* /ʏ/, *Buhle* /u/, *Bulle* /ʊ/.

It is most important that lip-rounding should commence *during* the articulation of the preceding consonant, otherwise the pronunciation of French *pu*, for example, is likely to resemble that of English *pew*. This point can be usefully underlined by reference to an experiment (reported in the *Guardian*) in which informants were shown a film of a person pronouncing *ga-ga*, but on the sound track was recorded *ba-ba*. Only 2 per cent of informants reported hearing *ba-ba*, presumably because the consonant is bilabial but no lip contact was apparent on the screen. The remaining 98 per cent reported hearing not *ga-ga*, but *da-da*, an alveolar sound midway between velar [g] which they saw and bilabial [b] which they heard. Visual information affects aural perception to a surprising degree, and so the English learner who neglects to 'pull faces' while speaking does so at the risk of being misunderstood.

A further problem is that of the *tenseness* of vowel articulations in French, Spanish, German and Russian. The vigorous lip-spreading of [e, ɛ] and rounding of [o] is not made; consequently, what should be a monopthong is often realised as a diphthong [ei] or [əʊ] and French *né, naît* and *beau* sound like *nay* and *bow*. The final vowel in the English borrowing *fiancé* is usually diphthongised, while in its French pronunciation the vowel quality remains constant.

A third difficulty stems from the absence from French and Spanish of strongly marked word stress. Words like *suppórter, Interzônenhandel* and *соуча́ствовал* ('participated') have one prominently stressed syllable. The vowels in the unstressed syllables tend to be *centralised* and assume the value of [ə] (see vowel position (xii) on Figure 8.3). Thus we have [sə'pɔtə, ɪntər'tsonənhandəl, sau'tʃastvəvəl]. In contrast, French and Spanish maintain the full value of every vowel (use of [ə] in French is restricted to final *mute e* and the article *le*). The English speaker must here resist the temptation – especially strong with cognates of words like *interesting* and *supposition,* which are very close to their French and Spanish equivalents – to make one syllable prominent and centralise the other vowels.

The final question to be examined under this heading is that of the French *nasalised vowels* / ɛ̃, ɑ̃, ɔ̃ /. These contrast with the corresponding oral vowels in words like *fait:fin* / fɛ:fɛ̃/, *gras:grand* /grɑ:grɑ̃/ and *dos:don*/do:dɔ̃/. Since these do not exist in English, the natural tendency is to produce an oral vowel followed by a nasal consonant. However in so doing the learner will obliterate the phonemic contrast which should exist between such pairs as *vient:viennent* /vjɛ̃:vjɛn/, *paysan:paysanne*/peizɑ̃:peizɑn/ and *bon:bonne*/bɔ̃:bɔn/. If the task of producing a nasalised vowel is in itself not easy, that of keeping the three vowels apart is all the more difficult. But many distinctions between very common words rest on these contrasts, for example *sein:son:sang* /sɛ̃:sɔ̃:sɑ̃/.

8.5.2 Consonants

Figure 8.5 displays the consonantal phonemes of the five languages. The asterisks immediately highlight points of contrast between the phonemic system of English and those of the other four languages. We will look at just eight areas of common difficulty:

(1) The English unvoiced plosive phonemes /p, t, k/ are strongly aspirated in initial position in a stressed syllable, as in the word *king*. Aspiration also occurs in the same context in north Germany presenting no difficulty to the learner. However, this feature is not present in the other three languages. Therefore, to aspirate a French, Spanish or Russian plosive will lead to the perception of a marked foreign accent, but without causing any confusion of phonemes.

(2) The same is true of the alveolar plosives and nasals in French, Spanish and Russian which are *dental* rather than alveolar, and often mispronounced by English learners.

(3) The *'r' phoneme* is subject in a great many languages to considerable variation in its phonetic realisation. English, German, French and Russian have each only one 'r' phoneme. The notation /r/ could have been used in all four cases, but phonetic symbols have been retained in Figure 8.5 to show that the most common realisation of the English phoneme is a voiced alveolar frictionless continuant, while in French generally it is a voiced uvular roll, in Russian it is an alveolar roll, and in German a uvular fricative. The consequence of producing the normal English sound will be the same as in the cases of aspiration and dentality; it will be perceived as an unusual allophone of the foreign phoneme. The situation in Spanish is more complex in that the learner

Figure 8.5

Basic consonant systems

		plos	*affr*	*nas*	*roll*	*flap*	*lat*	*fric*	*cont*
English	*bil*	p b		m					w
	la-d							f v	
	dent							θ ð	
	alv	t d		n			l	s z	ɹ
	pa-a		tʃ dʒ					ʃ ʒ	
	pal								j
	vel	k g		ŋ					
	uvul								
	glot							h	
German	*bil*	p b		m					*
	la-d							f v	
	dent							* *	
	alv	t d		n			l	s z	*
	pa-a		* *					ʃ ʒ	
	pal							*ç	j
	vel	k g		ŋ				x	
	uvul							*ʁ	
	glot							h	
French	*bil*	p b		m					*ɥw
	la-d							f v	
	dent	*t*d		*n				* *	
	alv	* *		*			l	s z	*
	pa-a		* *					ʃ ʒ	
	pal			*ɲ					j
	vel	k g		*					
	uvul				*ʀ				
	glot							*	

		plos	*affr*	*nas*	*roll*	*flap*	*lat*	*fric*	*cont*
Spanish	*bil*	p b		m					*
	la-d							f *	
	dent	*t*d		*n				θ *	
	alv	* *		*	*r	*ɾ	l	s *	*
	pa-a		tʃ *					* *	
	pal			ɲ			*ʎ		*
	vel	k g		*				*x	
	uvul								
	glot							*	
Russian	*bil*	p b		m					*
	la-d							f v	
	dent	*t*d		*n				* *	
	alv	* *	*ts	*	*r		l	s z	*
	pa-a		* *					ʃ ʒ	
	pal							*	j
	vel	k g		*				*x	
	uvul								
	glot							*	

must not blur the contrast between the tap and trill phonemes which distinguish such words as *caro*:*carro* /kaɾo:karo/. The indiscriminate use of [ɹ] will result in the disappearance of phonemic contrasts. Moreover, the fact that this phoneme does not occur in word-final position in RP English (in American English it does) may cause the learner to neglect such distinctions as French *cas*:*car*/kɑ:kar/.

(4) The English phonemes /b, d, g, v, z, ʒ / tend to be *unvoiced* at the end of a word when the word itself comes before a pause. Thus, in *Wave your hand* the pronunciation [hant] is usual, whereas *Hand it to me* is pronounced [hand]. In French and Spanish these phonemes are always fully voiced whatever their position in the word and in the sentence, and the English learner must beware of transferring his L1 articulatory habits. This devoicing of word-final plosives and fricatives is found in German and Russian; in contrast to English these phonemes are *never* voiced at the end of a word, wherever the word may be situated in the sentence. We may say that the opposition between the features *voiced* and *unvoiced*, although distinctive at other positions within the word, is at this point *neutralised*. An English speaker will be prone to say [band] rather than [bant] in the sentence *Der Band ist gross*. This means, of course, that the words *Bund* and *bunt,* which are phonetically identical in native German speech, may be mistakenly distinguished. This error does not confuse meanings but is typical of a strong foreign accent in German and Russian.

(5) A major source of difficulty is the *'l' phoneme*. In English it has three allophones: a clear allophone [l] at the beginning and in the middle of the words – *look, glad, pillow;* a dark allophone [ɫ] after a vowel or when it constitutes a separate syllable – *feel, cold, camel*; and a voiceless allophone [l̥] after /p/ and /k/ – *play, clean*. French and German native speakers use only the clear sound, while Russians use only the dark sound. The English speaker must therefore guard against using [ɫ] at the end of *salle* or *Gabel,* and against using [l] in *ладно*. Spanish once again presents the risk of conveying wrong meanings rather than simply 'foreignness'. It has two lateral phonemes /l/ and /ʎ/ which serve to distinguish such words as *loro*:*lloro* and *calar*:*callar.* The same remarks apply here as with the case of /r/ and /ɾ/ above.

(6) *Palatalisation* (see 8.2.1), an incidental feature in English, can be phonemic in Russian. It is one basis, with word stress, of the distinction between *угол* ('corner') and *уголь* ('coal').

(7) A further problem concerns the correct distribution of the allophones of L2 phonemes in the appropriate contexts. In some cases this involves sounds not used in English, as the following examples from Spanish will illustrate. When the phonemes /b, d, g/ occur between vowels they are realised as fricatives rather than plosives. Thus *nada* is

pronounced [naða] in contrast to *dar* [daɾ]. The articulation of [ð] poses no problems to English speakers, for whom it corresponds to the initial sound in *thin*. But the pronunciation of *la gata, lago* [la ɣata, laɣo, *para vender* and *ave* [paɾa βendeɾ, aβe] necessitates the mastery of new articulatory habits.

(8) Finally, we consider the voiced velar fricative phoneme /x/ of Russian, Spanish and German. It is distinctive in such pairs as *ход* ('passage'):*год* ('year')/xod:god/, *lejos*:*legos* /lexos:legos/and *Sache*: *sacke*/zaxə:zakə/, and so must be kept apart from the velar phonemes /k/ and /g/ in those languages. In German /x/ is also distinguished from the voiced palatal fricative /ç/ – *Kuchen:Kuhchen*/kuxxn:kuxxn/ – a difficult task for the learner in an area where there is no phonetically similar phoneme or allophone of English. The /x/:/ç/ contrast is not widespread, so the practical consequences will be the projection of a poor accent rather than any confusion of meaning.

8.6 Intonation

The previous sections in this chapter have dealt with the description of speech sounds in isolation, their variation according to context, and their organisation into systems within particular languages. The largest unit considered has been the word. We now turn to the question of the *rhythm* of sequences of words in connected speech.

In 8.5.1 we noted that in English, German and Russian all words of more than one syllable have one most prominent, or *stressed*, syllable, the others being stressed weakly or not at all. In French and Spanish this prominence is not nearly so marked. This contrast in respect of stress provides the basis for classifying a language as *stress-timed* or *syllable-timed*. In stress-timed languages (among them English, German and Russian) the strongly stressed syllables of an utterance are spaced at regular intervals of time. This creates the impression of a rhythmic beat. The number of unstressed syllables intervening between beats may vary. In *Peter and | Paul | playfully | provided | the peeled | potatoes |* we have six stress groups of one to three syllables each. The fact that the three syllables of *playfully*, for example, have to be 'squeezed into' the same period of time as the single syllable of *Paul* accounts for the centralisation and devaluation of the unstressed vowels discussed earlier. In contrast, syllable-timed languages (including French and Spanish) give approximately equal time to each syllable in an utterance, irrespective of its prominence. The impression is that of an unbroken stream of sounds. To use stress-timing when speaking a syllable-timed language, and vice versa, creates a most unnatural effect which, although not seriously inpairing comprehension, detracts greatly from the authenticity of the learner's accent.

Superimposed on the sounds themselves and the basic rhythm of the utterance there are variations in pitch, known an *intonation*. We feel intuitively that intonation in our L1 follows patterns which are a rich source of information. There are two major intonation patterns, or *tunes*. The first signals that an utterance and, possibly, the speaker's turn in the conversation are complete; the discussion can take a new course. The second leaves an impression of incompleteness, indicating either that the speaker has not finished or that the addressee must immediately pick up the thread of the conversation. We call these tunes *conclusive* and *suspensive* respectively (MacCarthy, 1975, p. 29).

These tunes fulfil a number of functions, which we can categorise as either grammatical or attitudinal. The (rising) suspensive tune typifies questions which require a yes/no answer, including where the grammatical form of the utterance is that of a statement. It is also used in subordinate clauses prior to the main clause. The (falling) conclusive tune characterises straightforward statements of fact, perfunctory commands and WH-questions (How? What? Who? When?) which demand information from the addressee. Thus intonation can indicate the sentence type.

Another important grammatical function of intonation is to 'punctuate' the utterance, as we can illustrate with two examples. *The man who swore was angry* and *The man, who swore, was angry* are distinguished intonationally. A single conclusive tune spans the whole of the first utterance, but in the second utterance it is suspended by the insertion of another tune. Similarly, the intonation *Give me fresh eggs and milk* will consist of one or two tunes depending whether *fresh* is intended to qualify *eggs and milk* or only *eggs*.

The tunes may be modified by the speakers for emphatic or contrastive reasons. In *Fred fed the rabbit* any one of the words other than the article can be emphasised. If the tune is basically conclusive, this implies that the speaker is answering or contradicting the addressee as to *who* fed the rabbit, or what Fred *did* to the rabbit, or again *what* Fred fed. With a basically suspensive tune the implication is that the speaker is seeking confirmation of the 'who', the 'what' or the 'to whom'. Thus intonation is very important in signalling relations *between* utterances as well as within them (see 10.3).

The range of attitudinal information conveyed by different variations on the two basic tunes is vast and the task of linking each effect to a particular intonation pattern is a seemingly impossible one. From the speaker's intonation we sense interest or boredom, sarcasm or humour, warmth or suspicion, disbelief or condescension, and many other attitudes, perhaps more than one at the same time. In interpreting the speaker's real intention we draw on not only intonation but also the role relationship of the two parties (4.3), knowledge of the speaker's identity and personality (5.2), the form of the utterance, the vocabulary, any gestures (5.1) and any other situational features which we feel to be relevant.

Further reading

Introductions to phonetics are to be found in O'Connor (1973), which also covers acoustic and auditory phonetics, and Gimson (1962), which is an exhaustive description of English pronunciation. Both contain sections on intonation, but for fuller accounts see O'Connor and Arnold (1961), a practical introduction with exercises, or Crystal (1969), which is a comprehensive theoretical treatment of intonation and associated features in English. MacCarthy (1978) is designed for teachers, but the sections on foreign-language learning are of interest to students also. To correct the simplified accounts of French, Spanish, German and Russian presented here the reader should consult MacCarthy (1975), Macpherson (1975), Moulton (1962) and Ward (1958).

Suggestions for inquiry

1 Find out if the consonantal phonemes of English and of one of the foreign languages (Figure 8.5) can all occur: (a) at the beginning of a word, (b) in the middle of a word between vowels (c) at the end of a word.
2 Devise series of words analogous to *ten*:*den*, *eaten*:*Eden*, *hat*:*had* in order to contrast the phonemes of your foreign languages.
3 What combinations of consonantal phonemes can occur at the beginning of a word before the first vowel: (a) in English, (b) in your foreign languages?
4 Transcribe in phonemic notation a brief passage from an English or foreign written source.
5 Transcribe in phonetic notation the same passage recorded on tape.
6 Indicate with upward- and downward-sloping lines above the transcription the rises and falls in pitch.
7 Using the information given in Figure 8.5, predict the likely pronunciation errors of a foreigner learning English.

9

Words and Word Systems

When *I* use a word, Humpty Dumpty said, in rather a scornful tone, it means just what I choose it to mean – neither more nor less.

The question is, said Alice, whether you *can* make words mean so many different things.

The question is, said Humpty Dumpty, which is to be master – that's all.

Lewis Carroll (1872) *Through the Looking Glass*

When a tactical substitution is made during a football game, it is with the aim of changing the pattern of play by introducing a player with a role different from that of the man he replaces. As a result the distribution of roles throughout the team will change, just as it would if only ten men had to cover a space previously allocated to eleven. Similarly, we can consider that the words of a language form a structured system in which every word is linked, ultimately, to every other word and where the appearance or disappearance of a word causes restructuring rather than simple expansion or contraction. With such an image in mind it is possible to explore systematically the labyrinth of lexical relations in a foreign language in order to add to and refine one's 'word-power', and to pinpoint differences in lexical structure between L1 and L2.

9.1 Word types

If asked to count the number of different words on a page where both *buy* and *bought* occurred, should we consider them as two occurrences of the same word or as single occurrences of two different words? The same problem arises in other languages in cases like *Zahn:Zähne, viene: vino, beaux:belle*, *столу:столом*. It is helpful, therefore, to clarify what we understand by *word* by introducing a distinction between the *phonological word*, which is a 'shape' given a primary expression in sound or a secondary expression in writing, morse code, etc., and the *lexical word*, which is a vocabulary item with a specific meaning. Dictionary headwords are usually lexical words. The answer to our initial question, then, is that in each case we have two phonological words but only one lexical word. It would be a mistake, of course, automatically to consider *the runs* as simply the plural of *the run*. Lastly, we need to recognise the *grammatical word*, which is defined in terms of its functional role in an utterance, as a *noun, verb*, etc.

Obviously, the potential combinations of a word viewed as a syntactic item and its potential cominations as a lexical item are not independent. Sentences (1) and (2) are both grammatically acceptable and meaningful:

(1) He ate the butter
(2) He spread the butter

We can extend the pattern of *transitive verb plus object* to produce the acceptable sentence (3), whereas (4) is anomalous:

(3) He ate the meal
(4) *He spread the meal

Thus syntactic and lexical constraints operate together in determining the selection of a given word. A word's phonological properties are important for the poetic function of language (4.4.1).

For the rest of this chapter, by *word* we will mean *lexical word*, unless otherwise specified. A common definition of word is 'a group of characters occurring between two spaces'. Although this may be expedient for some counting processes, it overlooks the fact that there are groups of characters which include a space or hyphen yet which we intuitively class as a single unit – *lingua franca, running-board, flea-pit*. The French for *watershed* is *ligne de partage des eaux*. Five words or one? Less problematic are *va-et-vient* and *colin-maillard*. German offers *Zähl-apparat* but *Zählkarte*. If we compare some translation equivalents for *toothbrush* – or is it *tooth-brush?* – we find *зубная щётка, brosse à dents, Zahnbürste*. We can test the degree of internal cohesion of the component parts by attempting either to make substitutions for one part while retaining the others, or to insert an adjective. The unacceptability of **running wide board* points to *running-board* being a single lexical unit. Internal fusions of form attest to this semantic unity as we see in *fo'c'sle, bosun, vinaigre*. We must accept, therefore, that not all words will be simple units.

9.2 The nature of the word

Every word has two faces: a *content-plane*, which embraces its lexical and syntactic characteristics; and an *expression-plane*, which is that of its phonological realisation. The two are indissolubly linked, like the two sides of the same sheet of paper. We call the expression-face the *signifier* and the content-face the *signified*. A *stroop* is a potential English signifier but not a word since it lacks a signified. *Desk* is a word only by virtue of a social agreement on the association of this particular string of expression-elements with a particular set of content-elements when it is used in speech.

The expression-elements and the content-elements have both substance and form (see 1.3.2 for a discussion of substance and form). That the expression-substance, phonic or graphic, has form is evident in the inadmissibility of **pfum* in English – in German it would be allowable. The nature of the content-substance, which is composed of *semantic components*, and its form are the main topic of this chapter, and to which we will return shortly (9.4). Figure 9.1 sets out the relationships between the concepts discussed so far.

It is important not to confuse the word itself with the 'thing' it sometimes represents, and which we call the *referent*. The relationship between signified and referent is direct, but that between signifier and referent is indirect, or *arbitrary* (indicated by the broken line in Figure 9.2). If there were a necessary link between the concept 'table' and the form of its expression, then we would not have *table, Tisch, mesa* and *стол*. Even onomatopoeic words, whose expression we might expect to be directly motivated, vary from language to language. A Russian duck cries *кряк* (*kryak*), a French one *couac*. In England one awakens to *cock-a-doodle-doo*, in France to *cocorico*.

9.3 Meaning types

For a dictionary to say that *schwach* means *weak* may be of some limited practical help, but it does not get us very far. Moreover, it is misleading. The dictionary will provide its grammatical category *adjective*,

Figure 9.1
The word: content-plane and expression plane

CONTENT-PLANE			EXPRESSION-PLANE		
SIGNIFIED		+	SIGNIFIER		
Substance +	**Form**		**Substance**	+	**Form**
Semantic components	(Lexical and syntactic structures)		Phonic		(Phonology)
			Graphic		

Figure 9.2
Referent–signifier and referent–signified relationships

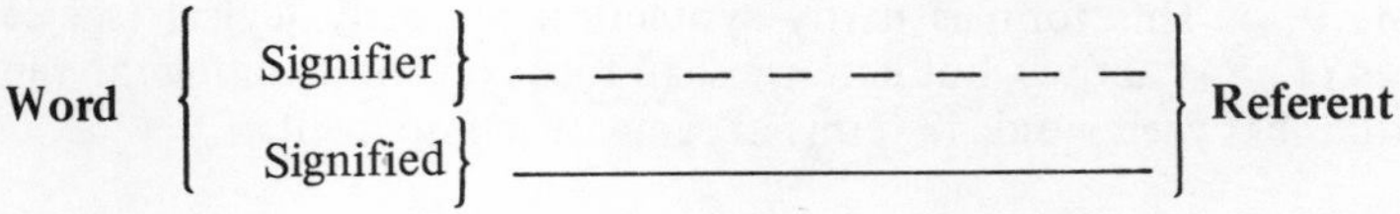

but this is only a gross indication of its potential use with other words, since we saw from sentence (4) above that grammatical categories need to be refined on semantic grounds. In this case we have *der starke: schwache Mann* but *der starke: dünne Kaffee*. And what does *bistro* or *bodega* mean – 'pub', 'cafe', 'bar'? It will be helpful to distinguish various types of meaning just as we recognised different types of word.

First, *syntactic meaning* is a product of the relationship between a word and its syntactic function in an utterance (see 1.3.1 and 9.1).

Second, *referential meaning* derives from the relationship between a word and its referent. This may, of course, be not an object like 'table' but an abstract concept like 'freedom', a mythical entity like 'hobbit' or a postulated phenomenon like 'black hole'. Even tables, found in all shapes, sizes and materials, have few absolute properties. Where is the dividing-line between *pond* and *lake, running* and *walking?* What is the referent of *long* or *low*?. A *white coffee* is not the same in colour as a *white shirt*, and *un steak bleu* should be anything but blue.

The third type of meaning, *sense*, compensates somewhat for the uncertainties above. It is a product of the relationships between words. Part of the meaning of *long* and *low* is their contrast with *short* and *high*. A coffee can be only *white* or *black*, perhaps *not too white* but never *grey*; shirts, however, come in all colours. Similarly, *terrier* is related to *dog, rise* to *fall, try* to *attempt* and *neigh* to *horse*. Reference and sense are part of the subject-matter of *semantics* (1.3.1).

Fourth is *situational meaning*, which arises from the relationship between a word and the situation in which it is uttered. A simple illustration is provided by *whatsit, Dings, Zeng, trasto* (physical objects), *chisme* (small things), *machin, bidule, truc, трюк, штука* and *штучка* which are understood only because speaker and listener share the information necessary to specify the referent. The role of situation in contributing to meaning and resolving ambiguity will be a recurrent theme (see 9.4 and 9.5), and is the concern of *pragmatics* (1.3.1).

Finally, words are related to the social and individual identities of their users and acquire a meaning of *social significance,* that is, they have an indexical (4.2) and thereby symbolic value (Chapter 5).

9.4 Lexical structure

Our task now is to give form to the elements of the content-plane (see Figure 9.1). This form is partly syntactic and partly lexical (see sentences (1)–(4) above), but here we shall focus on constructing the sense relations between words in terms of semantic components.

9.4.1 Lexis and vocabularies

If we were to be ambitious, we could try to relate to one another in an abstract system all the words of a given language at a given time, regardless of the situations in which they were or were not used. This we call the *lexis* of a language, and to create it we would be forced to make an arbitrary decision on when to accept no more words in our structuring since the stock of words is only theoretically finite (see 9.6). But we can further impose upon this situationally undifferentiated structure a 'grid' of social situations and establish lexical relationships *within varieties* (see 4.3.6). This is to create the *vocabularies* of a language. Not only are they more amenable to structuring, but they are of greater interest to the language learner since they directly reflect spheres of social activity.

Words that are part of one and the same variety, like *ami* and *camarade* of standard French, may be said to enter a relation of *opposition*, whereas the relation between words belonging to different varieties – *ami:pote* (colloquial), or *cigarillo* (standard):*cilindrín* (youth slang) – is one of *diversity*.

Some initial help in structuring the words of a language is to be found in the 'abbreviations' page of most dictionaries which presents the metalanguage used to categorise the entires.

Grammatical meaning is signalled by classifications into 'parts of speech', such as *adv., adj., n., f., pl.,* the lists being largely identical from one dictionary to the next. Few bilingual dictionaries seem to indicate explicitly sense relations like antonymy and synonymy. The words making up an entry for the target language are separated by commas or colons and it is up to the reader to decide what is the relationship between them. Is he to conclude from POMP, *s. pompe f, éclat m, splendeur f, appareil m, apparat m* that these five words have the same meaning? Dictionaries of synonyms and antonyms are, if anything, even less helpful. Ordinary dictionaries usually provide limited contexts to make clearer the use of a given word: POLISH [pɔliʃ] *v. tr.* I. *Polir* (*le bois, le fer*); *brunir* (*l'or, l'argent*); *cirer* (*des chaussures*). In dictionaries produced specifically for foreign learners these contexts can be quite extensive and oppositional relations figure more prominently.

Diversity is reflected in three main ways. First, we can distinguish indications of the speech-communities in which a word is used – *American, British, N. Italian, Spanish-American, Sicilian,* etc. Second, there is usually a very extensive list of spheres of activity – *aer., admin., agr., aviat., arch.*, etc. Third, there are indications of the 'level' of usage, again usually quite extensive – *colloq., pej., rhet., slang., vulg.*, etc.

This is not to say that the situational distribution of words will not change over time; of course it does. Science is an area where words are constantly being coined, and many enter general usage: *input* from computer science, as a synonym for 'contribution'; *ensemble* from mathematics; *орбит* (orbit), e.g. *на орбите пятилетки* from space research. What was initially a metaphorical, marked use is assimilated over time into general usage.

With the advent of computers and their wider accessibility to researchers, it has become possible to carry out what would otherwise have been impossibly time-consuming calculations of word frequencies in different writings. Some of the early motivation came from a desire to establish the contested authorship of literary works, by establishing patterns of distribution between parts of speech and lists of the most frequent words used by a given author, and seeing if these patterns were consistent throughout his works. To see what were de Gaulle's ten most frequent words in his broadcasts to the nation in the period 1958–65 is indicative of the man no less than of the times – *la France, le pays, la République, l'Etat, le monde, le peuple, la nation, le progrès, la paix, l'avenir.*

A small point must be made here. The computer analyses only in so far as it performs operations of addition and comparison on human instruction. It does not recognise idioms or distinguish homographs (*fit*: 'assemble', 'match' or 'healthy'?) unless it is told how. The need to formalise instructions to the computer in the form of programs has made a tremendous impact on progress in linguistics. None the less, the question must be asked whether it is merely signifiers which are being processed and not words. In the field of science and technology, where terminology (see 9.4.4) figures with high frequency, a claim to capture something of meaning and not just expression is more justified.

To take but a single example of application, many word counts have been produced from scientific and technical texts to provide teaching materials, and it has been found that the 1,000 most common words cover about 90 per cent of the text. A knowledge of these enables students to deduce not only the meaning of unknown words but also the grammar. By comparing frequencies established for specialised texts, and comparing them with word-counts produced from general texts, a picture emerges of those words characteristic of a particular variety, provided the situation has been adequately defined. The *potential* vocabulary remains beyond reach.

Relative frequency may also be a factor distinguishing between what otherwise appear to be complete synonyms. For example, in the texts of French governmental *arrêtès* in many of its occurrences *sur* is synonymous with *relatif à*. However, the latter is must more frequent, and thus is more characteristic of this particular text type. The greater frequency at a point in time of one of a pair of synonyms may indicate that the less frequent word is disappearing from use. Guilbert (1967) shows how over a period of three years *cosmonaute* overtook *astronaute* in frequency to a point where the latter had virtually disappeared from use.

9.4.2 Componential analysis

The assumption underlying this analytical method is that the content-plane of a word can be described as a bundle of *semantic components*, each component being a value of a universal semantic feature. The parallel with the phonetic components of phonological analysis is obvious (see 8.4), and componential analysis has the same universalist goals, that is, to establish a finite set of features, at some suitably abstract level, in terms of which all words of all natural languages can be specified, 'a universal inventory used in particular ways by individual languages' (Bierwisch, in Lyons, 1970, pp. 181–2). Further, this is a consequence of the hypothesis that 'all semantic structures might finally be reduced to components representing the basic dispositions of the cognitive and perceptual structure of the human organism' (ibid). Seen in this light componential analysis is striving towards the same goals as Chomsky and others in their inquiries (see 1.3.3). The number and status of the features postulated is of crucial theoretical importance.

Our aim is much more modest. There is no question of providing an encyclopedic definition for words under consideration. The sets of components can be devised on an *ad hoc* basis by the learner-analyst to cope with a specific group of words, and their adequacy is to be judged by the usefulness of the insights they may offer into the structure of L2.

The first step is to select a set of words which seem interrelated. We may call this a *conceptual field*. Comparing *gnome* with *set-square* will lead nowhere. Fields already investigated include colour, kinship, spatial, temporal and sound terms, verbs of motion, cooking and judgement. On a very practical level (when consulting a dictionary) one might be confronted with a set of words – for example, *pompe, éclat, splendeur* above. Assuming they are in the same field, the aim is to specify what space each occupies within the field and to what extent they overlap, if at all.

Next, it is necessary to form analogies among the words selected. Let us take as an example the words *man, woman, boy, girl*. The following analogies can be formed:

(5) Man:boy :: woman:girl
(6) Man:woman :: boy:girl

The common differentiating factor in (5) above is one of adultness, while in (6) it is one of sex. Establishing two features, ADULT and FEMALE, we can specify the words (Figure 9.3a). Each word has a different representation and is thus distinguished from the other three by the use of just two features. They all have a theoretical common or *generic* component + HUMAN, but it is unnecessary to introduce it, unless the pair *dog:puppy* are introduced, for example (Figure 9.3b). (The symbol ± indicates that a feature is indeterminate.) The generic component could now be, for example, +ANIMATE.

Pottier (1974) provides a sample illustration for French (Figure 9.4a). However, establishing contrastive components for foreign-language data is problematic, in that the learner usually lacks the native speaker's intuition born of long experience of the words in use. But this can be compensated by careful consultation of a comprehensive dictionary (and, ideally, corroboration from L2 native speakers). *Le Petit Robert* offers the following definitions:

Figure 9.3

Contrastive components (example 1)

(a)

	Female	**Adult**
Man	–	+
Woman	+	+
Boy	–	–
Girl	+	–

(b)

	Female	**Adult**	**Human**
Man	–	+	+
Woman	+	+	+
Boy	–	–	+
Girl	+	–	+
Dog	±	+	–
Puppy	±	–	–

Figure 9.4
Contrastive components (example 2 – French)

(a)

	Urban	Two exits	Spacious	Right of Way
rue	+	+	±	+
route	–	+	±	+
avenue	+	+	+	+
impasse	+	–	–	+

(b)

	Tree-lined	House-lined	Major	Urban	Two exits	'Voie'
rue	±	+	±	+	±	+
route	±	±	+	±	+	+
avenue	+	±	±	±	±	+
impasse	±	+	–	+	–	+

(c)

	Tree-lined	House-lined	Major	Urban	Two exits	'Voie'
rue	–	+	–	+	+	+
route	–	–	+	–	+	+
avenue	+	–	–	–	+	+
impasse	–	+	–	+	–	+

(d)

	Urban	Two exits	Spacious	Right of way
A	–	+	+	+
B	–	+	–	+
C	–	–	–	+
D	+	+	–	+

rue – voie bordée . . . de maisons, dans une agglomération
route – voie . . . de première importance
avenue – voie . . . plantée d'arbres qui conduit à une habitation
impasse – petite rue qui n'a pas d'issue

From them we can establish features and draw up a table of components (Figure 9.4b). The dictionary definitions have allowed us to establish that all four words are included in the class VOIE, in itself an interesting fact since English does not appear to have a corresponding generic term. *Right of way* is much more specialised. However, only *impasse* is uniquely identified, because for those entries marked ± we are not sure if both values, or only one, are permissible. By interpreting *bordée de maisons, plantée d'arbres, de première importance* and *dans une agglomération* as *specific*, defining components rather than *optional* components, each word is uniquely identified, and the table can be simplified (Figure 9.4c).

Returning to the simplest matrix (Figure 9.4a), we might ask ourselves if any other words participate in this lexical set by virtue of possessing a different combination of values for the four features (Figure 9.4d). That is, we create a configuration of components and inquire of a native speaker whether it is associated with a signifier and constitutes a word of the language. In the event we would discover that *A* is again *route, B* and *C* correspond to *chemin* and *D* to *ruelle.* Thus we have extended the set by two members and discovered that a non-wide, non-urban thoroughfare is indifferently *chemin* or *route*.

The distinction between the *generic* and *specific components* on one hand and the optional, or *potential components* on the other – together constituting the substance of the signified – is an important one which corresponds to a distinction between denotation and connotation (Figure 9.5). *Denotation* is a stable, socialised condition, whereas *connotation* is unstable and subject to variation from individual to individual or from group to group. To call the stem of a flower a *green fuse* was personal to Dylan Thomas; to talk of the *head of the group* is to use a metaphor which is in the competence of the whole community. Culture is shared connotations. The problem for anyone describing language use is to decide how far a component is idiosyncratic or, on the contrary, cultural. Tests have been devised to measure connotative meanings. For example, *mother* consistently scores highly on ten-point scales *good–bad* and *warm–cold*, while *woman* is rather neutral. Sentences (7) and (8) could provide another measure of how far connotations are shared:

(7) He was ugly but intelligent
(8) He was handsome but intelligent

Figure 9.5

Denotative and connotative components of the signified

SIGNIFIED

Denotation –	Generic components	+	Specific components
Connotation –		Potential components	

Ultimately, however, the set of features for a given word must be considered open, allowing a gradual 'drift' of meaning as individuals' connotations become generalised. Only then are they recorded in the dictionary. For example, *track* meaning 'one out of several items recorded on a disc' figures in only recent dictionaries. Thus the expression *lay tracks*, dated at 1874 for railway construction, has come to mean 'make recordings'.

In nomenclatures and terminologies, however, the avoidance of any possible ambiguity is of key importance to the specialist – and to the translator or interpreter – and thus where terms are concerned at one-to-one relationship between signifier and signified is the ideal. Yet with researchers in different parts of the world making the same discoveries unknown to one another, competing terms inevitably proliferate. From a componential viewpoint a term should be definable by a unique and closed set of components not displaying the indeterminacy of *day:night*, where *day* may either include *night* or be opposed to it.

9.4.3 Combinatorial lexical relations

In (9) it is not the banal co-occurrence of *gulp* and *gin* or even of *gulp* and *elephant* that strikes our attention:

(9) The elephant gulped the gin

It is the unexpected co-occurrence of *elephant* and *gin*, even though it is not semantically anomalous. A banal co-occurrence is often a predictable one, which indicates that the speaker is choosing from a limited pool of words at that point in the speech chain. This is not true of (10), where reference to almost any observable entity can be inserted –

(10) He saw a small --

but it is of (11) where *egg* is the sole possibility:

(11) He sniffed the addled --

The same is true of the Spanish *huevo huero*, of *прогорклое* ('rancid') which occurs only in the context — *масло* ('butter') and of *saur* which occurs only after *hareng*. Between these two extremes there is a scale of preferential co-occurrence between word pairs which manifests itself in general usage and which is called *collocation*.

This is not to say that the L2 learner should opt always for the banal, but to achieve special effects - for example, *He shouted softly* - he must first know the norm he is departing from. Furthermore, the collocational ranges of words allow the establishment of specific and generic semantic components (Figure 9.5), and are rarely identical for words given as equivalents in a bilingual dictionary. For example, *shrug* is restricted to *shoulders* - to specify *shoulders* is therefore redundant - but *encojer, schütteln* and *hausser* each has an extensive set of co-occurrents.

The extreme case of collocation involving groups of words is that of *idioms*, which function as a single unit not amenable to variation and whose meaning cannot be inferred from the meanings of their constituent parts. *He kicked the bucket* allows the idiomatic interpretation 'he died', whereas *he kicked the red bucket with sand in it* permits only a literal interpretation. *He's flogging two dead horses* and *il a un autre chat à fouetter* might conceivably have an idiomatic force, with humorous or other overtones, but we are again in the realm of pragmatics.

We now turn from the axis of combination to that of opposition.

9.4.4 Contrastive lexical relations

We will distinguish five different sense relations - hyponymy, homonymy, polysemy, antonymy and synonymy - descrbing them in terms of relations between sets of components.

Hyponymy. This is a relation of inclusion, like that holding between *furniture* (the *superordinate*) and *chair, wardrobe, table,* etc. (its *hyponyms*). Co-hyponyms are by definition part of the same semantic field, sharing a generic component, which in this case we could term + FURNITURE. Some sets of words have no superordinate: *No cycles, mopeds or motorbikes* is economically expressed by *Interdit aux deux-roues. Geschwister* has the same detonation as *siblings*, but without the sociological connotation.

Each hyponym will comprise all the components of the superordinate plus additional specific components which distinguish it from its co-hyponyms. The oppositions are not always clear (Figure 9.6 represents a fragment of the field of 'movement'), but the hierarchy does bring out the unilateral implication between superordinate and hyponym: to stroll is necessarily to walk but the reverse is not true.

The hierarchies vary from language to language. In English *greens* are included in the class of *vegetables*, whereas in Spanish *legumbres* and

Figure 9.6
The lexical field of 'movement'

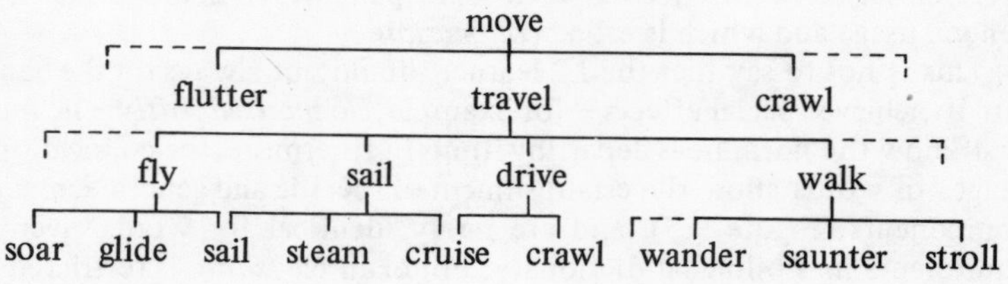

verdura are in opposition. Similarly, *Kartoffeln* are not *Gemüse*, and a German ordering his meat and two veg may be surprised to see peas and potatoes on his plate. The same form may serve as both superordinate and hyponym, as with *dog–dog:bitch*. This is the case with German *Schaf–Hammel:Schaf*, whereas English has *sheep–ram:ewe*.

Homonymy. Homonyms are words which have no common components and are therefore unrelated in meaning but which coincide in phonic and/or graphic form.

The pair *flour:flower* (*homophones*) will cause no confusion in a written text, nor will the recognition in speech of *refuse 1* (noun) and *2* (verb), which are homographs. The former can be a source of difficulty in aural comprehension, the latter in reading out loud, but these difficulties, even with complete homonyms like *bank 1* ('finance house') and *2* (of a river), tend to be minimised by a combination of grammatical, contextual and situational information. The French conjunction *car* ('for') and the noun ('coach') have different distributions in the sentence. Gender – *le:la vase, der:die Kiefer* – and stress – *зáмок:замóк* ('castle':'lock') – may also be differentiating factors. *Son 1* ('sound') collocates with *émettre* and *entendre, son 2* ('bran') with *manger*, etc. The ambiguity of (12) will probably be resolved by background information:

(12) Il s'est suicidé au café

('In the cafe', 'at coffee', 'by an overdose of coffee'?)

Polysemy. This is a relationship commonly known as 'shades of meaning' between related, overlapping sets of components and a single signifier. *Arm* could be assigned differing components on the basis of its occurrence in *John's arm, arm of the chair, arm of the sea*. Should the fact that *eat* collocates with *soup, ice-cream* and *toffee* force us to distinguish three verbs, that is, to say we have homonymy? The decision is ultimately an arbitrary one. The *Oxford English Dictionary* chooses

Figure 9.7
Adjectival polysemy

TIGHT

fast	*constricting*	*miserly*	*drunk*
serré	*étriqué*	*radin*	*plein*
fest	*eng*	*geizig*	*blau*
apretado	*estrecho*	*agarrado*	*borracho*
плотный	*тесный*	*скудный*	*пьяный*

to group the above three senses of *arm* under a single heading *arm 1*, while the sense 'weapon' is treated separately under *arm 2*.

In L1–L2 translation difficulties can arise from mis-consultation of the dictionary or from inadequate contexts, sometimes given in the wrong language. The problem can be particularly acute with adjectives (see Figure 9.7).

The plurality of reference afforded by homonymy and polysemy is exploited by advertisers and comedians in creating puns.

Antonymy. Opposites are related to the same scale, which supplies a common component (e.g. *high:low*, +VERTICALITY), but have opposite values in respect of some other feature (e.g. HIGH).

The number of absolute opposites is limited. Even the logical polarity of *dead:alive* (*dead* entailing *not alive* and vice versa) is denied by the expression *half-dead*. To grade absolutes – *very dead* – produces a marked use. The fact that the components –ADULT and +ADULT contribute to the semantic definition of *girl* and *woman* respectively (see Figure 9.3) should not polarise our view of general usage, which commonly distinguishes – with some indeterminacy – *girl, lass, teenager, young woman*. Although the stimulus *hot* will usually prompt *cold, not hot* does not entail *cold* because these two words do not cover between them the whole of a scale which ranges through *warm, cool, tepid,* etc. This means that antonyms are gradable without any resultant markedness. Even *black* and *white* have a mid-term *grey*, and to say *a whiter wash* is not felt to be unusual. In fact, *wide:narrow, tall:short, old:young* are implicitly graded by the noun which they qualify. A small giant is still larger than a big dwarf.

European languages seem to share an absolute preference for using the 'higher-value' word as the unmarked term, though the French prefer not to prejudge the reply by asking *Ça mesure combien?,* while an Englishman would ask *How tall:high:long is it?* To ask *How narrow is the plank?* implies that the plank's lack of width has already been noted.

A further illustration of oppositeness is *buy:sell, borrow:lend*. In both (13) and (14) Mary is the creditor, John the debtor:

(13) Mary lent John five pounds
(14) John borrowed five pounds from Mary

Parent:child and *husband:wife* exhibit a similar relationship of converseness.

Finally, there are pairs like *tie:untie* and *commander:décommander* where the prefix indicates a reversal of the initial act.

Synonymy. Sameness of meaning, defined by identity of the components associated with two signifiers, is a disarmingly simple relation. We concluded earlier (9.4.2) that the set of features which could be used in defining a given word is potentially open. This was a consequence of our recognition of several types of meaning (9.3). Even if we accept that *remarquer* and *constater* have the same denotation, they do not entertain the same sense relations – *remarquer quelqu'un* but not **constater quelqu'un*. It is also possible that a situational frequency count might reveal preferential usage of one or the other (see 9.4.1). All words will have a different potential at the level of connotation – *hide: conceal, liberty:freedom,* for example. Other 'synonyms' clearly stand in a relation of diversity (9.4.1) – *hayrick:haymow* are indicators of regional origin, *pass away:snuff it, mourir:crever, bouche:gueule* indicators of social class or simply familiarity.

There would appear to be no absolute synonyms, then, and in terminologies we have seen that synonymy is undesirable. But in general usage speakers can be very conscious of a norm which requires variety of vocabulary. Logically superfluous, synonyms fulfil a psychological need. It is reasonable, therefore, to consider that in certain situations features which are distinctive elsewhere are no longer felt to be so. In other words, we admit the possibility of *neutralisation* of semantic components just as we did for phonological features (see 8.5.2). Thus we may use either *boat* or *ship* in the context *We went to America by* —, but only *boat* in *He sailed his* — *in the bath.* Similarly, in the contexts — *militaire* and — *chirurgicale* the words *opération* and *intervention* can be regarded as having identical components, since when qualified by the same adjective they are not contrastive. Synonymy is, then, a relation dependent on verbal context and non-linguistic situation.

Figure 9.8 represents some of the lexical relations in which *car* participates.

9.4.5 The realness of lexical relations

Tests have been employed not only to assess the generality of conno-

Figure 9.8
Some lexical relationships for 'car'

Generic components (superordinates)
+MACHINE, +VEHICLE (machine, vehicle)

Specific components (denotation)

+4 WHEELS	+PRIVATE	+MOTOR	+PASSENGER
motor-bike	taxi	pram	tractor
moped	coach	wheelchair	lorry
scooter	bus	cart	van

CAR

Hyponymy	*Diversity*
saloon	automobile (American)
sports-car	jalopy (dated slang)
coupe	motor (current slang)
hatchback	private motor vehicle (official)

Potential components (connotation)
+METAL, +VIRILE, +WASTEFUL, +CONVENIENT . . .

CONTRASTIVE

COMBINATORIAL

run	fast		run
drive	economical	**CAR**	break down
repair	reliable		skid

tation (9.4.2) but also to explore the psychological reality of some of the meaning relations discussed above. In a word association test in which 1,008 informants were given the stimulus *long*, 758 responded *short*, while only nine responded *john* and eleven *fellow* (Clark and Clark, 1977, p. 478). Adults tend to make more contrastive responses (*dog*:*cat*) while children tend to combinatorial responses (*dog*:*barks*). Stress and phonological similarities can be influential – *sheep* may elicit *sleep* – but there are usually semantic ties also. The consistency of responses over a period of time indicates that words are stored in the brain in (relatively) stable sets. Slips of the tongue are further evidence of the structured nature of our mental 'word-banks', as (15)–(21) show:

(15) These were the worst years for beer – I mean wine
(co-hyponym selection)

(16) The dissertation's too short – long
(antonym selection)

(17) . . . in our academic ivy league (*for* ivory tower)
(collocation selection)

(18) . . . the lady with the Volkswagen (*for* dachshund)
(component selection)

(19) . . . his husband
(pronoun selection)

(20) populution (*population – pollution*)
(blend)

(21) game (*goal – aim*)
(blend)

9.5 Sentential relations

Relations between word meanings have repercussions on relations between sentences. This is a vast topic which we can no more than allude to here. The relation of entailment between hyponym and superordinate makes possible syllogisms like (22), provided the premise is accepted:

(22) Kelly is a red-head: red-heads are beautiful: Kelly is beautiful

He ran to town entails *He went to town* (which could be considered situationally synonymous), but is inconsistent with *He walked to town*. Sentences (23) and (24) are tautologies:

(23) A pound is a pound
(24) My sister is not a boy
(–MALE) = –(+MALE)

This is not to say that they convey no new information when uttered in a particular situation with a particular illocutionary force (4.4.3).

Polysemy – multiple lexical and grammatical meaning – can engender ambiguity, as in (12) or in *No tipping* and *Changing rooms can be unpleasant*.

9.6 Productivity

So far we have been concerned with describing the componential make-up of existing words, while noting that this is liable to shift over time. Their grammatical function, too, can change, so that we hear such expressions as *He was stretchered off the pitch* and *to 747 to New York*.

This trend is widespread in French, as is shown by *une départementale, un salarié, le dire, un faire-valoir.*

A trend to economy is apparent in German, where many long compound nouns are shortened in speech, and also in Russian, where, for example, *коллективное хозяйство* ('collective farm') becomes simply *колхоз*. An extreme example of economy is that of acronyms such as *UNESCO, GATT, UNO* which can be pronounced as words in their own right, unlike *USA, EEC* and others. French *URSS* shows fluctuation, being either pronounced as a single syllable or spelt out as four letters. In an inflecting language like Russian such acronyms-become-words are declined. *Вуз (Высшее Учебное Заведение* – 'institute of higher education') can appear as *вузах* and, incidentally, is *masculine*, while the full form is *neuter*.

Two words may be deliberately blended to evoke two sets of components, as in *smog, stagflation, brunch, nostalgérie* and *Kurlaub.* Speakers add to the lexis by creating new compositions of existing elements which are not always themselves words, as in *thermoplastics, aérogare* and *télécommander.*

Words can be subject to derivation by means of numerous prefixes and suffixes which generate antonyms (e.g. *in-* or *im-, nicht-* or *un-*) and adverbs, adjectives, nouns and verbs from other parts of speech. Some of these models are very productive. Spanish *-ar* allows the formation of verbs from nouns, such that *plastiquear* could conceivably be coined to mean *hacer artículos de plastico*. In Russian *-ость* ('quality') is highly productive, as are *-ение* ('process'), *-ка* ('end-product') and *-(ир) овать* ('verbal'), while in German *-isierung* is often added to a foreign root to create a noun like *Egalisierung, Rationalisierung*. French *schtroumpf* resurfaces as *schtroumpfer, schtroumpfant* and *schtroumpfement*. Prefixes like *mini-, super-, under- de-* are also productive and all find their parallels in other languages. French offers examples of adjectives and nouns derived from acronyms – *onusien* (*ONU*), *cégétiste* (*CGT*), *hachelemisation* (*HLM*).

The stock of potential words is therefore without limits, but not all of them actually occur. For example, to *schwarz* and *blau* correspond *die Schwärze* and *die Bläue,* but *die Grüne* does not exist. Spanish has *envidiable* but not *inenvidiable*, French dictionaries list *mésaventure* but not *mésaventurer*.

Our competence allows us to relate to the lexicon in some way – phonologically, grammatically or semantically – the poetic creations of Henri Michaux, like *s'espudriner* and *gobasse*, and the *slithy toves* of Lewis Carroll's *Jabberwocky*. To have in his competence the means for coining new words is an asset to the inventive learner, on condition he heeds Alice's question to Humpty Dumpty.

Further reading

Alternative treatments of much of the material in this chapter are to be found in Lyons (1968), Pottier (1974) and Palmer (1976), which is the most accessible introduction. Leech (1974) provides a more far-reaching view of semantics within a componential framework. The most comprehensive discussion of this area is in Lyons (1977), and Ullmann (1962) is of interest for diachronic studies. Nida (1975) provides an excellent practical introduction to componential techniques. Galisson (1970) applies them to French lexis, and Gak (1977) compares the lexical structures of French and Russian. Vinay and Darbelnet (1971) is a source of material for French and English, Malblanc (1963) for French and German. Adams (1973) looks at productive patterns of word-formation in English.

Suggestions for inquiry

1 Taking a list of 'synonyms' offered by an L2 synonym dictionary, try to establish, by using an L2 monolingual dictionary, relations of diversity of oppositions.
2 Find out if two noun 'synonyms' will collocate with the same range of adjectives and verbs.
3 Establish a list of ten acceptable contexts for an adjective and see if all the antonyms listed for it in an antonym dictionary can occur in the same contexts.
4 Take ten words in a semantic field like verbs of motion, sounds, verbs of speaking and devise semantic components to identify uniquely each word. Compare L1 and L2 results.
5 Taking a scale such as temperature, examination performance, solidity–liquidity, lightness–darkness, etc., establish the conventional number of points on it.
6 Using the information given on a dictionary's 'abbreviations' page, establish its classification of language varieties. Compare the result with the model presented in Chapter 4.
7 Taking any L2 noun, find ten more nouns in the same conceptual field and ten adjectives or verbs which collocate with them.
8 In how many of their English contexts can *head, arm* and *eye* be translated 'literally' into L2?
9 Starting from an L2 noun, find five nouns at a greater level of abstraction and five hyponyms.

10 Replace all occurrences in an L2 text of the equivalents of *big, small, good, bad, a lot, do, thing* by other words.
11 Using comics and cartoons, contrast the onomatopeic words of English and an L2.
12 Choose an L2 affix and specify its meaning and the class of roots to which it can be added.
13 Pick out any puns and unusual collocations from advertising copy and analyse them using componential techniques.

10

Text Structure

Language is a joint game by speaker and listener against the forces of confusion.

Norbert Wiener (1954) *The Human Use of Human Beings*, p. 82

We presented in 7.1 a model of language in which sound substance was related via lexical and syntactic form to situation. The utterances which speakers produce in situation are bound together in a manner which is by no means random. Thus in order to account for the ties existing between sentences in the grammar of a language, linguists have advanced the notion of a unit *text*. This chapter attempts to define the nature and meaning of the devices which enable speakers to create texts.

10.1 What is a text?

Text is 'language in operation' (Halliday, 1978, p. 130). It may be realised by speaking or writing; it may involve any number of participants – even a public debate has some kind of 'unity' and rules, otherwise hecklers would not be defined as such; and it may be of any length, from *Danger* or *Trespassers will be prosecuted* to a novel or an encyclopedia. Text is more, however, than the actualisation of content and role-relations; it is their *organised* expression. Consider the following string of sentences:

(1) Murky is a day outside, and it is the window that a sudden squall of rain lashes. But in the glow cheerful of the flames am I sitting, eating toast that over the fire has just been made by me

The content remains recognisable, yet it has been somehow 'scrambled', with the result that it can be retrieved by the reader only at the cost of a greater than normal effort. In terms of the semantic components of systemic grammar which were briefly outlined in 7.2.3 we can say that 'language can effectively express ideational and interpersonal meanings only because it can create text' (ibid). This enabling function is played by the *textual component* of the grammar. Like the other two components, it is conceived as a potential – a network of options, whose possible realisations are described below.

It is important to remember that the textual function is semantic, that is, it interfaces with social setting. Text is therefore, by definition, situationally *relevant*. The following, much-quoted extract (Labov, 1978) from a conversation with a schizophrenic illustrates the inappropriateness of utterances which do not respect the requirement of relevance:

(2) A: What is your name?
B: Well, let's say you might have thought you had something from before, but you haven't got it any more
A: I'm going to call you Dean

A regular correlation with the components of the speech situation (4.3) and an absence of any such incongruities will normally allow a text to be characterised as belonging to a particular type. In addition to their external relevance, texts display internal consistency *between* sentences, which we call *cohesion* (10.2): '"Cohesion" is defined as the set of possibilities that exist in the language for making text hang together: the potential that the speaker or writer has at his disposal' (Halliday and Hasan, 1976, pp. 18–19).

Cohesion is not the only factor which contributes to the impression of unity gained by the participants in the text-creation process (reading and interpreting text is an activity no less creative than writing); but it is the most significant since it operates beyond the limits of the sentence. Within the sentence itself we can discern the level of organisation of *information focus* (10.3). Also, we are aware of the existence of *generic structures* (cf. 4.3.7, on *genre*) which specify the 'skeleton' of such modes of social meaning as the ballad, the sonnet, the fable, the tall story, the joke or the legal hearing (10.4). Together, generic structure, cohesion and information focus – each at its respective level – confer upon text its 'text-ness', or *texture*.

We must expand a little further on the dynamic aspect of structuring texts. The 'forces of confusion' to which Norbert Wiener refers above are many. They may be noise in the literal sense of the word – a passing bus which drowns conversation; in an extended understanding it may be 'noise' in the form of a blurred photocopy. Then, again it may stem from the absence of shared knowledge, as in a learning situation, or from the absence of a common language, as when two foreigners try to converse. In the essentially interactive process of conversation the interlocutors try to establish what is 'common ground' in order to bridge the disparities in their knowledge and to exchange meanings effectively. Wiener's image of a 'joint game' is a good one, provided the participants are seen as playing on the same side (let us set aside instances of deliberate obtuseness on the part of some speakers). First of all, unless there is good reason to believe otherwise, listeners assume that speakers try to co-operate with them by being informative, truthful, relevant and clear. Thus, although the two parts of (3) are not overtly related, the listener will assume that some connection is intended by the simple fact that they are uttered 'in the same breath':

(3) Malcolm dropped by earlier. Do you fancy a drink?

If the listener also knows that Malcolm is not averse to a glass of beer, then the inference that they are to have a drink with Malcolm seems perfectly plausible. Second, text creation is interactive in that speakers usually have at the outset a game strategy which they then tend to adjust tactically in the light of changing circumstances. They do so as they modify their perceptions or presuppositions of what constitutes shared knowledge. In (4) the speaker has mistakenly supposed that the identity of the 'thing' in question is obvious:

(4) A: Have you seen my thing?
B: What thing?

In writing, where direct feedback (4.3.10) is not forthcoming, it is necessary for the author to question very carefully his presuppositions if an exchange of meanings is effectively to take place. Finally, as more and more text is created, so it becomes possible for the speaker to make an increasing number of references to the text itself. In a book such as this the 'cross-references' point both backwards and forwards, while in conversation speakers are less apt to refer to what they intend to say than what they have said. It is now time to look more closely at the devices for textual 'cross-referencing' between sentences, which come under the heading of cohesion.

10.2 Cohesion

We now know what cohesion does – it makes texts hang together; underlying this function is the concept of presupposition which we have just touched upon. Two examples will clarify the argument:

(5) Then he won't
(6) Einstein formulated the theory of relativity

On the one hand, (6) can be directly *interpreted* – that is, it can be directly related to the outside world and our knowledge of the identity of Einstein and the nature of his theory. However, (5) can only be interpreted if we can first discover the linguistic forms to which *then, he* and *won't* relate. These could equally well be (5a) as (5b):

(5a) John said he wouldn't go
(5b) Do you think Peter will play the piano tomorrow?

Presuppositions, then, are of two kinds: those involving a knowledge of the world, and those involving a knowledge of the linguistic system. The first kind is linked with a desire to 'pitch it at the right level', which requires that a speaker *memberships* his listener (Coulthard, 1977, p. 82). We have a good idea of what our intimate friends do or do not know, what their prejudices and opinions are; we can accordingly membership them as football fans, Marxists or art-lovers and assume certain knowledge on their part. A television newscaster, on the other hand, can assume little familiarity on the part of his mass audience with the items he is announcing, and must therefore be quite explicit in his account. The second, or linguistic focus of presupposition is the one which interests us here, and it allows us to state a general condition for cohesion: 'Cohesion occurs when the *interpretation* of some element in the discourse is dependent on that of another. The one *presupposes* the other, in the sense that it cannot effectively be decoded except by recourse to it' (Halliday and Hasan, 1976, p. 4). Thus the intrinsic continuity of cohesion ensures that information can be retrieved from the preceding text in order to fill in the 'missing pieces'. We distinguish four types of cohesion: *reference; substitution and ellipsis; lexical;* and *conjunction*.

10.2.1 Reference

If we imagine three different situations in which *This is it* can occur, we can detect different functions of *it* in each case:

(7) This is it
(*finds object he is searching for*)
(8) (I've been wanting a new toy . . .)
This is it
(9) This is it
(. . . the chance you've all been waiting for)

Whereas in (7) *it* refers to something in situation, the reference item in (8) – *toy* – and (9) – *chance* – is linguistic, within the text. Textual reference can either be retrospective (*anaphoric*), as in (8), or prospective (*cataphoric*), as in (9). The meaning of reference can be glossed as 'supply the referent in this instance' (for *referent*, see 9.2), and we rarely make mistakes in correctly identifying which referent to retrieve. For example, there will be general agreement that in (10) Spain were the winners, and that in (11) it was Paula's bike that was taken:

(10) France played Spain. They lost
(11) Paula arrived, and Mary took her bike

In fact, the use of anaphoric reference is so frequent that when it does not occur in (12), we suspect that two Johns are being identified –

(12) *John took Mary to a dance. John was left on his own*

– and not that 'John took Mary to the dance and was then ditched'.

Personal pronouns and their associated adjectives (*I, my, mine, you, your, yours*, etc.) are a major set of exponents of reference. It is worthwhile to reflect at this point on the 'meaning' of personal pronouns. Who is *I*? The answer is: the speaker. *You*, then, refers to a person or persons in the speaker's presence, and *I–you* constitute a reciprocal couple which switches every time the turn shifts within an interaction. The absence of any fixed referent for *I–you* makes their acquisition by children particularly troublesome (3.1). And as we saw in 5.4.1 different languages offer varying options of second- and even third-person pronoun forms, depending on role relationship. It is the *I–you* pair which determines, by exclusion, *he, she* and *they. We* includes at least the speaker – the 'royal we' – while *one* may or may not do so. Thus pronouns can only be interpreted by reference to the situation in which they are uttered, and they are allotted according to the allocation of speech roles. Discourse is very much an egocentric activity, so that even *He is tall* is, implicitly, *I say that he is tall* (cf. 4.4.3).

Also relative to the time and place of the speaker's speaking are the advervials *now, then, here, there* and the demonstratives *this, that, these, those*. In contrast to English, French, German and Russian, Spanish encodes three ranges of proximity: *este* ('this here'), *ese* ('that') and *aquel* ('that over there').

Considering the phrase *She lost her necklace*, it is interesting to note that the English *that* can refer to a single noun (13) or to an extended stretch of discourse (14):

(13) That was valuable
(14) That was silly

It is the nature of the adjective which allows us as readers to grasp the difference and also to reconstruct from there the contrasting intonation contours. French, however, employs different presupposing elements to mark the differing status of the presupposed elements:

(13a) Il était précieux
(14a) C'était idiot

A final means of establishing identity of reference is the definite article. To take an example from text B (at the end of Chapter 7):

(15) After pouring the batter into a hot pan, tilt the pan . . .

we notice that *the* identifies the pan in question as the hot one into which the batter has been poured. *A* selects one from a class, while *the* preserves identity of reference. Hence the opening line of the novel *Jaws* – *The great fish moved silently through the night water* – simultaneously fosters curiosity and complicity in the reader by identifying a single fish – *Which fish? What has happened already?* This device is not uncommon in novels; the opening of *One Flew Over the Cuckoo's Nest* is even more enigmatic – *They're out there*.

The presupposing element need not be identical in reference to the presupposed; the latter may simply be used as a reference point, as with *more oil* in (16):

(16) . . . add more oil to the pan (*text B*)

In this category can be placed comparatives and superlatives. For instance, *farther out into space* (text C) refers back to *the moon*, and *smaller sum* (text D) takes as its point of reference *that sum* which is not *less than one-half the Hire-Purchase Price*. The presupposing element may be seen as *different, other, similar, same*, etc., with respect to the presupposed.

10.2.2 Substitution and ellipsis

Whereas reference requires the listener or reader to supply semantic information from elsewhere in the text or situation, substitution and ellipsis require that they 'supply the appropriate *word* or *words* already available' (Halliday and Hasan, 1976, p. 226):

(17) Do you want the black or the red pen? – The black one

In (17) *one* is cohesive in that it is a substitute for *pen* in the previous sentence. In (18) *so* substitutes a whole clause –

(18) Is it raining? – I think so

– and in (19) *doesn't* substitutes a verb:

(19) He likes Mahler – No he doesn't

Substitution provides an overt cue to search for a preceding word, but ellipsis involves the total deletion of an element. Ellipsis is very far-reaching in English and can affect almost any part of speech:

(20) Bob goes on Mondays, Tony on Tuesdays (*verb*)
(21) Tom had four pints, Frank five (*noun*)

It is particularly widely used in question–answer sequence, where the missing words are immediately recoverable:

(22) Who's going to do the shopping? – Muggins is (*clause*)

In some instances the speaker has a choice between substitution and ellipsis:

(23) Has he finished? He has done/He has

Yet these possibilities vary from language to language; *one* is obligatory in (17), whereas French, Spanish, German and Russian allow the elliptical use of the adjective: *le noir, la negra, die Schwartze, чёрное*. Russian and Spanish permit the ellipsis of the subject of the verb: *¿Adónde* (*tu*) *vais? Куда (ты) идёшь?* ('Where are (you) going?). However, a Russian will often respond to a yes–no question by reiterating the verb used by the questioner: *Вы понимаете? – Понимаю* ('Do you understand?' – 'I understand'), rather than *Да* ('Yes').

10.2.3 Lexical cohesion

We saw in 9.4 that it is possible to structure the vocabularies of a language on socio-semantic grounds and that the types of relation suggested – hyponymy, synonymy, antonymy – have some psychological validity. When more than one member of a particular lexical set appears in a given text – especially if these words are highly related – then inevitably their inherent semantic 'closeness', once mapped on to the structure of that text, reinforces its cohesiveness.

Text A (at the end of Chapter 7) provides an excellent illustration of this phenomenon. As we would expect with a set of instructions for a piece of equipment, we have a number of terms which are closely related, primarily because the parts which they denote are themselves closely related. For instance, there is a part–whole relationship linking *lid, goblet, sealing ring* and *base* – all *parts* – to *liquidiser. Dismantle* is an antonym of *assembly, assemble, fitting* and *fit* which are themselves referentially synonymous. So, too, are *screw* and *turn*, which, moreover, both collocate within their respective sentences with *clockwise*. We must mention, also, the graded series *warm, hot* and *boiling*, all collocating with *water*, which in turn collocates with *rinse, soak* and *dry*. To sum up, a number of abstract semantic relations – both contrastive and combinatorial – are actualised in text with the result that the web of these relations threads almost invisibly through the text as a whole. In addition, the 'raw' reiteration of a number of words – *goblet, cover, base, liquidiser, clockwise, water, soak* – sets up further echoes which resound throughout the text.

It is worth recalling the class of 'general nouns' alluded to earlier (9.3) which play the role of superordinates defined by one or two generic components: *person, man* [+HUMAN]; *thing, object* [–ANIMATE, +COUNT]; stuff [–ANIMATE, +MASS]; *business* [–ANIMATE, +ABSTRACT], etc. The behaviour of such nouns verges on that of the elements we discussed under the heading of substitution.

We should not overlook the role the phonological dimension of the word has to play in cohesion. T. S. Eliot's *Skimbleshanks: The Railway Cat* illustrates the point admirably:

(24) There's a whisper down the line at 11.39
When the Night Mail's ready to depart,
Saying 'Skimble where is Skimble has he gone to hunt the thimble?
We must find him or the train can't start.'

The high incidence of fricatives – /s, z, θ, ð, f, h/ – and plosives, especially the aspirated /p, t, k/, conjures up the hissing of steam escaping from the waiting locomotive. Rhyme and rhythm could also be further investigated, but they are beyond the immediate horizons of this chapter.

10.2.4 Conjunction

This is a salient cohesive device because of its function of specifying the semantic connection of a clause with the preceding text. There are so many expressions which serve to express conjunctive relations that it is not possible here to do more than exemplify each of the four categories which Halliday and Hasan (1976) adopt: *additive* (*and, nor, or*); *adversative* (*yet, however, in fact*); *causal* (*so, therefore, because*); *temporal* (*then, next, in short*). The learner can add to these lists with little difficulty.

At the same time, it is worth pointing out that some conjunctives can be 'activated' by two different semantic components:

(25) He missed the bus. So he took a taxi
(26) The taxi will be here soon. So get ready

In (25) *So* is located in the content of what is being said; in other words, it is activated by the ideational component. In (26) *So* is part of the saying; it is an assessment by the speaker of the necessity of action in that situation, and as such is triggered by the interpersonal component.

Examples of both types of usage are to be found in texts A–D at the end of Chapter 7.

10.2.5 Cohesive density

Cohesion distinguishes text from non-text. This is not to say, however, that all texts are equally cohesive or cohesive in the same way. The several cohesive phenomena described above are just so many dimensions along which texts can be contrasted. Where (non-linguistic) action is focal, reference will tend to be situational, as in (7) above. But when speech itself is the focal activity – as in a lecture – and creates its own perceptual environment (e.g. linguistic theory) which is relatively independent of the social environment (a lecture theatre), then the need for cohesion is much greater. Anaphoric (backward) reference is the most frequent, though a speaker who has sufficient status, or who is determined to hold the floor, can employ cataphoric (forward) reference – *I intend to make two points . . .* – to forestall interruptions.

Some segments of texts are more densely tied than others; the paragraph is probably a useful working unit to adopt for comparative purposes. Finally, the different modes of cohesion appear to operate over different text spans. Substitution, ellipsis and conjunction span the least distance:

(27) You may need to add more oil to the pan. If you do, add only a little (*text B, Chapter 7*)

Reference elements often form 'chains' which link sentence after sentence, as do *we, we, we, our, us, us, us, our, we, our* in text C. Lexical 'echoes', in contrast, may be separated by lines, paragraphs, even pages. Yet it is wise to point out that if a word occurs three times, say, in a text of 3,000 words, it is highly improbable that it will be found at 1,000-word intervals. More likely is it that the three occurrences will cluster together.

10.3 Information focus

Cohesion operates across sentence boundaries, information focus within them. This focus is realised not in lexis and syntax but in phonology and therefore in an overt feature of spoken language only. Let us expand on an example used in our brief discussion of intonation (8.6):

(28a) **Fred** fed the rabbit yesterday
(28b) Fred **fed** the rabbit yesterday
(28c) Fred fed the rabbit **yes**terday
(28d) Fred fed the **rab**bit yesterday

In each of these four sentences the speaker has organised the information differently; the shift of focus follows the most prominent syllable. The focal element is that which the speaker considers most *newsworthy*. The tunes of (28a)–(28c) are heard to be 'abnormal', or marked. Now, with a basically conclusive (affirmative) tune, we decided earlier that the speaker was contradicting a preceding statement by his interlocutor concerning the identity of the feeder, the act accomplished or the time of the act, respectively. It is the corrected element each time which receives phonological prominence; it is presented as being *new* information not derivable from the preceding discourse or situation. The validity of the remainder of the sentence is not brought into question; it is presupposed as shared – or *given* – information. We see, then, that presupposition underlies information focus as it does reference. If (28a)–(28c) are corrections, then they presuppose *Peter, skinned* and *this morning*, for example. If they are answers, they presuppose *Who?*, *What do?* and *When?* But this is not the case with (28d); there are no such presuppositions of *guinea-pig* or *What?* because it is simply the 'normal', or *unmarked* tune. Speakers rarely produce utterances which they do not consider newsworthy in some respect – they may be primarily phatic (4.4.1), of course – and in this particular case it is quite conceivable that to the addressee the content is all new. Thus, with unmarked information focus it is the *last lexical item* which is made prominent and the sentence remains unspecified with regard to presupposition.

This explains the use of the substitute *one(s)*, which avoids the necessity of resorting to marked information focus:

(29) Have you a tin of beans?
(29a) I've only got **small** ones left (*unmarked*)
(29b) I've only got **small** tins left (*marked*)

Very often the *given* elements are overtly anaphoric.

The given–new distinction also relates to reference:

(30) John caught a crab
(31) The crab was caught by John

The move from the indefinite article – which is not cohesive because it presupposes nothing – to the definite (cohesive) article parallels the switch from the focus on *crab* as new to its presentation as given.

In written texts the assumption is that the information focus is unmarked, unless the use of italics, capitals or special punctuation suggests otherwise.

10.4 Generic structures

Cohesion, with its multiple layers of structure, allows us to characterise text and describe *how text can cohere*. Cohesion can form a basis for contrastive analyses of written language and, considered together with information focus, of spoken language. But it is insufficient to enable us to specify *what text can be created*. This second goal requires that we make the link between generic structure (10.1) and its realisation in sound via the core of the grammar. The aim is ambitious, but this has not deterred research.

In the field of literature attempts at systematising the structure of folk-tales or short stories are not new. With scientific texts the emphasis has been on isolating sequences of speech acts (4.4.3) of the structures such as *cause* → *effect* or *denial* → *reason* → *correction*. An unusually clear illustration of not only a generic structure but also its typical realisation is provided by an examination of the verdicts of French courts of appeal. Their peculiar requirements of clarity and lasting authority mean that documents which have a legally binding force tend to adhere to a 'standard format':

1. *Specification of plaintiff(s) and plea*
   Requête de X tendant à l'annulation du jugement . . .;
2. *Legal references*
   Vu le Code rural . . .; l'ordonnance . . .; la loi . . .; (etc.)
3. *Consideration of circumstances giving rise to appeal*
   Considérant que . . .;
4. *Deliberation*
   Sur le moyen tiré de ce que . . .; Considérant que . . .;
   Sur le moyen tiré de ce que . . .; Considérant que . . .;
   (Etc.)
5. *Verdict*
   Considérant qu'il résulte de tout ce qui précède . . .

The structuring of conversational text is not so rigidly codified, but neither is it random. Researchers have been interested to find out how turns come to be allocated smoothly in conversation and how participants progress through transactions like question–answer or complaint–apology/justification. Some of the more revealing phases of conversation investigated have been opening and closing routines. A typical telephone conversation begins as follows:

1.	*Summons*		(*Ring*)
2.	*Answer*	A.	Hello
3.	*Identification*	B.	Is that John?
		A.	Yes
		B.	This is Jane
4.	*Greeting*	A.	Hello
		B.	Hello

We have already seen that the exchanges are organised differently in other cultures (4.4.2). As for the closing of conversations, it often follows a pattern like this (adapted from Coulthard, 1977, pp. 86–7):

1.	*Topic boundary*	A.	Well, things always work out for the best
		B.	Certainly do
2.	*Pre-closing*	A.	All right dear
		B.	Okay
3.	*Marked new topic*	A.	OH BY THE WAY I'd just like . . .
2.	(*Repeat*)		
4.	*Closing*	A.	Bye bye
		B.	Goodnight

The concluding example of efforts to relate situation and linguistic system comes from an analysis of linguistic interaction in the classroom by Sinclair and Coulthard (1975). The model they adopt is a systemic one, which can be represented as a network of options (Figure 10.1). The model distinguishes five ranks of unit at the level of classroom discourse. Discourse is situated at the interlevel of context (see Figure 7.1) between situation and form. These ranks are: lesson, transaction, exchange, move and act. The analysts do not succeed in describing the structure of a speech event (4.3) equivalent to the lesson. The highest rank at which this proves possible is that of transaction. These speech events take the structure PM(M_1, . . . , M_n)(T): an obligatory preliminary transaction followed by an obligatory medial transaction, after which may come any number of medial transactions and an optional, concluding terminal transaction. In Figure 10.1 the number of options available at the lower rank has been greatly reduced in order to account only for the transaction below. The reader can trace on Figure 10.1 the path of the options selected and so supply the steps which mediate between transactions in discourse and their lexical and syntactic realisations:

Text continues on page 184 beneath Figure 10.1

Figure 10.1
Discourse structures in the classroom

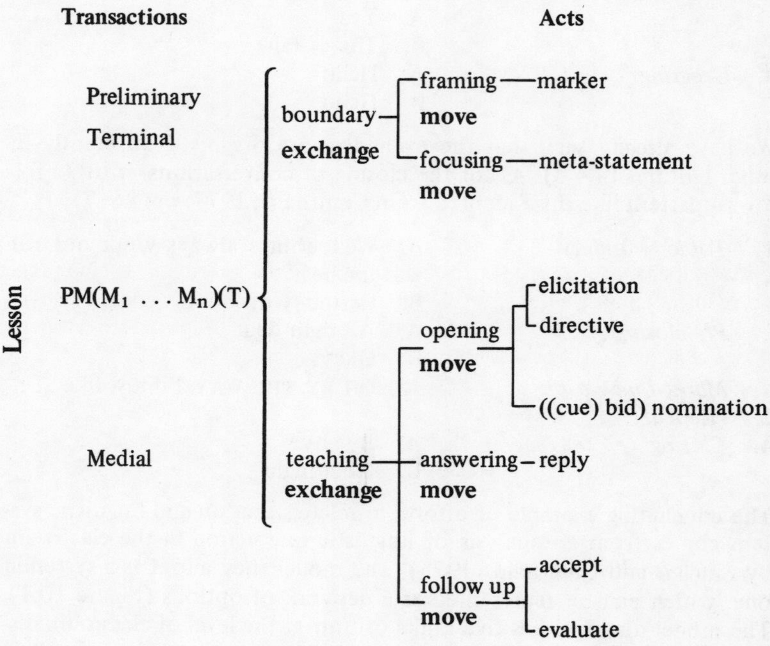

* * *

Discourse		*Syntax-Lexis*
P	*meta-statement*	Let's just look at these
M_1	*directive*	All eyes on me
M_2	*elicitative*	What's this?
M_3	*cue*	Hands up
M_4	*bid*	(*pupils raise hands*)
M_5	*nominate*	Janet
M_6	*answering*	(*Janet replies*) A paper clip
M_7	*evaluate*	A paper clip – good
M_8	*accept*	A paper clip
T	*marker*	All right

As a method of discourse analysis, it is rich in insights for linguistics. No less important observations, for pupils and teachers alike, can be made concerning 'who says what to whom when' in the classroom. It is the teacher who monopolises the floor. The pupils' linguistic reply is confined to Janet's *A paper clip*.

Further reading

Halliday (1978) defines the notion of text and sets it clearly in a broader theory of language. The most comprehensive work on cohesion is Halliday and Hasan (1976), while chapter 12 of Kress (1976) deals with information focus. References to these topics are also found in Lyons (1970) and Allerton (1979). A good introduction to speech acts, conversational analysis and discourse analysis with reference to language teaching is Coulthard (1977). The presentation by Sinclair and Coulthard (1975) of English used in the classroom is quite accessible to beginners. The classic work on generic structure in literature is Propp (1968).

Suggestions for inquiry

1 What is the function of *this* in the two sentences below?

This is what **puzzles** *me*
This *is what puzzles me*

2 Explain the different possible interpretations of:

John *is the leader*
The leader is **John**

3 Contrast texts A–D at the end of Chapter 7 on the basis of the cohesive devices employed.
4 What elements are used for reference in your foreign language? Contrast them with those of English.
5 List ten conjunctive expressions of your foreign language for each class of conjunctive.
6 Find four short foreign texts associated with different situations and contrast their use of cohesive devices as with the English texts above.
7 Using the analyses presented in 10.4 as a model, produce a generic structure for 'the joke'.

11

Analysis, Interpretation, Translation

> Such is our pride, our folly, or our fate
> That few, but such as cannot write, translate.

It is often said that translating is an impossibility. And so it is, if we are to define translating as the total re-creation in one language of a message first conveyed in another language. Given the considerable structural and cultural differences which separate languages, a translation can never be more than an approximation to the original message. But the yardstick of 'total transfer' is an unrealistic one. Translating is a particular kind of communication, and in *all* communication information is lost somewhere in the channel between sender and receiver. The fact of information loss is therefore no grounds for denying the validity of translating. Yet the theory of translating, unable to ally itself to any well-developed theory of language, lags far behind the practice of translating, which sees every day an increase in its importance and output. This is true not only of professional spheres in commercial and industrial enterprises and international organisations, but also of schools and universities where translating is a central activity in many teaching methods.

The aims of translating and the obstacles to them are often only vaguely formulated by the learner, even though he may be considering making a career of this activity. In this chapter we look to the accumulated experience of translators and to our discussion of aspects of verbal communication in the previous chapters in order to dispel some of this mystery.

Translating involves, most commonly, two distinct languages. We could, of course, envisage translating between two varieties of the same language – Jamaican English and Standard English, for example (although many may view these varieties as constituting separate languages). The speech-communities (2.3) in question may be separated not only culturally and linguistically but also temporally, as in the case of a modern translation of *Beowulf* or of *War and Peace*. These are all 'distances' with which the translator has to cope. Here we will assume two contemporaneous speech-communities using languages which are generally accepted as distinct.

Movement from one language to another can take place through the medium of either the written or the spoken word. We reserve *translating* for the former and *interpreting* for the latter. Each knows its own uses and constraints, and we will deal with them separately.

11.1 Translating

As a special kind of relationship between people, translating must be described within a sociolinguistic framework, such as the one outlined in Chapter 4. We can distinguish three *participants* (4.3.1) in this particular act of communication. the sender of the original text (10.1), the translator, and the receiver or receivers of the translated text. We also recognise two distinct but related texts, one in the *source language* (SL), the other in the *target language* (TL). The translator has a dual role - as a receiver of the SL text and the sender of the TL text - which is to bridge a gap between two groups of speakers. Consequently his task is twofold. On the one hand he has to analyse the form and interpret the force of the SL text. On the other hand he must decide what *purpose* the translation is to serve and formulate it as appropriate to that purpose and to his readership. The relationship between the two texts is best described, then, in pragmatic terms first of all (1.3.1). The translator's success in achieving his pragmatic goals will depend on the potential of the TL for expressing the meaning of the SL text, and on his own knowledge of the two languages. Inevitably there are cultural and linguistic obstacles which may make the desired effects difficult to achieve. Let us take these three factors in turn - purpose of translating, pragmatic relationships, cultural and linguistic obstacles - in order to see what abilities the translator should possess, and then we will sketch out some basic procedures.

11.1.1 Purpose of the translation

There are two main orientations in translating. The first, that of *formal equivalence*, aims primarily at enabling the receiver of the translated message to understand the content and particular structure of the original message and the bases of the reactions to it on the part of the SL community. Let us assume that our SL text is the transcription of a Tartar folk-tale from a remote part of the Soviet Union. A formally equivalent translation is of interest to a linguist who wishes to compare the structure of the Tartar language with that of his own or to that of a prospective learner of the language. It is also of use to the ethnographer interested in, say, the form of the ritual expressions (see 4.4.3) used in Tartar ceremonies or the way in which the culture and environment of the community are reflected in its language (see 6.1). In a more familiar context, translations of medieval French or German texts are often oriented towards formal equivalence. This may necessitate translating the SL units on a one-to-one basis, so that verb is rendered by verb, clause by clause and sentence by sentence in strict parallel. Another characteristic is the abundant use of annotations in order to explain the etymology of certain words, the fact that a pun is intended, the meaning of a literally translated idiom, or some feature of the language's cultural setting. In the last case, the footnote or paraphrase will seek to gloss SL word forms specific to that setting and which have been retained in the translation, such as *yurt*. It is via this route that many borrowings enter a language (6.2).

Such a translation makes great demands on the reader's concentration. First, the reader's attention may be constantly directed towards the explanatory notes. Second, he has to cope with a larger volume of information. For example, translating *Er sagt, dass er mir das Buch nicht lesen wird* by *He says, that he to me the book not read will* conveys information on both the content and the form of the German message which is not predictable to someone who knows nothing of German syntax. The more predictable a feature of a message is, the more *redundant* it is. In *She spend - every day skating at a nearby ---* the final *s* of *spends* is totally predictable and the reader anticipates one of a limited range of possibilities - such as *rink* or *lake* - to conclude the sentence (see 9.4.3). Normally redundancy in speech is about 50 per cent; in formal-equivalence translating it tends to be much lower.

The other main orientation in translating is towards *functional equivalence*. Its aim is that

> the receptor in the [target] culture should be able, within his own culture, to respond to the message as given in his own language, in substantially the same manner as the receptor in the [source] culture responded, within the context of his own culture, to the message as communicated to him in his own language (Nida, 1964, p. 149).

Let us take as an example *The quick brown fox jumps over the lazy dog*. One translation which respects normal French syntax and collocation is *Le rapide renard roux saute par-dessus le chien paresseux*. Yet this completely ignores the English sentence's function as a typing exercise employing all the letters of the alphabet. Its functional equivalent in French is *Zoé, ma grande fille, veut que je boive ce whisky dont je ne veux pas*.

To return to our Tartar folk-tale, a functionally equivalent translation would seek to recast the tale both in the TL idiom and within the bounds of the receivers' cultural knowledge. *Yurt* may be rendered by *animal-hide tent*, for example, and the translation of the German expression above will follow the predictable English word order. The result is naturalness of expression and enhanced readability thanks to a normal level of redundancy. While a functionally equivalent translation cannot communicate the same quantity of information about the source culture as can a formally equivalent translation, it can aspire to have an emotive effect on the TL readership.

We have contrasted the purposes of translating in somewhat polar terms in order to show that the often-cited conditions of faithfulness and accuracy are not absolutes but are determined in relation to the characteristics of the translation's intended public; translations are not all to be evaluated according to the same criteria. In practice, the two orientations are not mutually exclusive and the translator is usually required to render something of the 'atmosphere' of the source culture without sacrificing fluidity of style or equivalence of response among the target readers. The fact that speakers of different languages vary so greatly in their expression of the relationship between form and content means that the translator is constantly struggling to reconcile these conflicting requirements.

The discussion which follows places the emphasis on functional equivalence, the generally accepted canon of most translating practice today.

11.1.2 Pragmatic relationships

First of all we examine the relationships between (the original) author, his public and the text. The role relationship between author and public can be characterised on the scale *public–private* (see 4.3.1). The more it tends towards the *public* end of the scale, the more likely it is that the form of the message and the circumstances of its production will be governed by societal norms (4.3.4). This is true of articles of constitutions, legal judgements (10.4) and hire-purchase agreements, for example. A functionally equivalent translation must be modelled on an equivalent document in the target community.

On the other hand, the more the individuality of the author is stressed, the more likely it is that idiosyncratic preferences for certain forms of expression and even novel turns of phrase (see 9.6, for example) will appear. Despite this relative freedom of expression, the text may still clearly belong to a particular genre (4.3.7), such as 'the joke', 'the autobiography' or 'the after-dinner speech', by virtue of subscribing to the largely tacit conventions which apply in that situation. In this instance a judicious balance must be struck between the idiomatic translating of such genre markers as *Have you heard the one about . . .?* which belong to the public realm, and a more form-orientated translating of the author's personal style.

Moreover, the author writes with certain ends (4.3.9) in mind and certain perceptions of his public's general knowledge and likely reactions to his text (4.3.10). The final form of the text is a product of the interaction of all these factors, and the translator's first task is to analyse the variables just outlined.

Next we have the relationship between the translator and the text. The translator is, by profession at least, a member of the author's public. He may not correspond at all, however, to the typical reader envisaged by the author, since translators usually work into their L1 only and are often not permanent members of the source speech-community. But since language and society are inextricably linked, the translator must be as conversant with the source message's social functions as with its structural characteristics. He must be aware of any deviations from the expected pattern for special effect, of their acceptability or otherwise.

Finally, we consider the relationship between the translator, his public and the translation. It is already clear how far a difference of purpose can condition the final form of a translation. The translator has to make further adjustments in the light of his assessment of what his readers already know – should he use *métro, underground* or *subway* in translating from French? Acceptability is another important factor; some groups object to the use of borrowings (6.2.6), and certain topics may be subject to social taboo or official censorship. Irish blarney, English understatement and Gallic exaggeration may each call for adjustments to be made.

11.1.3 Cultural and linguistic obstacles

Communication between members of different cultures is possible because of an underlying sameness of human experience the world over and man's ability to adjust to new modes of behaviour. But we cannot for all that discount the serious difficulties posed to translators aiming at functional equivalence by the differences in the actual form taken by cultural institutions from one society to another. To translate *хлебосольство* by *hospitality*, as the dictionary suggests, loses the fact that it is a proud Russian tradition to extend a welcome to guests by placing bread (*хлеб*) and salt (*соль*) on the table. To translate literally into French *He waved two fingers at him* conveys nothing of the intended insult (see 5.1).

Even if the legal systems of the nations of Europe have more in common with one another than with the Muslim judicial system, they are far from identical. The French have no agent whose functions coincide with that of the English *solicitor*, nor does a *juge d'instruction* have a direct counterpart in English law. To translate them as *avoué* and *examining magistrate* is misleading, as the comparison of a good French monolingual dictionary with a good English monolingual dictionary will show. It is problems of this kind which have inspired the saying *traduttore, traditore* ('translator, traitor'); the betrayal is condonable in a translation of a detective novel, but not where a law textbook is concerned. Within the European Economic Community and the United Nations Organisation standard equivalents are laid down for translations relating both to each organisation's internal structures and to the institutions of the member countries. Cultural disparities present the greatest obstacle to function-oriented translating: 'Translation fails – or untranslatability occurs – when it is impossible to build functionally relevant features of the situation into the contextual meaning of the TL text' (Catford, 1965, p. 94).

Rooted in both culture and language is the social significance (9.3) of a particular word, utterance (4.4.3) or language variety (4.3.6). The evocation of Black English in *I asks Tom did he wanna go to the pictures* probably finds its closest French equivalent in the linguistic varieties used in Martinique; while Cockney rhyming slang would pass most naturally if its content and force are expressed in genuine Parisian *argot*. Let us take a final example from Uderzo and Goscinny's *Astérix chez les Bretons*, in which the authors convey the Englishness of the island's inhabitants by linguistic devices. When Astérix and Obélix burst into an English couple's home, the lady of the house exclaims *Je dis! Quelle est cette intrusion? Choquant!* This corresponds to a formal-equivalence translation into French of a stereotyped English remark. Aware of the connotations of the French, the translator has attempted to capture something of the response's humour and 'insularity' by substituting *I say! Don't you know a Briton's hut is his castle?* In short, the translator must appreciate the social evaluation given to linguistic stereotypes in both source and target communities.

We have already seen in section 6.1 that 'languages differ not so much as to what *can* be said in them, but rather as to what it is *relatively easy* to say in them' (Hockett, 1954, p. 122). Language can span the gulf between radically different cultures, but not always as elegantly as the translator would wish. The major linguistic obstacle to a natural translation is the obligation to specify certain features in the two languages involved (6.1.1–2 and 9.4).

In the first case features defined only poorly or not at all in the SL message are obligatory in the TL. In English verbs the specification of 'mode of locomotion' is optional, in contrast to German and Russian. Therefore, in translating *I went there yesterday* the German or Russian translator has to search elsewhere in the text for an indication of whether or not the speaker went on foot, and then translate accordingly. Imprecision may, of course, be deliberate, as the following dialogue illustrates:

- *Jane called earlier.*
- *Oh. Did she bring anything?*
- *She only phoned, she didn't come round.*

Call has two interpretations, both permissible in this context. The translator's job is to find a similarly ambiguous TL word. A further example is provided by address forms (5.4). If two adult female characters in an English novel address each other by their first names, the translator going into French, Spanish, German or Russian has no clear indication from this source whether to use T or V. In this age-group mutual FN is quite compatible with a certain distance, expressed by FN + V in the other languages.

A common fault when translating in the opposite direction (from 'obligatory' to 'optional') is to overtranslate by including too many optional features: a natural translation of *Ich werde dahin radfahren* is *I'll cycle there* or *I'll go there by bike*. To say *I'll ride there by bike* implies that the speaker is excluding the possibility of going on horseback, for example, while *I'll cycle there by bike* is so redundant that it is a tautology.

The final linguistic obstacles to translating to be mentioned here are ambiguity and the use of puns. In a pun two sets of features associated with two words which have identical or near-identical shapes are evoked simultaneously: that is, the author exploits a relationship of homonymy or polysemy (9.4.4). Some typical examples are *A funny accident can have you in stitches, Chasm is a nasty void* (an example from Brooklyn) and *A bigamist is an Italian fog*. They stretch the translator's ingenuity to the utmost. Ambiguity is more frequent in theory than in practice. As it stands *Time flies* allows two interpretations, but it is difficult to imagine that any ambiguity would surround its occurrence in a text. Two ambiguous, and genuine, examples of newspaper headlines are *Police death charge* and *Three Mile Island fuels rebellion in Yugoslavia*. The first hinges on whether *charge* means 'attack' or 'accusation', and the second on whether *fuels* is a noun or a verb. In both cases the story dispels the ambiguity. This is not to say that translation texts never contain inadvertent ambiguities, because they do. If the translator cannot discover which meaning was intended, by consulting the author, for example, then he has either to resolve the ambiguity himself, or to retain it, or to resort to a footnote.

Just as it is sometimes necessary to ascertain which features are relevant at a given place in a text by looking elsewhere in that text, so it is reasonable for the distribution of features in the TL text to be at variance with their distribution in the SL text. If we compare the two sentences *He cycled down to Nice* and *Il est descendu à Nice à vélo* we note that in both cases the idea of motion is conveyed by the verb. The English verb also specified the means of travel, whereas this is expressed in French by an adverbial phrase. Where the direction of travel is concerned, the distribution is just the reverse. Nevertheless, no one would deny these two sentences the status of translation equivalents.

11.1.4 Scientific and literary translating

In the world of professional translating the overwhelming volume of work is in the scientific and technical field, yet most schools and universities tend to concentrate on literary or non-technical journalistic texts. It is instructive to compare the two varieties in order to see how each presents different problems and calls for different orientations in translating.

Scientific texts place the emphasis on unambiguous information. The author, often *we*, does not intrude in the 'objective' presentation of the facts of the reported experiment. The readers are members of the same scientific community whose horizons are being extended. The assumptions as to their prior knowledge of the subject are made explicit in the bibliographical references. Idiosyncratic stylistic expressions are eliminated by the issue of editorial 'style sheets' which prescribe norms of length, layout, punctuation and the presentation of references, among other features. The unobtrusiveness of the author results in a high frequency of passives (*The experiment was conducted* . . .) and nominalisations (*The verification of the results* . . .) which do not require the identity of the 'conductor' or the 'verifier' to be specified. Another feature of English scientific style is the use of the future tense as well as the present tense to indicate predictable behaviour (*The solution will deteriorate if stored at low temperature*). In addition, a precise terminology relating to the field in question is used, and any new terms or unusual uses are clearly defined. Awareness of the norms governing scientific writing in his own language is essential to the translator. The style of the original does not concern the readers of the translation, who require simply to be clearly informed of the new findings. They are likely to tolerate a higher than normal information load.

The literary author, in contrast, seeks recognition of an identifiable 'style', the trade-mark of his individuality. His assumptions as to his readers' background are unlikely to be made explicit; indeed, the readership may not be clearly delimited at all. His purpose may be to persuade, to shock, to amuse or to do all three. He is less bound by norms and may even be intent on defying and redefining the norms of a particular genre. The range of subject-matter is virtually unlimited, and there may be frequent use of puns, unusual word associations, incongruous images and ambiguity. In short, form may be as important as content, if not more so, and the unpredictability of the whole rules out the possibility of a translation oriented towards function alone.

The connotations of a scientific text are no more than 'authoritative'. Those of a literary work may be various and highly individual, hence the proliferation of criticism generated by literature and the number of competing translations, each claiming to be 'more accurate' or 'more sensitive' than the others. A scientific text is rarely translated more than once into a given language.

Scientific writing has sub-varieties, such as instructions or patents, but again these tend to be governed by fairly rigid norms. Poetry imposes on the translator its own special constraints of metre, alliteration and rhyme. In the work of some poets the layout of lines on the page itself conveys a message, effectively restricting the translator to a fixed number of characters per line if the 'silhouette' is to be preserved.

11.1.5 Adequacy

First of all, is the translation adequate? 'The needs of the user must obviously be the decisive consideration' (Pinchuk, 1977, p. 205). The user must be able to understand the communicative intention of the original author and, in the case of a functionally equivalent translation, be moved to a response similar to that of the target public. All this must be achieved with optimum efficiency – 'maximal reception for minimum effort' (Nida, 1964, p. 182) – which means achieving a normal level of redundancy in order neither to overload the reader nor bore him by wordiness.

Second, is the translator adequate? We have alluded at several points to his necessary qualities, which must be a match for the complex tasks described. He must be sensitive to the denotations and connotations of words, structures and styles in two languages, and to the choices available. He must also be able to write creatively in one of them within the limits set by the situational norms and the original author's idiosyncratic style.

11.2 Interpreting

The interpreter requires all the linguistic and situational sensitivity of the translator, and more besides. Working through the medium of the spoken word, he must be capable of understanding a wide range of accents in the source language while being himself an accomplished speaker with an acceptable pronunciation (see 5.2). He must also be able to exploit intonational and paralinguistic information. The other main difference between translating and interpreting is the time available for the two tasks. Translators work to deadlines, of course, but they have time to consult dictionaries and colleagues and their pace is leisurely compared with that of interpreters, who are nevertheless expected to meet stringent requirements of accuracy. Although the bulk of the subject-matter is in the diplomatic and scientific-technical fields, speakers often make literary allusions or quote from legislation. The range of varieties is therefore no less wide than that encountered by translators. In fact, the latter tend to specialise in a particular, albeit broad, technical field in order to achieve a level of expertise sufficient to avoid misunderstanding the original, and to become familiar with the relevant terminology in two or more languages. Interpreters may find themselves dealing, in successive meetings, with hot-house tomatoes and pyjamas with sewn-in feet.

There are two principal modes of interpreting. In *consecutive* interpreting the interpreter makes notes to assist his memory of the speech, and when the speaker has concluded his contribution or a part of it the interpreter supplies the TL rendition. The interpreter is usually in the presence of the participants in the discussion. In *simultaneous* interpreting the interpreter, isolated in a booth, speaks at the same time as the orator, maintaining a brief time lag to allow the processing of the original speech. The audience follows the interpretation through headsets. The simultaneous method is most widely used in international conferences since the speaking time, especially when there are six working languages, is simply that of the delegates themselves. Consecutive interpreting increases the time required by 50 to 75 per cent, since more or less everything is said twice (although the interpretation is quicker than the original and removes hesitations, false starts and unnecessary repetitions). Both modes place a heavy burden on the interpreter's short- and medium-term memory.

Consecutive interpreting is slightly more analogous to translating than is simultaneous interpreting in that the interpreter has time during the original speech to marshal his notes, his thoughts and his vocabulary. He has the advantage of hearing a complete argument before speaking, even if he has not the possibility of reading back over various parts of it before giving his interpretation. He can, however, ask for clarification if necessary and he receives definite feedback on his performance by way of audience reaction or even questions. The simultaneous interpreter, even working in a team, has little chance of obtaining information outside of the original speech. Unknown TL equivalences have to be conveyed by paraphrases and unknown SL words guessed from structure, content and situation. Since the pace is dictated by the speaker, a polished style is less feasible than with consecutive interpreting or translating. Priority is given to the presentation of accurate information in a manner which may not be elegant but must be readily intelligible.

The main difficulty in simultaneous interpreting is remaining far enough behind the speaker to allow proper planning of a coherent interpretation, yet without losing track of the original speech. The variability of word order in Russian, the placing of German subordinate verbs at the end of the sentence, and the noun-adjective order of French and Spanish all force the interpreter to 'wait and listen'. Words like *éléments* may be interpreted as *members* or *information* according to the context, but the correct choice may not become apparent until later in the sentence in which the word has been uttered. Intonation carries a heavy load in both original and interpretation, and the fact that patterns usually span at least a clause allows the interpreter to anticipate sentence structure and even semantic contrasts. On the other hand, the interpreter must 'keep his distance' in order to have the information for planning his own intonation a clause in advance. Lagging too far behind may mean that the reaction of those members of the audience dependent on the interpretation is disconcertingly out of phase, like poor subtitling on a film.

Neither of these professions is always held in high esteem, as the epigram heading this chapter so clearly illustrates. Translators and interpreters are often blamed for errors which stem from poorly prepared originals, and the true complexity of their task is little appreciated. Whether he or she has one of these professions in mind or has an interest in languages for another reason, the learner might be encouraged by Steiner's remark (1975, p. 473): 'To a greater or lesser degree, every language offers its own reading of life. To move between languages, to translate . . . is to experience the almost bewildering bias of the human spirit towards freedom.' Follow that.

Further reading

Based on a long experience of Bible translating, Nida (1964) provides an excellent discussion of the subject, and is the source of several themes in this chapter. Catford (1965) is a slim but dense introduction to translating. Mounin (1963) offers many problem examples from less familiar languages. Pinchuk (1977) is a readable treatment of scientific translation with examples primarily from German. Herbert (1952) is a brief practical guide to the interpreter, offering some hints on note-taking, as does Rozan (1965). Seleskovitch (1968) gives a fuller account of the process and profession of interpreting. Steiner (1975) is a theoretical and philosophical investigation of meaning and translation.

Suggestions for inquiry

1 Take a brief passage of dialogue from a classic play in one of your foreign languages. Translate it, in keeping with the status of the characters, into (a) the English idiom of that period, and (b) contemporary English.
2 Produce also a formally equivalent, annotated translation.
3 Using the same dialogue: (a) lower the speakers' status, (b) raise it, and translate accordingly.
4 Repeat the process with an English source text.
5 Translate back into the SL a translation done by a friend. Compare the re-translation with the original.
6 Compare the translating style of a 'parallel text' edition of original text and translation with that of a translation published separately.

Bibliography

Adams, V. (1973) *An Introduction to Modern English Word-formation* (London: Longman).

Aitchison, J. (1976) *The Articulate Mammal* (London: Hutchinson).

Aitchison, J. (1978) *Linguistics*, 2nd edn (London: Hodder & Stoughton).

Allen, J. P. B. and Corder, S. P. (eds) (1973) *The Edinburgh Course in Applied Linguistics*, vol. 1 (Oxford University Press).

Allerton, D. J. (1979) *Essentials of Grammatical Theory* (London: Routledge & Kegan Paul).

Ammon, U. (1972) 'Zur sozialen Funktion der pronominalen Anrede in Deutschen', *Linguistik und Literaturwissenschaft*, II, 7, 73–88.

Anderson, J. M. (1973) *Structural Aspects of Language Change* (London: Longman).

Ardener, E. (ed.) (1971) *Social Anthropology and Language* (London: Tavistock).

Argyle, M. (1975) *Bodily Communication* (London: Methuen).

Augst, G. (1977) *Sprachnorm und Sprachwandel* (Wiesbaden: Athenaion).

Austin, J. L. (1962) *How to Do Things with Words* (Oxford University Press).

Bell, R. (1976) *Sociolinguistics* (London: Batsford).

Berry, M. (1975–7) *Introduction to Systemic Linguistics*, 2 vols (London: Batsford).

Birdwhistle, R. L. (1971) *Kinesics and Context* (London: Allen Lane).

Brown, R. (1976), *A First Language: The Early Stages* (Harmondsworth: Penguin).

Brown, R. and Ford, M. (1961) 'Address in American English', *Journal of Abnormal and Social Psychology*, 62, 375–85.

Brown, R. W. and Gilman, A. (1960) 'The Pronouns of Power and Solidarity', in T. Sebeok (ed.), *Style in Language* (Cambridge, Mass.: MIT Press) 253–76.

Burling, R. (1970), *Man's Many Voices* (New York: Holt, Rinehart & Winston).

Catford, J. C. (1965) *A Linguistic Theory of Translation* (Oxford University Press).

Cherry, C. (1978) *On Human Communication*, 3rd edn (Cambridge, Mass.: MIT Press).

Chomsky, C. (1971) *The Acquisition of Syntax in Children from 5 to 10* (Cambridge, Mass.: MIT Press).

Chomsky, N. (1959) 'Verbal Behaviour', *Language*, 35, 26–58.

Chomsky, N. (1965) *Aspects of the Theory of Syntax* (Cambridge, Mass.: MIT Press).

Christopherson, P. (1973) *Second-Language Learning* (Harmondsworth: Penguin).

Clark, H. H. and Clark, E. V. (1977) *Psychology and Language* (New York: Harcourt Brace Jovanovich).

Corbett, G. (1976) 'Address in Russian', *Journal of Russian Studies*, 31, 3–15.

Corder, S. P. (1973) *Introducing Applied Linguistics* (Harmondsworth: Penguin).

Coseriu, E. (1967), 'Lexical Structure and the Teaching of Vocabulary', in Council for Cultural Co-operation, *Linguistic Theories and their Application* (Strasbourg: AIDELA) 9–52.

Coulthard, R. M. (1977) *An Introduction to Discourse Analysis* (London: Longman).

Cruttenden, A. (1979) *Language in Infancy and Childhood: A Linguistic Introduction to Language Acquisition* (Manchester University Press).

Crystal, D. (1969) *Prosodic Systems and Intonation in English* (Cambridge University Press).

Crystal, D. (1971) *Linguistics* (Harmondsworth: Penguin).

Crystal, D. (1974) *What is Linguistics?*, 3rd edn (London: Edward Arnold).

Crystal, D. and Davy, D. (1969) *Investigating English Style* (London: Longman).

Culler, J. (1976) *Saussure* (London: Fontana–Collins).

Dittmar, N. (1976) *Sociolinguistics* (London: Edward Arnold).

Edwards, A. D. (1976) *Language in Culture and Class* (London: Heinemann).

Etiemble, R. (1973) *Parlez-vous franglais?*, rev. edn (Paris: Gallimard).

Ferguson, C. A. and Slobin, D. I. (1973) *Studies of Child Language Development* (New York: Holt, Rinehart & Winston).

Fishman, J. A. (ed.) (1968) *Readings in the Sociology of Language* (The Hague: Mouton).

Fishman, J. A. (1970) *Sociolinguistics: A Brief Introduction* (Rowley, Mass.: Newbury House).

Fishman, J. A. (ed.) (1971–2) *Advances in the Sociology of Langauge*, 2 vols (The Hague: Mouton).

Foster, B. (1970) *The Changing English Language* (Harmondsworth: Penguin).

Fowler, R. (1974) *Understanding Language* (London: Routledge & Kegan Paul).

Fromkin, V. and Rodman, R. (1978) *An Introduction to Language*, 2nd edn (New York: Holt, Rinehart & Winston).

Gak, V. G. (1977) *Sopostavitel'naya leksikologiya* (Moscow: Mezhdunarodnoye Otnosheniya).

Galisson, R. (1970) *Apprentissage du vocabulaire*, 2nd edn (Paris: Hachette).

Gardner, R. C. and Lambert, W. E. (1972) *Attitudes and Motivation in Second Language Learning* (Rowley, Mass.: Newbury House).

Giglioli, P. P. (ed.) (1972) *Language and Social Context* (Harmondsworth: Penguin).

Giles, H. and Powesland, P. F. (1975) *Speech Style and Social Evaluation* (London: Academic Press).

Giles, H. and St Clair, R. (eds) (1979) *Language and Social Psychology* (Oxford: Blackwell).

Gimson, A. C. (1962) *An Introduction to the Pronunciation of English* (London: Edward Arnold).

Guilbert, L. (1967) *Le vocabulaire de l'astronautique* (Rouen: Université de Rouen).

Gumperz, J. J. and Hymes, D. (eds) (1972) *Directions in Sociolinguistics: The Ethnography of Communication* (New York: Holt, Rinehart & Winston).

Halliday, M. A. K. (1975) *Learning How to Mean* (London: Edward Arnold).

Halliday, M. A. K. (1978) *Language as Social Semiotic* (London: Edward Arnold).

Halliday, M. A. K. and Hasan, R. (1976) *Cohesion in English* (London: Longman).

Harper, R. G., Wiens, A. N. and Matarazzo, J. D. (1979) *Nonverbal Communication: The State of the Art* (New York: Wiley).

Hartmann, R. R. and Stork, F. C. (1972) *Dictionary of Language and Linguistics* (London: Applied Linguistics).

Hatch, E. N. (ed.)(1978) *Second Language Acquisition* (Rowley, Mass.: Newbury House).

Herbert, J. (1952) *The Interpreter's Handbook* (Geneva: Librairie de l'Université).

Hinde, R. A. (ed.) (1972) *Non-verbal Communication* (Cambridge University Press).

Hockett, C. F. (1954) 'Chinese versus English: An Exploration of the Whorfian Theses', in H. Hoijer (ed.) *Language in Culture* (University of Chicago Press).

Hughes, A. and Trudgill, P. (1979) *English Accents and Dialects* (London: Edward Arnold).

Hymes, D. (ed) (1964) *Language in Culture and Society* (New York: Harper & Row).

Hymes, D. (1972) 'Models of the Interaction of Language and Social Life', in Gumperz and Hymes (eds), *Directions in Sociolinguistics*, 35–71.

Jakobson, R. (1973) *Main Trends in the Science of Language* (London: Allen & Unwin).

Joos, M. (1961) *The Five Clocks* (New York: Harcourt Brace & World).

Katz, J. J. (1977) *Propositional Structure and Illocutionary Force* (Brighton Harvester Press).

Katzner, K. (1977) *The Languages of the World* (London: Routledge & Kegan Paul).

Kostomarov, B. G. (1967) 'Russkii rechevoy etiket', *Russki Yazyk za Rubezhom*, 1, 56–66.

Kress, G. (ed.) (1976) *Halliday: System and Function in Language* (Oxford University Press).

Krysin, L. P. (ed.) (1974) *Russkii yazyk po dannym massovogo obsledovaniya* (Moscow: Nauka).

Labov, W. (1978) *Sociolinguistic Patterns* (Oxford: Blackwell).

Lambert, W. E. (1969) 'Psychological Studies of the Interdependencies of the Bilingual's Two Languages', in J. Puhvel (ed.), *Substance and Structure of Language* (Berkeley: University of California Press) 99–126.

Lambert, W. E. and Tucker, G. R. (1976) *Tu, Vous, Usted: A Social-Psychological Survey of Address Patterns* (Rowley, Mass.: Newbury House).

Laver, J. and Hutcheson, S. (eds) (1972) *Communication in Face to Face Interaction* (Harmondsworth: Penguin).

Leach, G. (1974) *Semantics* (Harmondsworth: Penguin).

Lockwood, W. B. (1972) *A Panorama of Indo-European Languages* (London: Hutchinson).

Lyons, J. (1968) *Introduction to Theoretical Linguistics* (Cambridge University Press).

Lyons, J. (ed) (1970) *New Horizons in Linguistics* (Harmondsworth: Penguin).

Lyons, J. (1977) *Chomsky*, rev. edn (London: Fontana–Collins).

McLaughlin, B. (1978) *Second Language Acquisition in Childhood* (Hillsdale: Erlbaum).

MacCarthy, P. (1975) *The Pronunciation of French* (Oxford University Press).

MacCarthy, P. (1978) *The Teaching of Pronunciation* (Cambridge University Press).

MacPherson, I. R. (1975) *Spanish Phonology* (Manchester University Press).

Magee, B. (1973) *Popper* (London: Fontana–Collins).

Malblanc, A. (1963) *Stylistique comparée du français et de l'allemand*, 2nd edn (Paris: Didier).

Matthews, P. H. (1979) *Generative Grammar and Linguistic Competence* (London: Allen & Unwin).
Morris, D., Collett, P. and O'Shaughnessy, M. (1979) *Gestures: Their Origin and Distribution* (London: Cape).
Moulton, W. G. (1962) *The Sounds of English and German* (University of Chicago Press).
Mounin, G. (1963) *Les problèmes théoriques de la traduction* (Paris: Gallimard).
Nida, E. A. (1964) *Towards a Science of Translating* (Leiden: Brill).
Nida, E. A. (1975) *Componential Analysis of Meaning* (The Hague: Mouton).
O'Connor, J. D. (1973) *Phonetics* (Harmondsworth: Penguin).
O'Connor, J. D. and Arnold, G. F. (1961) *Intonation of Colloquial English* (London: Longman).
Oller, J. W. and Richards, J. C. (eds) (1973) *Focus on the Learner: Pragmatic Perspectives for the Language Teacher* (Rowley, Mass.: Newbury House).
Palmer, F. R. (1976) *Semantics: A New Outline* (Cambridge University Press).
Piaget, J. (1960) *The Language and Thought of the Child* (London: Routledge & Kegan Paul).
Pilch, H. (1976) *Empirical Linguistics* (Munich: Francke Verlag).
Pinchuk, I. (1977) *Scientific and Technical Translation* (London: Deutsch).
Pottier, B. (1974) *Linguistique générale: théorie et description* (Paris: Klincksieck).
Pride, J. B. and Holmes, J. (eds) (1972) *Sociolinguistics* (Harmondsworth: Penguin).
Prichett, V. S. (1954) *The Spanish Temper* (London: Chatto & Windus).
Propp, V. (1968) *Morphology of the Folktale* (Austin: University of Texas Press).
Robins, R. H. (1971) *General Linguistics: An Introductory Survey*, 2nd edn (London: Longman).
Robins, R. H. (1979) *A Short History of Linguistics*, 2nd edn (London: Longman).
Robinson, W. P. (1972) *Language and Social Behaviour* (Harmondsworth: Penguin).
Rozan, F. (1965) *La prise de notes en interprétation consécutive* (Geneva: Georg).
Sapir, E. (1921) *Language* (New York: Harcourt Brace & World).
Saussure, F. de (1974) *Course in General Linguistics*, rev. edn (London: Fontana–Collins).
Scheflen, A. E. (1972) *How Behaviour Means* (New York: Interface).
Scherer, K. R. and Giles, H. (eds) (1979) *Social Markers in Speech* (Cambridge University Press).
Sebeok, T. A. (ed.) (1968) *Animal Communication* (Bloomington: Indiana University Press).
Seleskovitch, D. (1968) *L'interprète dans les conférences internationales* (Paris: Lettres Modernes).
Shuy, R. Y. and Fasold, R. W. (eds) (1973) *Language Attitudes: Current Trends and Prospects* (Washington: University of Georgetown Press).
Sinclair, J. McH. and Coulthard, R. M. (1975) *Towards an Analysis of Discourse: The English Used by Teachers and Pupils* (Oxford University Press).
Slobin, D. I. (1971) *Psycholinguistics* (Glenview, Ill.: Scott, Foresman).
Smith, N. and Wilson, D. (1979) *Modern Linguistics: The Results of Chomsky's Revolution* (Harmondsworth: Penguin).
Steiner, G. (1975) *After Babel* (Oxford University Press).
Stephens, M. (1976) *Linguistic Minorities in Western Europe* (Llandysul: Gomer Press).
Stork, F. C. and Widdowson, J. D. A. (1974) *Learning about Linguistics* (London: Hutchinson).

Trudgill, P. (1974) *Sociolinguistics* (Harmondsworth: Penguin).
Trudgill, P. (ed.) (1978) *Sociolinguistic Patterns in British English* (London: Edward Arnold).
Trudgill, P. and Giles, H. (1976) *Sociolinguistics and Linguistic Value Judgements* (Trier: Linguistic Agency, University of Trier).
Ullman, S. (1962) *Semantics: An Introduction to the Science of Meaning* (Oxford: Blackwell).
Vinay, J. P. and Darbelnet, J. (1971) *Stylistique comparée du français et de l'anglais*, rev. edn (Paris: Didier).
Ward, D. (1958) *Russian Pronunciation* (Edinburgh: Oliver & Boyd).
Weinreich, U. (1963) *Languages in Contact* (The Hague: Mouton).
Whorf, B. L. (1956) *Language, Thought and Reality* (Cambridge, Mass.: MIT Press).
Wilkins, D. (1972) *Linguistics in Language Teaching* (London: Edward Arnold).
Willis, F., Doble, G., Sankarayya, U. and Smithers, A. (1977) *Residence Abroad and the Student of Modern Languages* (University of Bradford).

Index

For convenient reference, the page number in the text at which each glossary-type term is most clearly defined is printed in **bold**.

FOR READER'S NOTES

FOR READER'S NOTES

FOR READER'S NOTES

FOR READER'S NOTES

FOR READER'S NOTES